# Islamic Legal Principles and Intellectual Property Rights in the Gulf States

# Middle Eastern & Islamic Studies at Gerlach Press

**Mehmet Asutay and Abdullah Q. Turkistani (eds.)**
**Islamic Finance – Political Economy, Performance and Risk** (3 vols. set)
ISBN 9783940924124, 2015

**Esther Peskes (ed.)**
**Wahhabism – Doctrine and Development** (2 vols set)
ISBN 9783940924506, 2016

**Afreen Siddiqi and Laura Diaz Anadon (eds.)**
**Science and Technology Development in the Gulf States: Economic Diversification through Regional Collaboration**
ISBN 9783959940023, 2017

**Frauke Heard-Bey**
**Abu Dhabi, the United Arab Emirates and the Gulf Region: Fifty Years of Transformation**
ISBN 9783959940009, 2016

**Nikolay Kozhanov**
**Russia and the Syrian Conflict: Moscow's Domestic, Regional and Strategic Interests**
ISBN 9783940924728, 2016

**David Price and Alhanoof AlDebasi (eds.)**
**Intellectual Property Rights: Development and Enforcement in the Arab States of the Gulf**
ISBN 9783959940108, 2017

**Tim Niblock with Degang Sun and Alejandra Galindo (eds.)**
**The Arab States of the Gulf and BRICS: New Strategic Partnerships in Politics and Economics**
ISBN 9783959940085, 2016

**Carool Kersten (ed.)**
**The Fatwa as an Islamic Legal Instrument: Concept, Historical Role, Contemporary Relevance** (3 vols. set)
ISBN 9783959940207, 2018

**Marc Owen Jones, Ross Porter and Marc Valeri (eds.)**
**Gulfization of the Arab World**
ISBN 9783959940320, 2018

**Yesenn El-Radhi**
**Economic Diversification in the Gulf States: Public Expenditure and Non-Oil Economic Growth in Bahrain, Oman and Qatar**
ISBN 9783959940528, 2018

**Tim Niblock with Talmiz Ahmad and Degang Sun (eds.)**
**The Gulf States, Asia and the Indian Ocean: Ensuring the Security of the Sea Lanes**
ISBN 9783959940580, 2018

**David Heard**
**Oil Men, Territorial Ambitions and Political Agents. From Pearls to Oil in the Trucial States of the Gulf** (2 vols. set)
ISBN 9783959940641, 2019

**Asma Hilali, S. R. Burge (eds.)**
**The Making of Religious Texts in Islam: The Fragment and the Whole**
ISBN 9783959940702, 2019

**Abdulrahman Alebrahim**
**Kuwait's Politics Before Independence: The Role of the Balancing Powers**
ISBN 9783959940726, 2019

**J. B. Kelly, edited by S. B. Kelly**
**Desert Dispute: The Diplomacy of Boundary-Making in South-Eastern Arabia** (3 vols. set)
ISBN 9783959940788, 2019

**Degang Sun with Dandan Zhang**
**Diplomacy of Quasi-Alliances in the Middle East With a Foreword by Tim Niblock**
ISBN 9783959940740, 2020

**David Heard (ed.)**
**The Trucial Coast Diaries (1948-1957). On the Way from Pearls to Oil in the Trucial States of the Gulf**
ISBN 783959940801, 2020

**Noel Brehony and Clive Jones (eds)**
**Britain's Departure from Aden and South Arabia: Without Glory but Without Disaster**
ISBN 9783959940825, 2020

**Tore T. Petersen and Clive Jones (eds.)**
**Grand Strategy in the Contemporary Middle East: The Concepts and Debates**
ISBN 9783959941563, 2022

**Sujata Ashwarya, Mujib Alam (eds.)**
**The Arab Spring: Ten Years On**
ISBN 9783959941587, 2022

**www.gerlachpress.com**

Nadia Naim

# Islamic Legal Principles and Intellectual Property Rights in the Gulf States

Gerlach Press

First published 2023
by Gerlach Press
Berlin, Germany
www.gerlachpress.com

Cover Design: Frauke Schön, Hamburg
Set by Anne Jeschke, Gerlach Press
Printed and bound in Germany



British Library Cataloguing in Publication Data.
A catalogue record for this book is available from the British Library.

Bibliographic data available from Deutsche Nationalbibliothek
http://d-nb.info/1272807606

ISBN: 978-3-95994-162-4 (hardcover)
ISBN: 978-3-95994-163-1 (eBook)

# Contents

# Abstract

This monograph aims to examine the intellectual property regimes in the Gulf Co-operation Council (GCC) states and assess the relationships between legislation, enforcement mechanisms and sharia law. The GCC states, currently Bahrain, Oman, Kuwait, Saudi Arabia, UAE and Qatar, all have varied mechanisms in place for both the implementation and enforcement of intellectual property rights. The monograph pays close attention to the evolution of intellectual property laws and regulations in the GCC states with particular interest directed towards the development of national intellectual property laws within the GCC states from the 1970's onwards*.

Intellectual property protection in the GCC states is considered from two perspectives. The first perspective addresses the international demand for higher standards of intellectual property protection in the GCC states. The second perspective defines intellectual property within the laws of Islam and explores the relationship between Islam and intellectual property. The latter part analyses religious influence, societal and cultural norms, economic reality and the developmental stage of each GCC state. It is an important area of study as developing Muslim countries are struggling with meeting international standards and a successful integrated framework will impact not only on GCC states but other Islamic states and as a result could potentially lead to more informed negotiation in trade agreements with developed states. The research argues there are systematic flaws in the GCC states adopting intellectual property laws which are in essence a procrustean modification of foreign laws which have developed from colonial occupation or laws taken from donor countries. The GCC legal systems of the states have evolved utilising different sets of legal principles and therefore it could be argued the foreign laws that have been adopted are somewhat unsuitable for the GCC states. With the advent of frontier technologies and artificial intelligence, unless Muslim countries take more of an active role in intellectual property development, the influence of Sharia principles will only continue to diminish.

The research has focused on the implications of the national and international legislative regimes on the protection of intellectual property rights on the GCC states. Consideration is given to compliance, mainly how compliant the GCC is to its World

* See Chapter 1 (1)-(9).

Trade Organisation (WTO) membership and Trade Related Intellectual Property Rights (TRIP's) Agreement and to what extent the European Union (EU) and the United States (US) influence the intellectual property protection regimes in the GCC. The research has examined the development of the GCC in three distinct stages; pre-TRIPS, TRIPS compliance stage and TRIPS plus.

Furthermore, the monograph argues that the somewhat simplistic formula of the GCC states passing a large number of intellectual property laws to appease the EU and US does not have the significant economic impact on the GCC economy as the international agreements would suggest. Not all trade is intellectual property related and not all foreign direct investment is contingent upon intellectual property protection. However, as the GCC states are largely oil dependent, they do need to diversify their trade and as such an intellectual property protection model that accounts for international intellectual property law and the bespoke cultural and religious views amongst GCC citizens can produce tangible results for both the GCC and its trading partners. What sets the research apart from previous research is two-fold. Firstly, the research is qualitative and has scratched beneath the surface of intellectual property law in the GCC and examined in detail the Islamic law principles that have been used to justify sharia compliance, the western perspective on international intellectual property and the impact of multilateral trade agreements. Secondly, the analysis of Islamic finance and the application of successful sharia compliant models in Islamic finance to intellectual property is innovative as it acts as a springboard to creating a modified sharia compliant intellectual property protection model. Finally, the monograph will conclude by making a series of recommendations to develop an integrated approach to intellectual property rights which takes into account; the structure of the GCC states, international agreements and pressures, the international institutions, Islamic finance and both societal and religious views.

KEYWORDS: INTERNATIONAL INTELLECTUAL PROPERTY, GULF CO-OPERATION COUNCIL (GCC), ISLAMIC LAW, ISLAMIC FINANCE, INTELLECTUAL PROPERTY RIGHTS PROTECTION RECOMMENDATIONS, TRADE RELATED INTELLECTUAL PROPERTY RIGHTS (TRIPS), INTERNATIONAL TRADE AGREEMENTS

# 1

# Introduction to the Examination of the Intellectual Property Regimes in the Gulf Co-operation Council (GCC) States

## 1 Introduction

The Co-operation Council for the Arab States of the Gulf (GCC), namely UAE, Saudi Arabia, Qatar, Oman, Kuwait and Bahrain, are a six-nation union dealing with a range of political and economic matters. The GCC was formed in response to three main issues; the perceivable security threats to the different Gulf Arab regimes from the Iran – Iraq conflict around the time of formation, the Soviet communist threat from Afghanistan and to be better protected against security threats[1].

The GCC states are geographically placed in close proximity to each other, and the entire GCC member states fall under the Arabian Peninsula. Yemen shares borders with the GCC states and falls under the same region, however it is not, as of yet, a GCC member state[2].

## 2 Purpose of Monograph

The research focuses on the intellectual property developments made by the member states of the GCC and how intellectual property development and subsequent deployment can act as a catalyst for financial prosperity. The main purpose of this work is to analyse and examine the intellectual property provisions currently in existence within the six states of the GCC and agreements entered into by the six states collectively under the GCC Union. The aim is to provide recommendations to improve the current level of intellectual property protection at both a national level and at a state level in the GCC through an integrated intellectual property protection model.

There have been three main stages in the development of intellectual property in the Gulf states; a pre Trade Related Aspects of Intellectual Property Rights (TRIPS) stage, the current level of TRIPS compliance and a push towards TRIPS Plus. To date, each individual Gulf state has developed its intellectual property laws at varying rates. Post 2000, the Gulf states all display a set of intellectual property laws that are largely compliant with TRIPS. Therefore a question arises as to how much scope there is in the current laws to accede to more stringent intellectual property provisions. The monograph will show this is a key question for the GCC, its international partners and the wider trading communities of the WTO.

There is a widening gap between the level of intellectual property standards that are demanded by developed countries and the capability of the GCC states to enforce these standards as will be discussed in Chapter 5[3]. Through intellectual property the region is opening itself up to further foreign direct investment which can lead to a positive impact on the economy[4]. The underlying theme behind the legislative changes that have taken place in the GCC, is the influence of sharia law[5]. The research will assess the impact of sharia law on the decisions taken by the GCC in intellectual property law development. It is an important area of study as developing Muslim countries are struggling with meeting international standards and a successful integrated approach to intellectual property rights could impact on a number of countries and trade agreements with developed states[6].

Where the study of intellectual property developments and Islamic law becomes multi-faceted is when consideration is given to the dichotomy that has arisen between the levels of intellectual property legislation in the Gulf states against the pressures from international states to increase intellectual property enforcement mechanisms. There are international pressures on the GCC states to adopt enhanced intellectual property laws for which they lack the necessary expertise, infrastructures and judicial experience to implement[7]. The integrated approach to intellectual property has

## 3 Research Questions

How can the GCC states satisfy international demands for better intellectual property protection without compromising their Islamic values and traditions?

Do the GCC states have the necessary capacity both in their legal structure and internal institutions to increase their levels of intellectual property protection?

What recommendations can be made to develop an integrated approach to intellectual property rights in the GCC taking into account: the structure of the GCC states, international agreements and pressures, the relevant international institutions, Islamic finance and both societal and religious views.

## 4 Research Objectives

The research objectives addressed are split across the remaining chapters:

### *Chapter 3*

- To identify the sources of Islamic law that justify intellectual property protection and analyse the influence of sharia law on intellectual property protection in the GCC states.
- To find differences/similarities between sharia law principles and intellectual property law to make recommendations on intellectual property development in the GCC.

### *Chapter 4*

- To provide a background to the western development of intellectual property rights to gain a holistic view of the international intellectual property industry.
- To review the role of US international institutions such as the Office of the United States Trade Representative (USTR) and its influence on the GCC states.
- To review the role of EU international institutions such as the European Patent Office (EPO) and the European Patent Convention (EPC) and its influence on the GCC states.
- To review the current international intellectual property legislation, policies, free trade agreements, bilateral agreements and enforcement mechanisms that exist in the EU and US and their influence on the GCC states. Substantive provisions from the free trade agreements on intellectual property law and protection will be considered.

### *Chapter 5*

- To investigate the development of intellectual property in the Gulf Co-operation Council (GCC) countries from pre-TRIPS, TRIPS and TRIPS Plus.
    - The Pre TRIPS analysis will focus on the level of intellectual property protection that existed before the GCC states began assenting to international treaties and agreements, covering a time period that runs from 1970 to 1990.
    - The TRIPS compliance stage will be considered as it occurred at different times for all six states and the timeline examines the sheer amount of changes that took place from 1990 to 2010[8].

    - Trips Plus provisions will be examined to understand how they go beyond the standards set at TRIPS level and the overview for TRIPS Plus follows on from when the TRIPS agreement was decided by the GCC states to the current state of play.
- To understand the intellectual property development of each GCC state as to be able to inform the set of recommendations to be made for the overall purpose of an integrated intellectual property approach concerning how intellectual property rights protection can be improved.
- To investigate the role sharia law can play in intellectual property development and what the key issues are.
    - To gain an understanding of Islamic law to provide support for the protection of intellectual property law.
    - To identify the provisions that protect intellectual property rights with the aim of increasing innovations and stimulate economic development
    - To address the doctrine of public interest and how to create better recognition and acceptance of intellectual property by the GCC citizens.

### *Chapter 6*

- There will be an in-depth analysis of the following key research areas: TRIPS Plus as a higher set of standards for intellectual property protection, the significant provisions of TRIPS Plus that impact on the GCC states, the various proposed implementation clauses in TRIPS Plus and what the potential ramifications of the TRIPS Plus provisions are for the GCC states.
- To review the role of international organisations on law making in the GCC countries such as the World Intellectual Property Office (WIPO), World Trade Organisation (WTO), the European Patent Office (EPO) and the Office of the United States Trade Representative (USTR). To assess the impact of the current international dispute settlement mechanisms on the GCC states outside of the WTO remit. The main mechanisms to consider are bilateral state agreements and investor to state dispute settlements.

### *Chapter 7*

- To analyse the success of Islamic finance, in particular the creation of sharia-compliant frameworks as an alternative to conventional banking and the role of sharia boards.
- To apply lessons learnt from the successes achieved in the Islamic finance sector to the development of an integrated approach to intellectual property rights protection.

### *Chapter 8*

- To make a series of recommendations based on the findings of the above research objectives in the development of an integrated approach to intellectual property rights. The aim will be for the research to set the ground for a novel approach to intellectual property protection in the GCC which takes into account the structure of the GCC states, international agreements and pressures, the relevant international institutions, Islamic finance and both societal and religious views.

## 5 Research Process

The research is non-empirical and theoretical in nature, it lays the foundations for further research in this area and for empirical research that could be carried out in the future. The research process has utilised a range of existing empirical studies in the field and the purpose of this chapter is to both outline and define the research process for the monograph. The research problem is focused on how to improve the international standard setting of intellectual property rights in the GCC states, with a close analysis of the role of sharia law in the future of intellectual property as well as the conflicting influences of international trade agreements. Further, the research analyses the role that Islamic finance can play in giving the intellectual property protection agenda an enhanced platform. The research questions are designed to provide the theoretical basis to provide a solution to the research problem[9].

Steps in designing the research process have followed a qualitative data analysis model.

The aim of qualitative analysis is to perform a selective process of representation of a given phenomenon with the overall objective of highlighting some of its properties[10]. The research process for the purpose of this research can be summarised as; searching the data, critical analysis of the data, data combination and synmonograph, followed by an analysis of results and findings as established by Hart (2001)[11] and Strauss and Corbin (2007)[12].

## 6 Proposed Methodology

The research design is a paper and online data collection method to find literature to date on intellectual property law development in the GCC states, the role of Islamic law in intellectual property rights protection and the development of the modern day Islamic finance industry. The literature is a collection of secondary sources from paper and online data collection and every attempt has been made to ensure the mainstream existing work in this area is accessed and analysed. Existing work from different databases will be used to identify relevant sources where data can be is available in relation to the GCC states. In respect of the Islamic sources, to confine the data to a timeframe is difficult as Islamic sources are by their nature historical and date back to when the Quran was first introduced. Therefore the Islamic sources will not be limited to a timeframe as such and will be accessed on the basis of relevance. Literature specific to intellectual property and sharia law can be placed in a timeframe as pre TRIPS there was not much by way of research in the area, however as the Gulf states started to gain independence from colonialization and develop their economies, there was more of an impetus towards knowledge based economies such as intellectual property rights. Consequently, a timeframe for the literature on the relationship between intellectual property law and sharia law as well as Islamic finance can be set from 1970 to the present day.

The sample size is a census sample as all literature available through paper data collection and online searches in this field is collected and then selected based on its relevance to the research. The data collected has come from policy documents, legislation, statistics, books, peer-reviewed articles, press reports, internet based materials, research studies, scholars in the fields of intellectual property and Islamic finance as well as relevant theory[13]. The data will be analysed through a variation of the grounded theory method whereby data collected will be analysed to produce a theoretical framework that encompasses Islamic law and intellectual property law as set out by Strauss and Corbin (1990 and 1998)[14].

The research methodology and data collection is split into three distinct categories:

- International intellectual property law development in the GCC in line with WIPO, international trade agreements, TRIPS provisions and the impact of corporate sovereignty and investor state dispute settlements in the GCC.
- Analysis of the protection of intellectual property rights in Islamic law, the sources of Islamic law and their application to intellectual property.
- Analysis of the protection of intellectual property rights through Islamic finance, how Islamic finance adheres to sharia law and how this can be applied to intellectual property protection.

The main research questions are to be answered through a theoretical analysis of secondary data across the different disciplines of intellectual property law, Islamic law and Islamic finance. It is essential to get an in-depth knowledge of the existing principles of intellectual property law from a GCC perspective and a western perspective in order to inform a series of recommendations for an integrated approach to intellectual property rights protection in the GCC. The founding principles of Islamic finance and the sharia compliant structures that exist within Islamic finance will be researched from a qualitative and exploratory approach in order to gain better understanding of Islamic finance, and in turn be able to apply the research findings to developing an integrated intellectual property framework. This is a theoretical investigation as to date, the role Islamic finance can play in the development of intellectual property rights protection has not yet been explored, thus the research is a qualitative study exploring new phenomena. For the GCC states, Islamic finance is not a new phenomenon in itself, nor is intellectual property. A new perspective on the research area will be identified through the relationship between Islamic law and intellectual property rights protection while taking into account; the structure of the GCC states, international agreements and Islamic finance. This therefore highlights the novel contribution the research will make in amalgamating different research strands to propose a set of new recommendations for the protection of intellectual property rights.

## 7 Grounded Theory Methodology

Grounded theory is a general methodology for developing theory that is grounded in data that is systematically gathered and analysed. Grounded theory originates from the mid-1960s with the pioneering work in medical sociology by Barney Glaser and Anselm Strauss[15]. This led to the subsequent publication of *The Discovery of Grounded Theory* by Glaser & Strauss in 1967. Grounded theory is a general method of comparative analysis that discovers theory within four main areas; the general work, the relevance of the work in creating an understanding, how fit for purpose the existing work is in terms of validity and modifiability. The last area is the main focus of the research as the purpose of the research is to make recommendations to modify the approach taken by the GCC states in protecting intellectual property rights. It requires an interpretation of Islamic sources, intellectual property laws and developments and an understanding of Islamic finance.

In essence, the methodology is predominantly based on the grounded theory method as the research is qualitative, however there is some deviance from the method to account for Islamic law. The data collected will inform the substantive qualitative theory development on the influence of sharia law on international intellectual property protection in the GCC. What makes the grounded theory method the closest option for the research is that there is a continuous interplay between data collection and data analysis. For example, in Chapter 3, data is collected from the different Islamic sources and then analysed from the accepted translators to infer intellectual property reasoning.

Grounded theory alone is insufficient for the research as its ultimate aim is to provide a systematic generation of theory from research. Although the research will lead to the emergence of conceptual categories, these concepts are limited in their application across all the research areas as theoretical explanations on Islamic sources are confined within the four sources of sharia. Therefore the research will follow the desk based research approach in gathering data from existing research and theory to be able to analyse international intellectual property development and the impact of TRIPS provisions on intellectual property rights protection in the GCC. In relation to sharia law the precepts of Islamic jurisprudence in relation to the relevant areas of sharia law, from the four main Islamic sources, will be applied as set out below.

## 8 Islamic Law Sources

There are four main schools of Islamic jurisprudence: Hanbali, Shafii, Maliki, and Hanafi. Hanbali is followed by Saudi Arabia and is the strictest of the four schools, adopting a literal interpretation of the Quran and Sunnah. The Shafii school of thought is more widely accepted as it allows the application of secondary Islamic sources to make legitimate analogies. The Maliki school differs slightly from the other schools as it relies on historical customs and practice and is observed in Kuwait, Bahrain and the United Arab Emirates.

The four main schools are followed by Sunni Muslims although there is a minority population of Shia Muslims who follow a different school of thought. Islamic jurisprudence from the Shia Muslim perspective is beyond the scope of the research, although it is an area that could potentially influence further research. The sources cited below are the established sources approved by the four main schools of Islamic jurisprudence.

### *The Quran*

The main accepted source for the Quran is available at www.quran.com. Data sources for the website include Tanzil, QuranComplex, Zekr and Online Quran Project. Translations are provided by seven authors as approved by Saudi Arabia; Sahih International, Muhsin Khan, Pickthall. Yusuf Ali, Shakir and Dr. Ghali. The reason there is more than one single approved translator is because there is a general consensus among all Islamic scholars that the Quran cannot be completely translated into another language because it was written for the Arabic language. This is largely because the stylistic and syntactic properties of the Quran are language-specific.

As a result, sharia scholars are able to consider translations from authors that have been approved by Saudi Arabia; however, the most widely accepted translations to date come from Sahih International and Muhsin Khan.

### *Sahih International*

Sahih International is an approved translation by Saudi Arabia and is available at the King Fahad National Library in Saudi Arabia[16].

### *Muhsin Khan*

Muhsin Khan's translation is the most widely disseminated Quran in most Islamic bookstores and Sunni mosques throughout the English-speaking world and is approved by both the University of Medina and the Saudi Dar al-Ifta in Saudi Arabia[17].

### *Pickthall*

Mohammed Marmaduke Pickthall's translation is entitled The Meaning of the Glorious Koran and was first published in 1930[18]. It is less common than Sahih International and Muhsin Khan, nonetheless it is an accepted translation available at www.quran.com.

### *Yusuf Ali*

Yusuf Ali's translation was first published in 1934. In 1989, Saudi Arabia's Ar-Rajhi banking company financed the US based Amana Corporation's project to revise the translation to reflect an interpretation more in conjunction with the line of Islamic thought followed in Saudi Arabia. Ar-Rahji offered the resulting version for free to mosques, schools, and libraries throughout the world[19].

### *Shakir*

The works of the translator Muhammed Habib Shakir are also available at www.quran.com and he is one of the recognised translators of the Quran[20].

### *Dr. Ghali*

Dr. Ghali was the head of the English language department in Al-Azhar University in Cairo. He spent around 15 years to finish his translation of the Quran. While working at King 'Abdul- 'Azeez University, Dr Ghali, along with a committee of further twelve professors, was assigned to revise the most prominent translations of the Quran into English[21].

## 9 The Sunnah

Sahih Al Bukhari is the approved author of Sunnah sources. The Sunnah is often described as the practical companion to the Quran, demonstrating in practical terms the meaning behind the Quranic verses. Validity of the Sunnah is very important as a source of Islamic law as the Sunnah was in essence the acts, practices and statements attributable to Prophet Muhammed, which were recorded and recapitulated for the Muslim world to follow.

Sahih Al Bukhari's Sunnah sources have received certificates of approval from: Sheikh 'Abdul 'Aziz bin 'Abdullah bin Baz, Dar-ul-Ifta', Presidency of Islamic Research, Ifta', Call and Propagation, Kingdom of Saudi Arabia, Sheikh 'Umar Muhammad Fullata, General Secretary of Islamic University, Al-Madina Al-Munawwara and Dr. Muhammad Amin Al-Misri, Head of Higher Studies, Islamic University, Al-Madina Al-Munawwara.

The English translation of Sahih Al Bukhari Hadith is by Muhsin Khan who is an approved translator of the Quran. The translation is further approved by three scholars who have undersigned the translation. They are; Shakir Nasif Al-'Ubaydi, M.A. (English), Vanderbilt University, U.S.A., Teacher of English: Baghdad University & College of Education, Makka, Dr. Mahmud Hamad Nasr, Graduate of Khartoum University, Physician: King Hospital, Al-Madina and Dr. M. Taqi-ud-Din Al-Hilali, PhD, Berlin University, Germany, Professor: Muhammad V University, Morocco, Islamic University, Al-Madina[22].

## 10 Western Methodology Considerations

### *Social Constructionism*

Social constructionism stands out as a relevant method for the research. In terms of the knowledge matrix, social constructionism falls within an epistemology of interpreted realism[23]. Social constructionism focuses on how individuals and groups participate in their creation of perceived reality and their shared social constructions of meaning. Gergen defines social constructionism as "the terms on which the world is understood are social artefacts, products of historically situated interchanges among people"[24]. The discussion on language, discourse, society and knowledge is pertinent to the research as how language is interpreted under sharia law has a bearing on the level of intellectual property rights protection that a GCC state will allow. The theology expanded upon Burr's work that "If we accept the view… that a multitude of alternative versions of events is potentially available through language, this means that, surrounding any one object, event, person etc., there may be a variety of different discourses, each with a different story to tell about the object in question, a different way of representing it to the world"[25].

## 11 Discourse Analysis

The discourse analysis has three strands: content, linguistic and narrative. Content analysis can be quantitative or qualitative, linguistic analysis is concerned with early structuralism and narrative analysis is based on stories. There is an argument that the discourse analysis on the research in question falls under both content and narrative analysis. The content analysis can be linked to western intellectual property rights principles and the discreet Islamic law principles of property rights can be better understood through the narrative analysis of the stories that support Islamic jurisprudence.

Although both social constructionism and discourse analysis can be shown in this work, they are not fit for purpose as the aim of the research is to make a set of recommendations on how to approach intellectual property rights protection through an integrated framework of established Islamic law principles. Therefore the research methodology will apply the grounded theory method to the research area. The research will follow the four criteria as outlined above of; discover a new set of recommendations within the general work in intellectual property, the relevance of the work in creating an understanding of intellectual property in the GCC, how fit for purpose the existing work is in terms of validity and making proposal for modification of the intellectual property systems in place. There is a deviation from classic grounded theory methodology as the research aims to investigate the research question through three distinct strands: intellectual property, Islamic law and Islamic finance.

## 12 Data Collection

Data has been collected through different strands: legislation, case law, governmental resources and international agencies, Islamic sources, scholarly work and publications by expert authors in their field. The data collected is split in to the three categories of data collection as outlined this chapter (4); intellectual property data, Islamic sources and Islamic finance.

## 13 Legislation

Legislation is easily accessible for each GCC state via the WIPO and from the official publications of each GCC state on their e-government websites. Intellectual property legislation from the six GCC states is covered in Chapter 2. Legislation is easily accessible and available in English. Legislation is also considered from western states, predominantly from the US and EU which is readily available from legal research sites such as Lexis Library, Lawtel, Brill Online and various other government websites.

## 14 GCC Case Law

GCC states do not have an online repository that archives case law as would be found in the EU or US. Therefore, access to case law is problematic and provides a limitation to the research. In an attempt to overcome the limitations, reports produced by the GCC states such as annual crime and safety reports have been used. Also, quantitative research reports have formed part of the data collection process.

The enforcement mechanisms in operation within the GCC states have been assessed through statistical data, border measures statistics, crime reports and cases reported in the media. As the focus of the research is on making a set of recommendations for an integrated intellectual property protection approach, relevant international case law has been considered.

## 15 Intellectual Property Resources

Intellectual property resources have been accessed under four main categories; the GCC, the US, the EU and other resources. The main data collection has taken place from the resources listed in appendix 1. For the GCC, these include: the GCC Charter, the GCC Patent Office, the Saudi Embassy, the Ministry of Information, Sultanate of Oman, Arab Human Development Reports, the constitutions of GCC states, Kuwait Programme on Development, Governance and Globalisation in the Gulf states, Political Economy of the Gulf Reports, Bahrain Economic Development Board, Gulf Research Center and the Emirates Center for Strategic Studies and Research.

## 16 Islamic Finance Methodology

The research into the structures of Islamic finance, the sharia boards and governance practices has followed a similar research process as intellectual property. It has been desk-based research with the gathering of data from the institutional databases of each individual GCC state, Islamic finance institutions, GCC Islamic banks, international financial organisations, Islamic finance scholars, articles by leading authors in the field of Islamic finance and the sharia sources as detailed earlier in this chapter.

## 17 Islamic Finance Resources

Islamic finance is a well-regulated industry with a number of key organisations and institutions both at a government level and from the business sector that control and oversee the development of Islamic finance. The main resources that have been accessed are from; financial services authorities, financial services centres, national Islamic banks, federal laws, sharia boards, reports, articles and authored work.

## 18 Conclusion

The first chapter has set out the research proposal, the research objectives and outlined the methodology and research process. The research is non empirical and theoretical in nature as the monograph attempts to make a series of recommendations to develop an integrated approach to intellectual property rights which takes into account; the structure of the GCC states, international agreements and pressures, the international institutions, Islamic finance and both societal and religious views. The research objectives are novel and aim to provide a modified approach to international intellectual property rights protection. The intellectual property landscape is constantly changing, however at a time when new standards are being introduced, this research is very topical, shedding light on the international intellectual property standard setting debate.

Chapter 2 provides a background to the GCC states. It will discuss the reasons behind the formation of the GCC, the GCC charter, the political and religious structures that exist in the GCC states by way of a state by state analysis. The second chapter will also cover the national intellectual property laws in each GCC state as well as the international agreements that the GCC states are signatories to. It will also highlight the similarities and differences in individual state governance.

From Chapter 3 onwards there is a clear breakdown of the research objectives and relevant analysis to answer the overall research aim of making a set of recommendations to support an integrated approach to intellectual property rights protection in the GCC states. There will also be spillovers from the research findings for other developing countries that abide by sharia law at a constitutional level. Chapter 3 will also focus on the sharia law that exists in the GCC states and the development of intellectual property under sharia law principles. Further, consideration will be given to the specific idiosyncrasies that sharia law poses for intellectual property developments given the fact that the Quran makes no direct reference to intellectual property. However there are several inferences that can be drawn from the Quran and therefore all sources of sharia law, relevant to intellectual property, will be considered. An in-depth analysis of the four main sources of sharia law with specific reference to intellectual property protection will be carried out in Chapter 3.

Chapter 4 will answer the research objectives that concern outstanding free trade agreements with the European Union (EU) and the United States (US), the intellectual property perspective of the US and EU and the current phase of negotiations with the GCC. The chapter will highlight the working relationships the GCC states have with both the EU and the US and introduce key contentious issues around investor state dispute settlement mechanisms and corporate sovereignty.

Chapter 5 investigates the development of intellectual property in the Gulf Co-operation Council (GCC) countries from pre-TRIPS, TRIPS and TRIPS Plus. It analyses the level of intellectual property protection that existed before the GCC states began ascending to international treaties and agreements covering a time period that runs from 1970 to 1990. Then, leading on to the TRIPS compliance stage which occurred at different times for all six states and finally the impact of Trips Plus and the potential ramifications for the GCC states.

Chapter 6 analyses the key objectives concerning what the potential changes have been for the GCC states in order to increase compliance from TRIPS to TRIPS Plus. Building on from this are the benefits/pitfalls of international trade and the impact of ISDS on intellectual property rights in the GCC. The chapter highlights the need for ISDS to be compliant with sharia law, given there is a potential risk it could conflict with Islamic principles.

Chapter 7 explores the role the Islamic finance sector can play in improving intellectual property rights protection in the GCC. Thus, it will identify the main principles of Islamic finance and apply lessons learnt from Islamic finance success to intellectual property protection. The main sharia compliant areas that will be considered in Chapter 7 are musharaka, mudaraba, murabaha, istisna, ijara, salam and sukuk. The chapter will outline the founding principles of Islamic finance, specifically in relation to the sharia compliant frameworks, Islamic finance products, the role of sharia boards, governance and development. The chapter provides the foundations of the overall integrated framework for intellectual property protection from the perspective of Islamic finance success.

Finally Chapter 8 will be a comprehensive summary chapter with a very clear objective to set out the framework for a modified approach to intellectual property rights protection in the GCC states. The final chapter will recapitulate the main research findings from earlier chapters and make a series of recommendations to develop an integrated approach to intellectual property rights which takes into account; the structure of the GCC states, international agreements and pressures, the international institutions, Islamic finance and both societal and religious views. The research findings from the individual chapters will inform the overall content of the integrated approach to intellectual property rights protection in the GCC states through the three main research strands of intellectual property rights protection from the western standard setting perspective, intellectual property rights protection expedited by Islamic law and Islamic finance. Also, further research points will be outlined as given the theoretical nature of this work, there will be a number of areas with the potential for development into further research avenues of research.

# 2

# Background to the GCC States

## 1 Introduction

The GCC is a union of six states in the Middle East which have undergone many changes over the last thirty years. The purpose of this background chapter is to gain an understanding of the GCC as a union and as a collection of individual states, in terms of their political structures and legislative development.

The GCC union was founded on 26 May 1981 and the continued aim of the union is to promote coordination between member states in all fields in order to achieve unity. The main impetus behind the GCC union was in response to three main issues; the perceived security threats to the different Gulf Arab regimes from the Iran – Iraq conflict around the time of formation, the Soviet communist threat from Afghanistan, and to be better protected against security threats[26]. A failed coup attempt in Bahrain in 1981[27], a series of bombings in Kuwait in 1983[28], and the Iran-Iraq War caused regional instability and spearheaded the Internal Security Agreement in 1982[29].

Therefore, the International Security Agreement addressed a number of security concerns for the GCC states and enhancing security protection has been and continues to be a primary concern. Along with the geographical commonalities the GCC states share, they comprise the world's biggest oil producers and currently account for 29% of the world's proven oil reserves and 23% of global hydrocarbons reserves[30]. Collectively, the states are dependent, to varying degrees, on oil production[31].

## 2 The GCC Charter

The GCC Union is a co-operation agreement between the six GCC states that was established in 1981. The purpose of the GCC Charter was to set out the key objectives of the GCC states and to hold court in the international arena as a regional entity. The preamble to the GCC Charter is embedded with a statement outlining a respect for the shared religious views of its members stating: Each member state is *"fully aware of the ties of special relations, common characteristics and similar systems founded on the creed of Islam which bind them*[32]".

Before analysing intellectual property regimes in the GCC, understanding the structure of the GCC Charter is relevant to forming a complete picture of how deeply rooted in Islamic values the states are. The impact of religious beliefs on the GCC states is important as the GCC Charter deals with all aspects of business and commerce. For example, Article 4 of the GCC Charter lists the key field of its collective co-operation as: economic and financial affairs, commerce, customs and communications, education and culture[33]. The GCC Charter is a comprehensive document that sets out the charter over twenty-two articles and deals primarily with establishing a Council and the main objectives of the union. The GCC has its own Supreme Council, Ministerial Council and Secretariat General[34], Article 7 declares the Supreme Council as the highest authority in the GCC[35] and Article 8 lists the main functions of the Supreme Council. The Ministerial Council is formed of the Foreign Ministers of the member states or other delegated ministers; it is primarily concerned with proposing policies and recommendations[36]. The Secretariat General is led by a Secretary-General who is assisted by a number of staff and the Secretary-General is appointed by the Supreme Council[37]. Thus, despite the variances in the governance structures of the GCC states, there has been a conscious effort to develop a GCC Charter that is democratic and representative of all member states. The aim of the articles of the GCC charter is to set out how the states can collectively govern a single common market.

The GCC union recognised the need for more uniformity in regard to intellectual property rights and has its own patent office which acts as a regional patent office. What makes the GCC patent office such a landmark development in the region is that it secures legal protection of the inventor's rights in all of the GCC states with authority to grant a regional community patent. The main reason behind the GCC community patent was to make available a uniform patent and co-ordinate efforts in the area of patent protection to enhance technological advancement in support of their joint economic weight.

The GCC patent office is based in Riyadh, Saudi Arabia and has a basic system which has been inaugurated in a similar fashion to the GCC Charter with a set of articles that clearly define the community patent system in line with the objective of overall cooperation between member states. The basic system statute consists of 13 articles which establish the main functions of the GCC patent office and sets out the composition of the patent office, the roles and responsibilities of the board of directors and the director. The patent system develops on from the foundational composition of the patent office and consists of 34 articles dealing with the process of granting a patent, compulsory licensing, length and duration of a patent. From January 2021, the GCC patent office stopped receiving new patents and requires applications to be made to individual states[38].

The GCC states have their own domestic patent offices and intellectual property rights protection and enforcement institutions. Although the GCC states have a community patent, each GCC state has national intellectual property offices. Saudi Arabia, the largest of the GCC states, has a department set up at the King Abdul-Aziz City for Science and Technology to assess and grant patents[39]. Saudi Arabia, as will be seen in Chapter 2 (4) and Table 1, has invested heavily in improving its intellectual property protection and continues to adhere to international agreements. Saudi Arabia has one of the more established patent systems in the GCC, accepting online applications. Other GCC national patent systems are not as well developed; for example in Oman, the main patent office is the Ministry of Commerce and Industry of Oman and it has only recently started formal examination of pending applications. Qatar shares similarities to Oman as the Ministry of Justice has the role of granting patents and has also recently started accepting local applications. In the UAE, the intellectual property institutions are extensive as the Ministry of Economy has several divisions dealing with different areas of intellectual property. In Bahrain, the Ministry of Information and Ministry of Industry and Commerce are responsible for domestic intellectual property. In Kuwait, Ministry of Trade and Industry, Trademarks and Patents Department is responsible for granting patents. Many of the GCC states have opted to assign intellectual property matters to a ministerial department with the exceptions of Saudi Arabia and UAE[40].

The GCC has approved a unified GCC trademark law, which was issued in 2006 and after revisions, has now come into force[41]. The purpose of the trademark law is to bring together the common legislative features of all six states into one trademark law and to streamline the process; however there have been significant delays in bringing the GCC trademark law into force. The GCC trademark law is dissimilar to the GCC patent office as filing in each state will mean adhering to national level registration processes that could lead to lengthy delays[42].

## 3 Background to the GCC and International Relations

The GCC has made considerable efforts to develop international relations, most notably with the EU and US, along with others[43]. The GCC is currently the European Union's (EU) fifth largest export market and the EU is the GCC's second largest trading partner[44] and follows the main international provisions of the General Agreement on Trade and Tariffs (GATT), WTO and TRIPs. In the case of the GCC, these have been supplemented by further negotiations regarding international provisions concerning intellectual property.

The GCC has a strong desire to develop national laws and regulations in regard to intellectual property rights to bring it on a par with legislative and regulatory developments in the international arena. In the economic agreement between the GCC states, adopted by the GCC Supreme Council, the preamble states a desire to;

*"to enhance the economy of the GCC Member States in the light of recent global economic developments which require further integration among the Member States to strengthen their negotiating position competitive capacity in international markets*[45]*"*.

**Table 1: Gulf States and Ratified International Treaties**[46]

| Treaty | Kuwait | Bahrain | Oman | UAE | Saudi Arabia | Qatar |
|---|---|---|---|---|---|---|
| Berne Convention | | ✓ | ✓ | ✓ | ✓ | ✓ |
| Brussels Convention | | ✓ | ✓ | | | |
| Budapest Treaty | | | ✓ | | | |
| Hague Agreement | | | ✓ | | | |
| Madrid Protocol | | ✓ | ✓ | | | |
| Nairobi Treaty | | | ✓ | | | ✓ |
| Nice Agreement | | ✓ | | | | |
| Paris Convention | | ✓ | ✓ | ✓ | ✓ | ✓ |
| Patent Cooperation Treaty | | ✓ | ✓ | ✓ | | ✓ |
| Patent Law Treaty | | | ✓ | | | |
| Rome Convention | | ✓ | | ✓ | | |
| Trademark Law Treaty | | ✓ | ✓ | | | |
| UPOV Convention | | | ✓ | | | |
| WIPO Convention | ✓ | ✓ | ✓ | ✓ | ✓ | ✓ |
| WIPO Copyright Treaty | | ✓ | ✓ | | | ✓ |
| WIPO Performances and Phonograms Treaty | | ✓ | ✓ | | | ✓ |

The economic agreement covers trade, international economic relations, the GCC common market, scientific and technical research, development and infrastructure. In relation to international economic relations, the economic agreement focuses on securing better terms and more favourable conditions in their international economic relationships by conducting economic relations in a collective manner when dealing with other countries, blocs and regional groupings, as well as other regional and international organisations. The table below shows all international agreements that each GCC state is a signatory to and highlights the full spectrum of international intellectual property treaties and conventions from the most compliant of the GCC states to the least.

## 4 The GCC as a Collection of Rentier States

The six states have similar autocratic monarchies, political and cultural identities, which historically stem from Islamic beliefs. Unlike other international bodies, the GCC is unique in that all its member states are Islamic states. Each individual state has varying degrees of sharia law incorporated in their constitutions as seen below:

**Table 2: Impact of Sharia on GCC Constitutions**

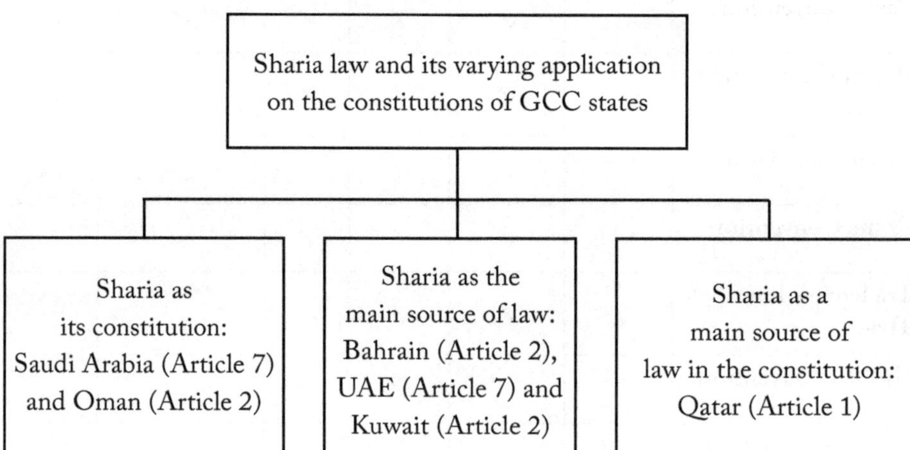


There are unique features that are associated with the GCC union states as it is the only union where member states share similar infrastructures. For example, a substantial part of the revenues derived by the GCC states are from oil and gas exports; they are essentially small populations and the governments are dependent on their large oil and gas reserves[47]. The GCC states are often referred to as rentier states because of their government structures and due to the fact they share certain commonalities such as providing economic necessities for citizens, no state tax and large populations of foreign labour in the private sector[48].

Each of the Gulf rentier states have undergone significant development since the early 1980s and continue to develop[49]. However each state differs in terms of governance, religious influence, intellectual property development and economic progression. Specific to intellectual property, all six states ascended to the WTO between a ten-year span, from 1995 and 2005. Whereas most of the GCC states became WTO members in close proximity to each other, Saudi Arabia lagged significantly behind by nearly a decade. Given Saudi Arabia has prominence within the GCC and several decision-making seats, the time Saudi Arabia took to reach a decision can be linked to the constitutional significance of sharia law. This is discussed further in Chapter 3[50].

Variations in economic progression are best seen through the ratio of government debt to gross domestic product (GDP) in each state[51]. It needs to be noted that there are a series of external factors which influence economic progression in a country and for the purpose of this research the focus is intellectual property; therefore the role of intellectual property in economic progression against other variables is outside the scope of this research.

Saudi Arabia and Kuwait are similar as they are at the lower end of both debt to GDP and international agreements. Qatar, UAE and Bahrain also show similarities in debt to GDP and international agreements, they have the three highest debt figures and more international treaties in place than Saudi Arabia and Kuwait. Oman is an anomaly in that its debt to GDP is low and it is a signatory to the most international treaties. There are other variables which contribute to a state's debt to GDP as intellectual property is one determinant for foreign direct investment. Other factors that impact on a state's GDP include human capital, physical capital, technology, fiscal productivity, research, labour productivity through exports and cost of imports.

## 5 Development of Intellectual Property Laws

To date, each individual Gulf state has developed its intellectual property laws at varying rates. The general pattern of change has been to deviate from a sharia based discretionary exercise of personal authority towards a codification of laws[52]. In theory, the Gulf states now display a set of intellectual property laws that are largely compliant with TRIPS. The GCC states have enacted detailed legislation to improve their intellectual property laws by introducing criminal prosecutions and civil sanctions. Intellectual property offices are set up in each GCC state offering intellectual property right holders a legal recourse where their rights have been infringed[53]. Further intellectual property laws have been enacted to meet TRIPS standards as seen later in this chapter[54].

In order to raise existing TRIPS provisions to TRIPS Plus standards, in line with international trade agreement requirements, the GCC states have to consider whether there is enough scope in their current laws to comply with TRIPS plus provisions. This is the fundamental question at the core of the TRIPS Plus dichotomy, do the GCC states further develop their intellectual property legislation as required in international trade agreements or do they reconsider their standpoint?

This is a key question for both the GCC states and their international partners as at the heart of all the developments in intellectual property is the potential to increase economic progression and foreign direct investment (FDI). Foreign direct investment is where a company is based in one country and makes an investment in a foreign country by setting up a subsidiary, a joint venture or an associate entity. The foreign company has a minimum 10% of the voting stock, and it invests equity and capital to generate earnings and contribute to the host country's fiscal developments[55].

Foreign direct investment is actively sought by the GCC states and forms part of the GCC unified economic agreement[56]. From an economics point of view, foreign investment is more likely to take place where host countries have strong intellectual property protection. This is largely due to gaining investor confidence by offering legal remedies that can reduce the risks of infringement and leads to an economic boost for protected products[57]. This has a positive effect on the volume of foreign direct investment (FDI) as foreign firms are able to compete effectively in developing countries knowing there are intellectual property laws in place to safeguard against infringement and offer remedies.[58]

Foreign direct investment is need driven, therefore it will always exist in some shape or form, even when intellectual property rights are not as developed as the foreign investors would require; however by increasing compliance, the path to economic progression has an increased chance of success.

## 6 Saudi Arabia

In terms of size, Saudi Arabia is the largest country in the GCC and is the world's largest oil exporter. It has 17% of the world's proven oil reserves and is the largest exporter of petroleum. Given its mass oil reserves and production, Saudi Arabia's economy is heavily dependent on oil income. Further, due to Saudi Arabia's extensive oil reserves, policies and procedures on export rules and tariffs are regularly reviewed as there is a direct impact on the global energy sector.

Saudi Arabia is an absolute monarchy which was ruled by King Abdullah bin Abdul Aziz Al Saud, who is now succeeded by King Salman bin Abdul Aziz Al Saud. Salman is the head of state and Prime Minister of Saudi Arabia. Article 1 of its Basic Law of Government states the Holy Qur'an is the constitution[59] while governance is according to Islamic law. Out of all the GCC states, Saudi Arabia's judicial system is the most reliant on sharia principles[60] in relation to decision making in its criminal and civil courts.

Although the Saudi Arabian judiciary claims an independent status, its decisions cannot contravene sharia law and must reflect sharia principles as set out in the constitution[61]. The majority of the Muslim population is Sunni Muslim, with the Saud family following Wahabbism[62]. In Islamic law, there are four main schools of jurisprudence; Hanbali, Hanafi, Shafai and Maliki[63]. The Saudi courts and judicial committees apply the Hanbali school of jurisprudence[64].

Saudi Arabia has a dual court system; the sharia courts and the board of grievances. Since 2007 Saudi Arabia has spent nearly $2bn on overhauling its judicial system in an effort to streamline the legal process. Under the Basic Law of Governance in Saudi Arabia, the King has ultimate authority over all branches of the State[65]. The executive branch has the King as the chief of state and head of government. The cabinet consists of a council of Ministers appointed by the monarch every four years and includes many royal family members.

Intellectual property legislation is a recent phenomenon for the GCC states and has brought about a vanguard of change in the intellectual property sector. Saudi Arabia had been negotiating its membership since July 1993; progress was slow in Saudi Arabia as a minimum level of TRIPS compliance was required to complete ascension to the WTO[66]. Saudi Arabia eventually joined the WTO in 2005[67]. Therefore, it took a twelve-year period for Saudi Arabia to develop from a pre-TRIPS model of intellectual property law protection to a TRIPS compliance stage[68]. Although this is not the longest time period for TRIPS compliance, the time taken by Saudi Arabia to reach TRIPS compliance was three times that of Oman. Despite the time taken to reach TRIPS compliance, Saudi Arabia does now have extensive national legislation covering intellectual property law[69].

## 7 Oman

Oman is a small province and Sultan Qaboos bin Said is the Head of State, Supreme Commander of the Armed Forces and Royal Oman Police[70]. As in Saudi Arabia, the constitution sets out very clearly that the basis of law is sharia law as stated at Article 2[71]. The majority of the Omani population follow the Ibadhi Muslim interpretation of Islam, with the remaining divided between Sunni, Shia and Hindu.

Oman has provisions in its legal system to allow non-Muslims to practice their religion which reflects the influence western laws have had on Oman[72]. The legislative structure has undergone reform, the Basic Statute of the State sets out at Article 58 that the Oman Council shall consist of the Shura Council[73] and the State Council[74]. The State Council's members include former ministers, undersecretaries, ambassadors, judges, senior officers and experts in specific fields.

The legal system in Oman is similar to the civil law system, heavily influenced by Egyptian and French law[75]. In 1981, the Sultan ordered the establishment of the Consultative Council to provide Oman's citizens with opportunities to participate in the country's government[76]. The legislative branch of the Omani Government consists of a bicameral body[77] comprising of two chambers. The upper house has 70 members appointed by the monarch and has advisory powers only[78]. The lower chamber of 84 members is elected by popular vote[79]. Under the Royal Decree 13/97 of 1997 commercial courts were established with a three-tier structure, with the Supreme Court in Muscat; six courts of appeals and 45 primary courts in various parts of the country[80].

In 1996, Oman joined the WIPO and the treaty came into force shortly after[81]. Oman achieved TRIPS compliance and WTO membership within four years of starting the process, achieving WTO membership in 2000. Oman entered into a Free Trade Agreement (FTA) with the United States in 2009[82], one of the key issues in the agreement being to strengthen intellectual property rights protection and enforcement[83]. Oman's intellectual property law has developed in line with western jurisdictions[84].

Currently, Oman has national legislation to govern a number of intellectual property areas including copyright[85], industrial property[86], protection of breeders' rights[87], consumer protection[88], civil and commercial procedure[89] and national heritage[90]. On an international level, Oman has ratified the highest number of intellectual property treaties followed closely by Bahrain[91]. Oman has good trade links with the US; the United States-Oman FTA 2006 built on existing FTAs to promote economic reform and to improve intellectual property rights protection and enforcement[92].

## 8 Bahrain

Bahrain is a small, independent Islamic Arab State which achieved independence from Britain in 1971 and has close ties with Britain and the US[93]. Given the historical presence of Britain in Bahrain, its legal system reflects traditional English law principles[94]. The US Navy has a long and established presence in Bahrain[95]. Bahrain, along with its oil reserves, stands out as a banking and financial services centre; its reasonably prosperous economy makes it less dependent on oil than other Gulf states[96]. However, given Bahrain does not have the same level of oil reserves as its neighbours[97], it is imperative for Bahrain to develop other areas to drive its economy.

The Bahraini government adopted a second constitution on 14 February 2002 which amended the first constitution of 1975, changing the country's name to the "Kingdom of Bahrain"[98].

The new constitution established a hereditary constitutional monarchy with a bicameral parliament[99]. The constitution has developed a doctrine of separation of powers with the formation of the National Assembly as it is responsible for regulating legislative powers through an elected lower chamber of parliament and an independent judiciary[100]. The elected Council of Representatives and the all-appointed Shura Council together establish the National Assembly[101]. The Supreme Council of the Judiciary was established by Decree Law No. 19 of 2000. The legal system of Bahrain is based on several sources, including customary tribal law (urf), Islamic law and civil law[102]. Sharia law is a principal source of legislation[103]. The civil courts comprise of a three-tier system: the Courts of Minor Causes, which have jurisdiction over civil and commercial matters, the Middle Courts, which have jurisdiction over criminal matters and at the top level is the High Court of Appeal[104].

Although Oman has the highest number of international agreements in intellectual property law, Bahrain has the most intellectual property legislation overall when compared to other GCC states, as it has legislated the most at the national level[105] and has ratified eleven treaties at the international level[106]. Bahrain was the first of the GCC states to agree a free trade agreement with the US, which came into force in 2006[107].

Bahrain is continually reforming and amending its intellectual property laws. Bahrain's Shura Council members have approved the amendments to the intellectual property protection law in relation to out of court settlements and exemptions for educational use of intellectual property[108]. Intellectual property protection is tasked to the Directorate of Industrial Property in the Ministry of Industry and Commerce to set up internal infrastructures to improve intellectual property rights protection.

## 9 Qatar

Qatar is another small GCC state and similar to Saudi Arabia in that it is rich in natural gas and oil reserves, which has boosted its economy[109]. It is an independent sovereign Arab State and has been ruled by the Al-Thani family since it gained independence from Britain in 1971[110]. Sheikh Hamad bin Khalifa Al-Thani was the Emir of the State of Qatar up until 2013 and has been succeeded by his fourth son, Sheikh Tamim bin Hamad bin Khalifa Al Thani. Qatar has a similar autocratic system to its neighbouring GCC states. The Qatari constitution sets itself apart from the other GCC states as seen in Table 2[111]. It is not exclusively sharia-based like Saudi Arabia and Oman, nor does it have sharia as a main source of law like the remaining GCC states.[112] Instead, it has sharia as a source of law as stated at Article 1 of the Qatari Constitution; "*its religion is Islam and Sharia law is a main source of its legislations*"[113].

The legislative authority in Qatar is developing towards a more semi-democratic model. The legislative branch of Qatar is established in the Advisory Council, which approves the general policy of the government and exercises control over the executive authority[114]. The Advisory Council consists of 45 members. Thirty of them are elected directly by secret ballot, while the remaining 15 are appointed by the Emir from among ministers or others[115]. Although the Constitution does not directly deal with the protection of intellectual property rights, Article 27 of the Constitution recognizes the right to private property. Also, Article 24 protects and encourages the dissemination of arts, science, national and cultural heritage[116].

Qatar shares similarities with Bahrain in terms of its national intellectual property legislation with a number of intellectual property areas covered by statute[117]. In 2009 Qatar set up the Centre for the Protection of Intellectual Property Rights. It operates within the Ministry of Justice and gives the justice minister the authority to appoint independent experts to help the centre carry out its functions.

## 10 The United Arab Emirates

The United Arab Emirates, (UAE), is a federation of seven monarchies[118]. Its main revenues derive from oil, construction industry and tourism. Free trade zones exist in UAE, whereby foreign ownership is permitted at 100 percent with zero taxation, to help diversify the economy. Outside of the free trade zones, any foreign investment must be owned by a UAE national by at least 51 percent of the business.

The system of governance is monarchic with the exception that there is a federal head[119]. Islam is the State religion and sharia is the main source of legislation[120]. Abu Dhabi has natural oil reserves that account for approximately 90 percent of UAE oil production and allows Abu Dhabi to take a leading role in political and economic decision-making[121]. The federal system of government is composed of a Supreme Council, the Council of Ministers, a Federal National Council (FNC) that acts as a parliamentary body and the independent judiciary through the Federal Supreme Court[122]. The Supreme Council is the highest constitutional authority; it elects a president and vice-president from amongst them to serve for a renewable five-year term in office[123]. The Supreme Council re-elected President Sheikh Khalifa bin Zayed Al Nahyan in November 2009; he is also the current ruler of Abu Dhabi.

The UAE joined the WIPO in 1974 and started addressing the issue of intellectual property protection[124]. National legislation exists in many areas of intellectual property including copyright[125], trademarks[126], industrial designs[127] and other areas[128]. The UAE patent system operates under two systems; the Patent Cooperation Treaty (PCT) system for domestic patents, and the GCC Patent system for regional patent applications[129]. The UAE is also a signatory to several international treaties which puts it on par with Qatar's international obligations but below Oman and Bahrain[130]. The UAE can be seen to value a knowledge-based economy as part of its strategy is to promote and enhance innovation, research and development by promoting and protecting intellectual property rights.

Further, the UAE is the first of the Middle Eastern countries to host the World Expo. It is a global event that spans several months and takes place every 5 years. It was initiated in London in 1851 and has continued to act as a global community conference to share business developments that impact global economy, sustainability and innovations. The World Expo exhibition is a catalyst to making progress on issues of international prominence such as economic transformation, cultural development and social regeneration[131]. Specifically for the UAE and the GCC region as a whole, hosting the World Expo further cements the region as a dynamic hub for global commerce and the link between the East and West. In relation to intellectual property development, the build up to 2020 was the optimum platform to drive innovation from local and international investors to meet consumer needs and increase infrastructure capacities at a national government level and regionally. By acting as a hub, Dubai has an opportunity to define its intellectual property future and by association that of the remaining GCC states, to develop an integrated working model of intellectual property rights protection that incorporates their traditional values with international obligations[132].

## 11 Kuwait

Kuwait is ruled by Amir Sabah al-Ahmad al-Jabr Al Sabah[133] and has a modest population size.

It is a hereditary Emirate, with all rulers chosen from the Al Sabah family. It has a substantial crude oil reserve, second in the region behind Saudi Arabia, with 10% of the world's natural oil reserves. Oil, at 90% of export revenues, is the main revenue for Kuwait. It is a fully sovereign state with sharia as a main source of legislation[134]. It was the first of the GCC states to have a constitution[135] and formed a precedent for other Gulf states[136]. It seeks to have a partly democratic composition in Parliament, similar to Qatar, as Parliament consists of fifty representatives who are directly elected; with a further fifteen members appointed by the Emir[137]. The Kuwait legal system is based on civil law jurisdiction[138] and has a clear system of separation of powers, distinguishing between the legislative and executive branches of government[139]. The Kuwait constitution does not refer to intellectual property, however Article 18 (1) of the Constitution refers to private property rights[140]. Intellectual property development in Kuwait is not at the same level of Bahrain, Qatar, Oman and UAE. Kuwait currently has four statutes dealing with intellectual property[141].

Kuwait is on the US Special 301 Report Watch List for its lack of progress on enforcement efforts against piracy and counterfeiting. The main shortcomings identified by the report were the failure of the judiciary to enforce penalties that were seen as severe enough to act as a deterrent to intellectual property infringement and the lack of legislative reform in Kuwaiti copyright law.

## 12 Conclusion to the Background of the GCC States

Intellectual property laws in the GCC states have a very clear development timeline. From the 1970s onwards each autocratic monarchy has developed its own national laws and generally they have all chosen to follow a Western style legal framework. The GCC focus is to develop international standards as this has become a growing challenge for the development and diversification of national exports and international trade[142]. Each state varies in its number of international agreements with Kuwait being signed up to one international treaty while Oman has 13 international treaties in force. The number of national and international membership for each State can be linked to the weight sharia holds in legislative matters. The six GCC states can be separated in respect to the level of sharia compliance observed. The strictest following of sharia law is by Saudi Arabia which cites sharia as the constitution of the state. Below Saudi Arabia is Oman which has sharia as the basis of legislation. Qatar follows behind Oman with sharia considered to be the main source of law and lastly Qatar, Bahrain and Kuwait have sharia as a main source of law.

Improvements in the enforcement of intellectual property rights and protection from infringement, from a GCC perspective, have been slow. In terms of patent protection, the GCC Patent Office started receiving applications for patents in 1998; however, given that it did not have TRIPS standards until 2001, the first patent application was not granted until 2002[143]. Of the patents granted by the GCC, the majority of the innovators are non-residents. Therefore, there is a much greater demand for intellectual property protection by non-residents than GCC nationals. This ties in neatly with the current demands on the GCC states to adopt more stringent intellectual property provisions under TRIPS plus as the protection is aimed at benefiting foreign innovators with the knock-on positive effect of increased foreign direct investment.

This chapter has provided a background overview of the six GCC states and the GCC itself. The brief historical look at the states adds context to the understanding of their infrastructure, governance and shapes current legislative procedures. The intellectual property issues that exist in the GCC states will be analysed and examined to reflect their developments to date in later chapters. However, before considering the intellectual property issues, there is an anomaly raised in this chapter which will be addressed next. All of the GCC states abide by sharia law as per their constitutions and all have adopted a suite of intellectual property laws without integrating sharia law principles. Therefore Chapter 3 will examine the relevant sharia law principles to intellectual property right protection in order to inform the main recommendations for an integrated approach to intellectual property rights protection.

# 3

# The Development of Intellectual Property under Sharia Law Principles in the GCC States

## 1 Introduction

This chapter will identify key sharia law principles to show that there are three key stages in the development of intellectual property in the GCC states; a foundation stage, a development stage and an advanced stage. This chapter will focus on the foundation stage and will show how intellectual property is justifiable under sharia law. The findings of the chapter will inform the content of the key research outcomes around; developing an integrated approach to intellectual property in the GCC and progressing from the foundation stage to a development stage that incorporates sharia principles with western style intellectual property provisions.

The GCC states are historically Islamic states and they have all incorporated sharia law into their written constitutions as discussed in Chapter 2[144]. The influence of sharia law principles is not ubiquitous among all six of the GCC states as each state is independent in how it governs and develops national laws. Among all the GCC states, the main primary source of sharia law is the Quran, however what weight sharia law has in influencing the law-making process and legislative developments differs from state to state. Saudi Arabia has sharia as the source of law[145], for Oman it is the basis of legislation[146] and for Qatar, UAE and Kuwait it is a main source of law[147]. This leaves Bahrain with sharia as a principal source of law at a constitutional level[148].

Despite the uniform banner of the GCC, how individual GCC countries observe sharia laws and incorporate religion into their intellectual property law development differs from state to state. Intellectual property law, in the GCC states, has developed in line with the WIPO and TRIPS standards and therefore the states have adopted a number of western style intellectual property laws[149]. To fully understand the influence of sharia law on intellectual property development, it is necessary to consider Islamic jurisprudence in this area and draw attention to the relevant intellectual property references from the four main sources of Islamic law[150].

Existing intellectual property laws in the Gulf have been criticised for lacking teeth and effective enforcement.[151] The study of sharia law in relation to intellectual property is key to the successful implementation of intellectual property as through Islamic principles citizens of Islamic states can identify with the rights as opposed to seeing them as principles imposed through western thinking and accompanying law making structures.

As the GCC states currently stand, they all have sharia enshrined in their constitutions and secular laws regulating intellectual property. Although sharia does not prohibit intellectual property protection or enforcement in the Gulf, the two concepts lack a catalyst principle to amalgamate the Islamic jurisprudence to enhance intellectual property development in the region and satisfy international agreements[152]. This is the main reason as to the intention behind proposing an integrated intellectual property framework in the GCC which can harmonise intellectual property with Islamic law through an Islamic law perspective as currently Islamic law is being forced to fit around international intellectual property laws, creating a square peg in a round hole scenario.

Intellectual property legislation has developed in the Gulf over a period of thirty years as has been discussed in Chapter 1. As the states do not lack minimum intellectual property legislation, the reason for analysing sharia principles is to address the lack of protection offered as opposed to the enactment of the laws[153].

In this chapter there are two main objectives:

- To give an overview of the principles of sharia law and analyse the influence of sharia law on intellectual property protection and enforcement. Primary and secondary sources of sharia law will be examined to draw clear conclusions on the influence of sharia law sources on intellectual property rights development.
- To consider the research to date on the relationship between sharia law and intellectual property to understand sharia law principles for intellectual property with specific reference to defining intellectual property within the laws of Islam and addressing the international demand for higher standards of intellectual property protection.

## 2 Overview of Sharia Law Principles

*"Classical Muslim methodology (usul) refers to the basic textual sources and methods used in producing Muslim attitudes in different spheres of life including international relations.*

*These sources are the Qur'an, Sunnah, ijma (consensus), and ijtihad (the use of human reason or aql) in elaboration and interpretation of the Shari'ah. Ijtihad includes the fourth major source of Muslim thought, the qiyas (analogy)*"[154].

Sharia law impacts on protection parameters in respect of copyright, patent and trademark protection[155]. The GCC states have enacted intellectual property laws in copyrights, trademarks, patents, trade names, integrated circuits, industrial designs and plant varieties on the stipulation that the intellectual property asset is not prohibited by Islam nor does it significantly harm the doctrine of public interest[156].

The influence of sharia on intellectual property is dependent on three main factors: applying Islamic law principles to support the protection of intellectual property law, identifying provisions to protect intellectual property rights with the aim of increasing innovations and stimulate economic development and assessing the effectiveness of intellectual property law against society both recognising and accepting it[157]. To address the three main factors identified above, the remainder of this chapter is dedicated to applying Islamic law principles to support the protection of intellectual property law through an analysis of primary and secondary sharia law sources. Secondly, provisions will be identified in Chapters 5 and 6 that can better protect intellectual property rights with the aim of increasing innovation and stimulate economic development[158]. Thirdly, an assessment of the dependence of intellectual property law development on society both recognising and accepting it will be carried out in Chapters 6 and 7[159].

The argument by some Islamic scholars against intellectual property protection is based on the principle that the level of effort invested in producing the intellectual property asset is heavily outweighed by the profit made, however the main counter argument for this is that not all the assets of an intellectual property right holder are profitable and therefore by denying a monopoly right, intellectual property development is hindered as innovation is stifled[160].

## 3 Primary Sources of Sharia Law

Sharia law is a legal framework developed primarily from the Quran and where the Quran is clear and unambiguous on setting a legal precedent, other sources of law are subordinate to the Quran. It is split into 114 chapters and is considered to be a compilation of the verbal revelations given to the Prophet Muhammad over a period of twenty-two years from God through the Angel Gabriel[161]. The chapters of the Quran are known as "surahs". Each chapter is broken down into "ayas" (verses) and has a specific title covering a particular topic. The structure of the chapters varies, the longest chapter being the second chapter, titled "*Al-Baqarah*" (Arabic for *The Cow*), containing 292 ayas and also containing the longest ayat at verse 282. The second chapter is relevant to intellectual property protection as it details Islamic jurisprudence on financial matters including debiting money, lending, borrowing and interest. The key ayas from the second chapter of the Quran that deal with business ethics are from verse 252 to 286. The Quran gives a moral framework for Muslims to abide by and integrates all aspects of life in to its 114 chapters[162]. The Quran is deemed authentic text by Muslims and as such no part, surah or ayat, can be amended or disregarded[163].

To supplement the Quran, the Sunnah is the second most important source of authority. The Sunnah is based on model behaviour of the Prophet Muhammed, statements and sayings which have been collected and recorded as short reports known as hadiths. The Quran and Sunnah are seen as primary sources of Islam whereas other sources, such as ijma and qiyas, are considered secondary. Unlike conventional primary sources of law, such as common law and legislation, the primary sources of Islamic law are based on a divine law. It does not have the same historical development linked with societal progression in western laws; there is no binding precedent or amendable legislation[164]. However, what the Quran and Sunnah do allow for is the interpretation of primary sources of sharia law in regard to translation and approval. The Quran is considered as the word of God, therefore it supersedes any historical law making that was in place prior to its revelation and cannot be altered[165].

From an intellectual property stance, the Quranic revelations were at a time when intellectual property rights did not exist. Thus, the Quran predates any cultural norm approach, within Islamic or western states, to intellectual property protection. Knowledge in the Quran is protected as the word of God and was revealed to the Prophet Muhammed as an intangible asset on the basis that is a divine asset that has been bestowed upon mankind[166]. The knowledge from the Quran was then extended upon by the Sunnah as a form of teaching how the Quran should be applied. For example, primary sharia sources on property rights are not expressly limited to tangible property and therefore Quranic references on proprietary rights have been extended to intellectual property rights, as will be discussed later in this chapter (8).

The source of law in the Quran, is God, as in Surah Yusuf, Verse 40, the text states; *"Legislation is not but for Allah"*[167] and therefore the Quran stipulates mankind to be a trustee of the knowledge passed down in the Quran. As the number of extensive legal references in the Quran and Sunnah are limited, secondary sources of Islamic jurisprudence have been developed over the centuries. Islam is established as a divine law encompassing belief (Imān), ethics and moral character (Iḥsān).

## 4 Overview of Secondary Sources of Sharia Law

The secondary sources of sharia law act as a framing device used to set precedents where the Quran and/or sunnah have not provided sufficient, if any, guidance to reach a consensus. The two main sources of secondary law are ijma and qiyas. Ijma, is a source of law that is applied when consensus on a point of law is needed that has not been adequately dealt with by the primary sources[168]. Qiyas is a form of analogical reasoning as Adigun describes qiyas as "… *a mode of reasoning to legislate for novel questions, to reveal the divine rule of law and to harmonize between divine legislation and human interests*"[169].

### *Ijma as a Secondary Source of Sharia Law*

Of the two secondary sources, Ijma is ranked as the third source of law due to it originating from a unanimous viewpoint, after the Quran and Sunnah. There are two forms of ijma. Firstly, the authentic ijma is the consensus of the Prophet Mohammed's companions. Second is a consensus of an interpretation of Islamic law scholars in a particular country, on a particular issue, in a specific moment[170]. A scholar also known as an "Ulama", when presented with an interpretation matter, applies ijtihad (their own reasoning) to come to an interpretation. The reason ijma is ranked as the third source is due to it originating from a unanimous viewpoint. There are references from the Quran to support the use of ijma. For example, Surah Imran at Verse 103 reads; "*hold fast to the rope of Allah, all of you, and do not split into factions*"[171]. The historic Sunnah reference used to reach a consensus and validate ijma is in the hadith of the Prophet Muhammed stating; "*My community will never agree upon an error*[172]".

### *Qiyas as a Secondary Source of Sharia Law*

Qiyas is a fairly limited concept and ranks as the fourth source of law. The literal meaning of qiyas is to ascertain the weight and quality of something. In terms of qiyas methodology, scholars apply it through four distinct areas; as an original case (Asl), a new case (Far), an effective cause (Illah) and a ruling (Hukm)[173]. The method is to find a verse in the Quran, in Sunnah or a rule on which consensus was achieved as the point of departure. The direct purpose must be determined, and the relationship between the rule, and the question considered in extending the rule, must be clearly explained to justify the extension of the rule.

A common example of qiyas is in the extension of the Quranic prohibition on drinking wine which is found in the Quran at Surah Maidah, Verse 90, which states; "*O you who have believed, surely wine…are only an abomination of Ash-Shaytan's (The all-vicious, the Devil) doing, so avoid it, that possibly you would prosper*"[174]. The point of departure can be established here as a ban on wine drinking. From the four essential areas of analogical reasoning, Asl has been applied to extend the original case, of a prohibition from wine, to a unanimous consensus by Ulamas to apply qiyas reasoning to extend the ban to all alcoholic drinks[175]. Qiyas are relevant to Islamic justification for intellectual property protection as analogical reasoning is applied to Quranic rules on proprietary rights, contract law, international transactions and public interest to justify intellectual property rights as will be seen later in this chapter (7)-(12). The relationship between sharia and intellectual property rights protection is further analysed in Chapters 5 and 7[176].

## 5 Criticism of Secondary Sources of Sharia Law

The main criticism of secondary sources has to be their lack of uniformity, the application of ijma and qiyas varies depending on the school of thought followed by each individual country and region[177]. There are four main schools of Islamic jurisprudence; Hanbali, Shafii, Maliki, and Hanafi. Hanbali is followed by Saudi Arabia and is the strictest of the four schools, employing Qiyas only as a last resort[178]. The Shafii school of thought is more widely accepted as it allows the application of qiyas to make legitimate analogies[179]. The Maliki school differs slightly from the other schools as it relies on historical customs and practice of the Medinan people as a source and is observed in Kuwait, Bahrain and the United Arab Emirates.

The final school, Hanafi, gives consideration to the four main sources as discussed above, however if a consensus cannot be reached then historical custom and practice is considered along with juristic preference (Istishan). In the GCC, intellectual property protection has been considered as sharia compliant although the approval is not attributed to any one school of thought[180]. There is criticism that the use of secondary sources for the basis of intellectual property laws should not be allowed as the Quran and Sunnah are a form of intellectual property from which new inferences should not be made[181]. The main argument against the use of secondary sources to justify intellectual property rights has always revolved around the fact that that intellectual property is a new concept that is not regulated by Sharia, and as a result, not protected according to its principles[182].

## 6 Conduct under Sharia Law

Once a relevant rule under sharia has been determined, the relevant conduct under the rule must then be determined[183]. There are five types of conduct under sharia: mandatory, recommended, permitted, recommended against, and banned[184]. As a result, some areas of law have been governed under a strong sharia influence and others have not. The table below highlights the main types of conduct and roles of sharia law:

**Table 3: The Five Types of Conduct under Sharia**

- Conduct under Sharia Law
  - Mandatory (*wajib*) acts must be followed with sources in Quran and Sunnah e.g. Criminal Law and Family Law
    - Permitted (*mubah*) e.g. Intellectual Property Law
    - Recommended (*mustahab*) e.g. Divorce Law
  - Banned (*muharam*) acts are prohibited in the Quran and Sunnah e.g. surrogacy, Interest and unjust enrichment in Contract Law, Business and Islamic Finance.
    - Prohibited (*makruh*) e.g. social issues

## 7 Classifying Intellectual Property Law

Intellectual property cannot be classed as mandatory or recommended as it is not mentioned in the primary sources of sharia law. Likewise there is an argument that it cannot be classed as recommended against or banned for the same reason[185]. This has left the majority of scholarly work in the area on whether intellectual property protection can be permitted under sharia law to draw inferences from sharia law on property law, contract law and public interest[186].

### *No Quranic Reference for Intellectual Property Law*

The Quran makes no reference to intellectual property law and therefore makes no legal provisions in its regulation[187]. In terms of applicability, there is an argument that there is an inherent weakness in producing new laws in areas where there is no Quranic or Sunnah reference[188]. Laws that can be identified from primary sharia sources have more weight in Islamic courts and in legislation. For example, punishments in criminal law can be found in both the Quran and Sunnah, as a result many Islamic countries still have capital punishment. It is generally accepted that an argument against intellectual property on the main ground that it is not mentioned in the Quran and Sunnah is weak given that there are several areas of law that are not expressly mentioned in the primary sources however secondary sources have been used to establish legal norms.

An example is in the use of qiyas in defining classes of women that are prohibited to a man for marriage. The Quran refers to certain women that a man cannot marry at Surah Nisa at Verse 23; "*prohibited to you [for marriage] are your mothers, your daughters, your sisters, your father's sisters, your mother's sisters, your brother's daughters, your sister's daughters, your [milk] mothers who nursed you, your sisters through nursing, your wives' mothers, and your step-daughters under your guardianship [born] of your wives unto whom you have gone in. But if you have not gone in unto them, there is no sin upon you. And [also prohibited are] the wives of your sons who are from your [own] loins, and that you take [in marriage] two sisters simultaneously*"[189]. The verse does not account for the father's aunt; however through jurist use of analogical reasoning, the father and mother's aunts are prohibited because the reasoning takes into account the close proximity in a blood relationship[190].

### *Inferential Reasoning for Intellectual Property Law*

Intellectual property has been understood using inferential reasoning as the topic is a new concept[191]. Legal reasoning in property law, contract law and public interest has formed the basis of sharia approval for intellectual property protection[192]. Islamic law on proprietary rights is the most obvious example of established law that can be manipulated to support intellectual property.

## 8 The Use of Proprietary Rights to Justify Intellectual Property Law

*"Property institutions fundamentally shape a society. These legal relationships between individuals, different sorts of objects, and the state are not easy to justify. This is especially true of intellectual property".*[193]

### *John Locke on Property as a Natural Right*

Proprietary rights in law have been in existence for many centuries[194]. Leading philosophers, Immanuel Kant and John Locke, have written significant pieces of work to influence and shape proprietary rights[195]. John Locke, in his work entitled *Locke's Second Treatise on Civil Government,* defines proprietary rights in its simplest form in the appropriation of an apple from a tree at Chapter 5. He ascribes the labour used to collect apples to a private right; "*the apples he gathered from the trees in the wood, has certainly appropriated them to himself. Nobody can deny but the nourishment is his. I ask then, when did they begin to be his? when he digested? or when he eat? or when he boiled? or when he brought them home? or when he picked them up? and it is plain, if the first gathering made them not his, nothing else could. That labour put a distinction between them and common: that added something to them more than nature, the common mother of all, had done; and so they became his private right"*[196].

From his initial work on property rights, Locke developed the labour theory that people have a right to the fruits of their labour. Locke believed that the labour right is a natural right, not dependent on the particular laws in a society[197].

## *The Sunnah on Property as a Natural Right*

The Sunnah also makes reference to property rights as a right under natural law[198]. The Sunnah is translated as the path to be followed by all Muslims based on the example of the Prophet Muhammad. The Quran stipulates such following at Surah Al Ahzab Verse 21; *"There has certainly been for you in the Messenger of Allah an excellent pattern"*. Given the Sunnah is based on the example, legislative actions, character, manners, and habits of the Prophet there is a large body of Sunnah from which specific references can be found to justify intellectual property rights protection. Examples from the Sunnah include: *"no person's property is lawful to be taken except by his consent"*[199] and *"he who cultivates barren land is entitled to the ownership of that land"*[200]. The barren land can equate to the idea in intellectual property which in itself is not protected, the cultivation of the barren land represented the expression of the idea and it is this expression that makes the inventor entitled to intellectual property protection.

Consent is also a key principle in Islamic property rights. Where consent is not given, a person looking after the property of another is a trustee of the property and on the trust that the property will be returned to its legal owner. Applying this to intellectual property, Muslims act as trustees of knowledge based asset, not owners of the protected knowledge and must use the asset with the permission of the right holder[201]. Therefore there is a strong equity analogy rooted in the Sunnah principles that have been written to establish property rights as natural rights. The right of a beneficiary under a trust allows action to be taken against people to impose sanctions or injunctions. The right of a beneficiary is a proprietary right because it is effective against third parties and therefore there are classes of proprietary rights which exist in Islamic law. The law of equity is instrumental in the creation of some intellectual property rights such as trademarks, equitable actions for breach of confidence and passing off. Equity therefore serves as a form of analogical reasoning, providing an effective cause between the original Islamic rights of property, Asr, aligned with a new case, Far, for intellectual property rights[202].

## *Quranic Proprietary Rights to Justify Intellectual Property Law*

Quranic verses make precise references to proprietary rights[203]. The common theme of the Quranic verses is to strive with your efforts in your property and has formed a basis for a similarity to the Lockean labour theory[204]. Theoretically there is a strong foundation of knowledge within the Quran and Sunnah in relation to property law which can be connected to intellectual property[205]. A Quranic reference is made in the Surah An-Najm, Verse 39, linking Locke's labour theory to Islamic proprietary rights; "*And that man hath only that for which he maketh effort*"[206]. Islam allows a person to own property, possess and enjoy wealth which has been acquired through lawful means and effort[207].

Therefore, a common analogy was to attribute Islamic principles of property to the protection of intellectual property. While this has a certain degree of standing, particularly in regard to appropriation, as the natural rights under Locke's labour theory, a distinction is drawn between tangible assets and intangible assets. How the two are measured can vary significantly and more relevant to the current economic climate, how the value of intangible assets can be assessed and protected can have a profound effect on economic growth potential. The Hedaya, a Guide on the Mussulman Laws, refers to historical Islamic text which was composed in the twelfth century and it set out the legal system which was central to the entrenchment of British rule in India.

It provided the framework for active control of civil administration and the courts and the first English translation was written in 1791 to aide British rule of India. Although the Hedaya is now superseded, it remains a valid document as it set out Islamic laws in key areas of; charity (zakat), marriage, fostering, divorce, slavery, oaths, and relevant to intellectual property, punishments. The Hedaya distinguishes between punishment for theft of a tangible as set versus an intangible asset and as such categorised incidents of theft which should lead to the amputation of a hand and those which should not. Relevant to the study of intellectual property in Islamic law, is the what the Hedaya states as the punishment for the theft of a book; *"the hand of a thief is not cut off for stealing a book, whatever be the subject of which it treats, because there the object of the theft can only be the contents, and that is not property"*[208].

The Hedaya states that the theft of a book would not lead to the amputation of a hand as the object of the theft is the content of the book and not the book itself, concluding amputation cannot take place for stealing ideas, as ideas are not property. This is found in an Islamic text which dates back to the twelfth century and translated into English in the eighteenth century. The same legal principle was heard in the English Criminal Appeal Court in 1979 where a Defendant could not be prosecuted for stealing an exam paper as the purpose of the theft was not to steal paper[209]. The Hedaya commentary further distinguishes the punishment for theft of a book stating the theft of a book of accounts would be theft of appreciable property as in this case the contents are not the object but the paper and other materials of which the book is composed.

Therefore the Hedaya predates anything of a similar nature in western texts, clarifying the Islamic justification for differences in the punishment applicable to theft of a tangible asset from an intangible asset. Therefore, the Hedaya concept of not allowing amputation for the theft of a book relates well with the foundational tenets of intellectual property as you cannot protect a physical book. Tangible assets are documented in detail in the Quran and greater inferences can be drawn from how property is protected in the sacred verses of the Quran and how the reasoning behind property protection can extend to intellectual property protection.

## *Quranic Reform on Property Law*

The principal Quranic reform in the area of property was the introduction of the doctrine of Istikhlaf developed from Surah Al Hadid, Verse 7 where the Quran declares that all property belongs to God, and that man has been made a successor of that property in his lifetime, in the capacity of a mere trustee[210]. The exercise of the right of ownership is subject to the public interest of society to be supervised by the government[211]. Where the interpretation of Islamic proprietary rights to intellectual property rights falls short is in establishing an Islamic principle to deal with economic free riders[212]. The issue of economic free riders in Islamic states has been raised by various scholars however there is no definitive Islamic doctrine resolving the issue[213].

## *Linking Theft of Property to Intellectual Property Infringement*

Theft of property is referenced in the Quran to prevent unjust use of property that does not belong to the perpetrator; "*And eat up not one another's property unjustly (in any illegal way e.g. stealing, robbing, deceiving, etc.), nor give bribery to the rulers (judges before presenting your cases) that you may knowingly eat up a part of the property of others sinfully*". The closest Quranic reference to intellectual property can be found in Surah Al-Nisa, Verse 29; "*O you who have believed, do not consume one another's wealth unjustly but only [in lawful] business by mutual consent*". This would support principles of intellectual property protection as when intellectual property infringement takes place; the loss of revenue for the right holder is against his permission. The punishment for theft of physical property in the GCC states is based on the severity of the crime and the loss incurred. In intellectual property law, the loss incurred is not always as clear. For example, speculative losses can be recovered as damages in intellectual property infringement cases however the damages sought cannot always be given a clear numerical value as easily as the theft of a tangible asset.

## *Sharia Principles on Mutual Consent*

Mutual consent is mentioned at Surah Al-Nisa Verse 29 as a piece of property cannot be stolen if there is mutual consent between the parties concerned on how the property can be used. Mutual consent can be extended to compulsory licensing as it gives an intellectual property right holder monopoly over his wealth (mal) in the form of a knowledge-based asset. Compulsory licensing allows the patent holder to be paid for authorised copies of the product and to be adequately remunerated when taking into account the economic value of the patent. The mutual consent can be inferred from governments allowing someone else to produce the patented product while adequately remunerating the patent holder[214].

A monopoly right generates wealth for the right holder, the intangible asset can thus be considered as the source of income for the intellectual property right holder for his invention. The economic value of any intellectual property asset can vary from a nominal amount to extremely high amounts, however the Quran stipulates against excessive wealth in the hands of a few and critics have raised this as a concern where a monopoly right can generate disproportionate wealth[215]. To allow intellectual property right holders overcome this barrier, the granting of a monopoly right is counter balanced by the publication of specifications in patents. Developing on from this are the legal remedies available to property right holders when intellectual property infringement takes place. Punishment for the theft of property is based on the severity of the theft. With intellectual property infringement, the GCC states have sought to pass laws that offer intellectual property right holders some recourse whilst keeping a distinction between property theft and intellectual property infringement[216].

## *Defining Intellectual Property Infringement*

There are some pitfalls with the inference that theft of intellectual property equates to theft of physical property. Firstly, where an intellectual property asset is used without the consent of the right holder, an infringement has taken place and not theft in the same sense as the theft of a tangible asset[217]. This is largely due to the fact that primary sources of sharia law have laid down criterion for assessing the severity of physical property theft and the subsequent punishments but not for the theft of intangible assets. Secondly, the intellectual property right holder's main concern is financial and therefore compensation as a remedy for infringement ties in more with Islamic principles on the remedies available for failure to honour contractual obligations, international business and trade than theft of physical property. For example, remedies sought by intellectual property right holders include prohibitory injunctions and where necessary interim injunctions, seizure of infringing goods, compensation, exemplary damages and in extreme cases imprisonment. In comparison, offences related to theft of tangible assets lead to a different set of sanctions with imprisonment at the forefront of the possible punishments. Therefore, defining violations of intellectual property assets as infringement is more appropriate than theft.

## 9 Sharia Sources on Contract Law

There are a number of Quranic references in relation to contract law. Quranic references attributed to contract law include Surah Al-Mā'idah, Verse 1, *"O you who have believed, fulfill [all] contracts"*[218]. Further references focus on honouring contractual promises and documenting the contract[219]. In considering contract law it is useful to have a comparator. In English contract law there are seven key elements which make up contract formation; agreement, consideration, intention to create legal relations, form, capacity, consent and legality. Even where all the required elements of a contract are met, a contract will not have legal effect under sharia law if it contains an attribute of gambling[220], alcohol[221] or forbidden meat[222]. Taking agreement first of all, in sharia law this is not as straightforward as one party making an offer which the other accepts given the influence of the doctrines of riba[223] and gharar[224]. *Riba* is the doctrine on the prohibition of interest payments, undue profits or excessive gain from a transaction and *gharar* deals with risk, speculative transactions, ambiguity or excessive uncertainty in contracts[225].

Two key elements of general theory of contract are evident at Surah An-Nisā', Verse 4, to have mutual consent and gainful exchange[226]. The Sunnah further expands on the obligations on contracting parties to fully disclose the value of their bargain and any defects that exist; *"both the buyer and the seller give the option of either confirming or cancelling the bargain three times, and if they speak the truth and mention the defects, then their bargain will be blessed, and if they tell lies and conceal the defects, they might gain some financial gain but they will deprive their sale of (Allah's) blessings*[227]." As the Gulf states have embarked on international contracts and treaties, *riba* and *gharar* have played a significant role in financial transactions[228], particularly in Islamic finance which will be considered in more detail later[229].

## 10 Sharia Sources on International Transactions

In terms of sharia references to international transactions and conducting business, the Quran has clear statements regarding honouring agreements and the need for certainty whilst forbidding riba and gharar[230]. The clearest reference can be found in Surah Al Baqarah at Verse 275; *"Those who consume interest cannot stand [on the Day of Resurrection] except as one stands who is being beaten by Satan into insanity. That is because they say, "Trade is [just] like interest." But Allah has permitted trade and has forbidden interest. So whoever has received an admonition from his Lord and desists may have what is past, and his affair rests with Allah. But whoever returns to [dealing in interest or usury] – those are the companions of the Fire; they will abide eternally therein*[231]*"*. Through trade, different models of contractual arrangements have emerged which although are sharia compliant, allow a trader or investor to earn some return on the capital that has been invested without breaching the prohibition on interest. It is the distinction between return on investment and interest that has been the cornerstone of the Islamic finance industry.

Therefore, the key to a successful application of intellectual property rights in the Gulf states is striking a balance between permissible trade and circumventing riba and gharar similar to how sharia compliant models have evolved in Islamic Finance. In an international context, intellectual property protection is at the heart of all trade agreements and the greater the protection, the more trade takes place through foreign direct investment[232]. When a developing country can demonstrate stronger intellectual property protection, there are obvious advantages as foreign companies and multinationals are more willing to invest where they have confidence that there is a legal recourse for intellectual property infringement[233]. This then has a direct impact on tax revenues and transaction costs as there is evidence of a viable legal structure to protect intellectual property and associated knowledge-based assets[234]. This is where an integrated approach to intellectual property is needed to marry sharia compliant intellectual property models to international standards, notably TRIPS and FTA's.

Along with the three areas of law considered in the primary sharia sources, there are a number of references to honouring obligations in treaties made irrespective of the religion of the contracting parties[235]. This principle has been extended to international treaties between Gulf states and non-Islamic states as can be seen in the many international agreements the Gulf states have with other countries and organisations[236]. There are also relevant references that can be found for moral rights. At the time of the Prophet Muhammed, both the Quran and Sunnah were recorded orally; as such there was a great need for exactness and accuracy in the sayings and for the sources to be attributed correctly[237].

## 11 Sharia Sources on Public Interest

Public interest, known as maslaha, is the third area of Islamic law that has been related to intellectual property protection[238]. Public interest aims to protect and progress the legitimate interests of the community within the recognised sources of Islamic law and secure public welfare through promoting the benefits of a rule or protecting against harm[239]. If public interest is applied broadly to intellectual property protection, there is a negative impact on protection for inventors as the argument would be that a monopoly right cannot be granted on public interest grounds[240]. Thus the relationship between public interest and intellectual property law has steered away from a broad application of the doctrine of public interest to allow sharia approval of intellectual property rights. However, if public interest is construed too narrowly, there would be a risk of harm to the public welfare[241]. This is especially apparent in new developing areas of intellectual property law such as corporate sovereignty and investor to state dispute mechanisms which will be considered in more detail in Chapter 6[242].

The purpose of Islam is to safeguard public welfare. Further research is needed on the impact public welfare provisions, from the four sources of sharia law, can have on intellectual property protection. Islamic scholars often apply analogical reasoning to address public welfare changes. When there are contradictions between laws and social norms, jurists reconcile such differences through principles of necessity and or expediency[243]. There is a significant gap between the enactment of intellectual property laws and acceptance of the laws by the general public. These lacunae can be addressed through further analysis of the importance of public interest in strengthening intellectual property protection and will be a contributing factor in the recommendations of an integrated approach to intellectual property rights in the GCC which takes into account Islamic principles from existing sharia compliant frameworks and international intellectual property rights obligations[244].

## 12 Sharia Sources on Economic Gain

A final important principle in the Quran that supports intellectual property protection is the doctrine of economic gain[245]. The Quran encourages economic prosperity where business transactions are made honestly and in line with the doctrine of fair dealings as seen at Surah Al-Anfal; *"do not betray Allah and the Messenger or betray your trusts while you know [the consequence]"*. The purpose of economic gain is linked to a person's right to reap the benefits of his hard work and to not be deprived of the subsequent wealth acquired from it[246]. Economic gain also correlates to the basic pillars of Islam which are cited as; the declaration of faith, five daily prayers, zakat, fasting and pilgrimage to Mecca[247]. Zakat is one of the five pillars of Islam and is a payment of 2.5% of a person's wealth towards the poor on an annual basis. This has a direct link to economic prosperity as the more income a person generates, the more Zakat payments they are obliged to make[248]. The zakat payments in turn ensure an improvement in the economic position of the poor; therefore can be linked to public welfare[249].

There are references in the Quran that prohibit false attribution and mutilation of someone else's work. Surah Al-'Aĥqāf at Verse 4 states the need for evidence in verifying a person's right[250]. Moral and conduct towards others is also evidenced in the Quran and is an all-encompassing statement that can be extended to conduct in business. There are references in the Quran which state the need for a moral and ethical code to be adopted in conducting daily tasks and activities[251]. References can be found in *Hadiths* that give prominence to moral and financial rights, further evidencing support for intellectual property protection[252].

## 13 Previous Work on Sharia and Intellectual Property Law

Previous work on the relationship of Islamic law and intellectual property law has developed under two main strands; defining intellectual property within the laws of Islam[253] and addressing the international demand for higher standards of intellectual property protection[254].

## 14 Sharia and Intellectual Property

Starting with the first strand, in ancient Islamic customs there was a system of knowledge acknowledgement known as ijaza (certificate). If a person is to teach, quote or reproduce certain Islamic knowledge, then he or she must obtain an ijaza from the author. This system of a chain of authority is designed to ensure authenticity in the passing of knowledge from one person to another and also as a form of respect for authors. Ijaza only protects the moral right of an author to a certain degree as it is believed that the knowledge itself belongs to God, not to any individual[255]. Al' Afghani (2005) distinguished ijaza from any association to copyright principles on the grounds that ijaza aims to ensure accurate passage of knowledge. Although, by applying inferential reasoning, if the moral rights of the author are protected within limitations then as a result, ijaza protects copyrightable material to a divine source, with an unlimited length of time.

Intellectual property protection in the Arab world is not a completely new phenomenon. Although legislative progress in the field of intellectual property law can be seen to have taken place very recently[256], informal tenets of intellectual property rights protection did exist. Poetry was highly regarded and copyright infringement of such works was heavily disapproved of[257]. Jamar (1992) examined the legal protection of intellectual property within the framework of Islamic legal structures and principles, while focussed on the role of government regulations and various substantive Islamic law principles. Jamar's suggestion of a three tier approach to Islamic law is widely accepted and cited by many authors[258]. They are: firstly areas in which Islamic law have spoken with a relatively full voice, such as spiritual duties, personal status, and inheritance. Secondly where it has provided some general principles as in contract law and thirdly where it is silent, such as in the field of intellectual property, where the ruler of the people is free to act provided that the laws promulgated do not run afoul of sharia prohibitions and are consistent with sharia principles. For example, this can be seen in the fundamental principles that states apply in their governance when balancing intellectual property rights and freedoms of its citizens.

Price (2009) highlights the tensions between safeguarding Islamic law values and pressure from developed countries to conform to pro-west standards[259]. Price's work focuses on the Gulf countries and in terms of subject matter, the countries are very interesting as not only are they revered Islamic states they have undergone dramatic intellectual property development in a short span of a few decades. Beltrametti (2010) raises an important question on the effectiveness of intellectual property laws that are made by Islamic states as despite the significant legislative changes that have taken place, issues of enforcement still remain[260]. Intellectual property law is evolving as international trade agreements are including intellectual property chapters, investors are able to challenge foreign governments through corporate sovereignty and investor to state dispute settlements. As such, the relationship between sharia law and intellectual property law could potentially change and this will be considered in more detail in Chapters 6 and 7[261].

## 15 The Religion Loyalty Index

El Bialy and Gouda (2011) developed a religious loyalty index that assessed the interplay between intellectual property violations in a given country and the importance of religion to the citizens of a given country. Muslim countries have the highest level of religiosity to Islam than other religions[262]. Their empirical research has found that Muslim developing countries have a high level of both intellectual property based piracy as well as a high level of religiosity to Islam[263]. Therefore, there is an anomaly between how Islamic law supports intellectual property and how citizens of Islamic countries with a high religiosity are high intellectual property infringers. The findings of Bialy and Gouda's research is not a new concept, a number of scholars argue the view that for citizens of Islamic countries, intellectual property is seen as a foreign concept, protecting western interests and benefits[264]. Consequently, many citizens of Islamic countries do not view intellectual property infringement as a crime in the same sense they would view theft of a tangible asset.

Bialy and Gouda argued sharia does support intellectual property protection as Muslim judges use *qiyas* in dealing with intellectual property piracy. The reasoning was based on the interpretation of property law which has been expanded to include intellectual property[265]. The main relevant finding of the empirical research was that Muslim countries were found to have a high level of religiosity to Islam and a high level of intellectual property infringement. This will be a running thread throughout the research as the argument for an integrated approach to intellectual property rights in the GCC is supported by the religion loyalty index as given the adherence citizens of Muslim countries have to religion, the role sharia law can potentially play in bridging the gap between religiosity and intellectual property infringement will be addressed further in Chapters 4 to 6[266].

## 16 Conclusion

The purpose of the chapter was to give an overview of the relevant principles of sharia law and analyse the influence of sharia law on intellectual property protection. In summary, although there are no primary sharia law sources that make reference to intellectual property law, there are relevant principles of sharia law that can be found in secondary sources. In terms of conduct under sharia law, intellectual property law is classified as permitted on the basis that the Quran is silent on intellectual property rights protection and therefore it cannot be mandatory, recommended, prohibited or banned[267]. The main sharia law principles that have been considered are; proprietary rights, contractual rights and public interest. The sharia principles on ownership of property, obligations on property right holders, remedies for property right holders and appropriation of property can justify the existence of intangible assets in intellectual property. Theft of property is also referenced in the Quran and carries a severe punishment however there is a distinction between intellectual property theft and infringement as the criterion laid down by primary sources of sharia law for assessing the severity of physical property theft and the subsequent punishment cannot be applied to theft of intangible assets. The second key distinction between intellectual property theft and infringement is the remedies sought by the intellectual property right holder[268]. The remedies for intellectual property infringement share more similarities to breaches of contract law whereby the primary remedies sought are financial and criminal prosecutions are for the most severe cases. Therefore, the remedies for infringement under Islamic law can be found in the primary sharia sources of contract law for failure to honour; contractual obligations, international business and trade agreements rather than theft of physical property[269]. The Islamic concept of contract law has been applied to intellectual property law as there are clear and unambiguous primary sharia law sources concerning certainty in contractual agreements and rules on honouring agreements. It strengthens the argument for intellectual property protection as principles of Islamic contract law can be seen in contractual agreements licensing the use of knowledge based assets and granting monopolies for a given time period.

The research to date on the relationship between sharia law and intellectual property has favoured sharia approval for the existence and protection of intellectual property rights. However at the heart of intellectual property protection, is acceptance by the public at large of intellectual property as predicated with Islamic law[270]. At present, laws exist without the necessary understanding or awareness for their existence. Empirical research by Bialy and Gouda has shown that Islamic countries display both a high affinity to religion and a high percentage of intellectual property rights violations. This leaves the relationship between sharia and intellectual property law at a developmental stage. The foundational stage has been met through the GCC states acceptance of the use of secondary sharia sources to permit intellectual property rights. However the development stage requires an integrated intellectual property approach to enforcement that is a hybrid of clear and unambiguous sharia principles and international intellectual property laws. The GCC states have chosen to adopt western laws on intellectual property rights protection and incorporated a number of laws as highlighted in Chapter 2 without paying attention to the role Islamic law can play in integrating intellectual property law in a the legal system of an Islamic state. There is therefore a need for a foundation of mutual understanding between a western philosophy on intellectual property law and Islamic concepts. An industry that has been successful in bridging the differences between western practices and Islamic principles is the Islamic finance industry where Islamic finance has its own set of sharia compliant financial products[271].

Continuing on the theme for a foundation of mutual understanding between western approaches on intellectual property law and Islamic concepts, Chapter 4 will consider international intellectual property laws and highlight the intellectual property stand point of the US and EU to then analyse the relationship between the two powerhouses and the GCC. The chapter will focus on the historical development of intellectual property in both the US and EU, the current international intellectual property law demands on the GCC states within the context of intellectual property protection and enforcement as this will facilitate a holistic approach to the development of intellectual property in the GCC and inform the series of recommendations for an integrated intellectual property model. It is imperative to understand the direction the EU and the US are coming from when they are demanding higher levels of intellectual property protection in the GCC as this will then influence how an integrated approach to intellectual property rights protection can take shape and evolve.

# 4

# A Foundation of Mutual Understanding: The United States and the European Union's Stance on Intellectual Property Protection

## 1 Introduction

At the heart of all trade agreements and negotiations between different states and blocs is one fundamental principle, to increase economic ties between the trading partners. Intellectual property infringement costs the G20 countries $125 billion annually; this includes losses in tax revenue from counterfeiting and piracy[272]. In terms of the global economy, the International Chambers of Commerce (ICC) estimates the losses to the global economy from intellectual property infringements at $1 trillion annually[273]. This chapter will analyse the intellectual property standpoint of both the EU and the US and the relationship each powerhouse has with the GCC. Further, the GCC also has pending trade agreements with other counties and therefore how the GCC handles its current negotiations with the US and the EU, will impact on the GCC's foreign trade and economic interests with other countries[274]. The GCC has outstanding free trade agreements with the European Union (EU) and the United States (US). The EU is a uniquely large economic and political partnership between 28 European countries that are collectively represented in the global arena[275]. The US has the largest economy in the world and, as do many of the EU countries, exports and imports goods around the globe. The US and the GCC have set up a joint committee since 2012 to examine opportunities for enhancing economic, commercial, investment and technical cooperation as set out in the framework trade agreement[276]. The US-GCC Strategic Cooperation Forum was convened in 2012 in Riyadh, Saudi Arabia with Secretary of State Hillary Rodham Clinton representing the United States and Foreign Minister Prince Saud Al-Faisal representing the Kingdom of Saudi Arabia. The main impetus for a trade agreement is largely due to an increased effort to raise the volume of trade and investment between the US and the GCC.

The negotiations for the trade agreement between the EU and the GCC began in 1988. The purpose behind the trade agreement is similar to that of the framework trade agreement between the US and the GCC, to harmonise investment rules in the GCC to allow corporations to participate more directly in oil, banking, investment and other industries; however political issues have slowed down the progress of the EU-GCC trade agreement[277]. To understand the individual relationships that both the US and the EU have with the GCC on international intellectual property protection, this chapter will analyse the development of intellectual property rights from the perspectives of the EU and the US to facilitate a meeting of minds between western intellectual property systems and the developing systems in the GCC.

The research objectives addressed in this chapter are:

- To provide a background to the western development of intellectual property rights to gain a holistic view of the international intellectual property industry.
- To review the current international intellectual property legislation, policies, free trade agreements, bilateral agreements and enforcement mechanisms that exist in the EU and the US and their influence on the GCC states.

## 2 Background to the US Intellectual Property Law

The US has been dealing with intellectual property protection from as early as 1790 when the first ever patent was granted to Samuel Hopkins for a process of making potash, an ingredient used in fertilizer[278]. The US Constitution protects two types of intellectual property, "Writings" and "Discoveries." At Article 1, section 8, the US Constitution states; *"To promote the Progress of Science and useful Arts, by securing for limited Times to Authors and Inventors the exclusive Right to their respective Writings and Discoveries[279]"*. In order to protect the writings and discoveries within the intentions of the constitution, the US Congress passed legislation to protect "writings" in the form of copyright law. In 1790, the US passed its first copyright law[280]. Similarly, the intention behind protecting "discoveries" was in essence patent protection, which led to the Patent Act of 1790 being passed.

From when these Acts were enacted to where we currently stand, the US has had over two centuries to extend and enhance the value of intellectual property assets. For example, in copyright law, the protection has developed significantly from written works and novels to computer programs[281]. Many landmark cases have originated from the US[282] and influenced international courts and policy making[283]. The US currently has thirty-six intellectual property related laws. The main legal provisions cover trademark law[284], copyright[285], patent law[286], trade secrets[287] and antitrust law[288].

The US government has set up specialist offices to regulate the different areas of intellectual property. The US Patent and Trademark Office (USPTO) is a highly skilled federal organisation that deals with all aspects of patents and trademarks from filing an application to infringement rights and policy development[289]. The USPTO works closely with the United States Trade Representative (USTR) and other United States Government (USG) agencies to review intellectual property policies and regulations in foreign countries to assess how key countries are tackling intellectual property infringement and how they are progressing with action plans to strengthen intellectual property protection nationally and in line with regulations worldwide[290]. Enforcing intellectual property rights through bilateral trade agreements has been a more effective method of raising international intellectual property standards than pursuing intellectual property rights as a standalone agreement. This is largely due to the unique trading commodity within intellectual property; knowledge as a good is far more difficult to protect than tangible assets[291].

## 3 The US and International Intellectual Property Law

Intellectual property rights granted to American inventors by US authorities are applicable across all US territories. However, these rights are ineffective outside of the US and an inventor who requires patent protection overseas must apply for his invention to be patented in the patent office of the foreign country or a regional office like that in the GCC, which is discussed further in Chapter 5. It is the question of how intellectual property right holders can protect their intangible assets in foreign territories that has led to the momentum behind developing minimum standards of international intellectual property laws. If the US can influence foreign intellectual property policies and enforcement, it can have a heavy impact on the establishment and progress of a global intellectual property market[292]. This is why a thorough examination of the development of intellectual property in the US is relevant to the GCC as in order for the GCC to meet its international obligations, it must first seek to understand the framework within which intellectual property has developed. This will give the GCC states a fighting chance of implementing rules and regulations that will be seen as a GCC state-led approach to intellectual property.

### *International Agreements*

The solution to protecting intellectual property rights overseas for the US and other developed countries has come in the form of international agreements[293] and treaty memberships[294]. Over the years the US, in its trade agreements, has incorporated a number of intellectual property provisions with many countries[295]. In respect of bilateral investment treaties, the US has thirty-nine agreements in force[296]. Although the US is in trade talks with all of the GCC states, Bahrain and Oman concluded their bilateral agreements with the US in 2006 and 2009 respectively.

Both FTAs have very similar provisions on substantive intellectual property law and protection. The US-Oman FTA provisions on intellectual property required Oman to accede to the Patent Cooperation Treaty (1970), the Convention Relating to the Distribution of Programme-Carrying Signals transmitted by Satellite (1974), the Protocol Relating to the Madrid Agreement Concerning the International Registration of Marks (1989), the Budapest Treaty on the International Recognition of the Deposit of Microorganisms for the Purposes of Patent Procedure (1980), the International Convention for the Protection of New Varieties of Plants (1991), the Trademark Law Treaty (1994), the WIPO Copyright Treaty (1996) and the WIPO Performances and Phonograms Treaty (1996)[297]. The US-Bahrain FTA agreed to ratify the same international agreements as Oman.

## 4 The US Approach to Intellectual Property

The driving force behind the emergence of international protection of intellectual property rights in the US came largely from the formation of an American Intellectual Property Committee (US IPC) in 1986[298]. The Committee was a US Coalition of its most powerful corporations across various industries, mainly; pharmaceutical, IT sector, entertainment, software industries, generic pharmaceutical industries and chemical companies[299]. CEOs of the twelve original corporations lobbied for standard setting in international property law to better protect their intellectual property assets on a global scale, particularly in developing countries[300].

In the 1980s, dominant organisations within the US IPC were frustrated with the lack of protection of their knowledge assets beyond the US, with the CEO of Pfizer accusing numerous countries of designing domestic laws that allowed them to "legally take" US inventions[301]. The US government sought to influence the WTO through its powerful position in global trade and by linking intellectual property protection and trade in the form of a trade agenda setting process. By 1994, the TRIPS agreement had been signed and the US seized the opportunity to be more active in forming bilateral agreements since TRIPS entered into force[302]. The US intellectual property strategy can be seen as a tiered plan, starting with an increase in bilateral agreements with developing countries and then to extend intellectual property protections through multilateral agreements[303].

The US strategy incorporated the creation of corresponding programs to safeguard intellectual property rights of international US corporations and further facilitate support mechanisms to help achieve the end result desired by the US IPC.

The main support mechanism created by the US was the special 301 program, which allows the USTR to monitor a watch-list of countries violating intellectual property rights, and depending on how substantial the violations are, trade sanctions can be applied against the countries with the most prolific infringement record.

## 5 The US and International Agreements

The US is pursuing international agreements that are binding and contain enforcement provisions. The stumbling block for the US and other developed countries, in raising the intellectual property protection bar in developing countries, has always been the infrastructures and level of technological and economic development of individual states[304]. For the US, incorporating intellectual property into trade agreements became a pressing matter as the US IPC, led by the US private sectors, campaigned to have intellectual property included in the Uruguay Round, 1986 Agenda[305], of the General Agreement on Tariffs and Trade negotiations, GATT[306]. Further, the US IPC lobbied to have intellectual property integrated into US trade law and other international agreements such as the North American Free Trade Agreement (NAFTA)[307].

Therefore, the force behind the inclusion and regulation of intellectual property into the international trade agenda was in fact the US IPC and a victory for multinational organisations within the US and ally organisations in Europe and Japan[308]. It is clear that the pressure on constantly improving intellectual property rights protection and enforcement will only increase with time. For the GCC states, as they walk the tight rope between TRIPS and TRIPS Plus compliance, understanding the basis of their international agreements and the structures that exist within the agreements will determine how successful they are in developing an approach to TRIPS Plus and intellectual property rights protection.

The TRIPS agreement is not without its critics with the United Nations Trade Conference on Trade and Development (UNCTAD), a report in 1977 branding the agreement as *"a reverse system of preferences granted to foreign patent holders in the markets of developing countries[309]"*. UNCTAD, which is governed by its 194 member states, is one arm of the United Nations with the responsibility of dealing with international trade development issues for all its member states[310]. This issue of introducing intellectual property legislation to fit the needs of foreign investors as opposed to intellectual property rights protection that is fit for purpose has been highlighted as one of the stumbling blocks of international intellectual property rights protection by the UNCTAD in its biannual investment forum reports[311]. How do the GCC states promote better intellectual property rights protection when the protections offered by the legal system are seen as giving preference to foreigners? This question can be answered by considering UNCTAD reports on how developing countries can improve domestic regulatory frameworks by introducing a set of rules and regulations which are more than simply a suite of foreign-based legislation and reflect the needs and development timelines of individual states[312].

## *The US and TRIPS Standards*

Given that developing countries seeking WIPO ascension imitated provisions of the Paris Convention to formulate national laws or continued with laws already laid out whilst under colonial rule, it can be argued that TRIPS started a mirror image phenomenon with the US wanting more and more reflection of its own intellectual property laws and enforcement mechanisms copied into the laws of its trading countries and other developing countries[313]. The counter argument to this theory is that, from the point of view of developing countries, they accept the restrictions placed upon their sovereignty on the basis that the protection from political and other business risks will lead to an increase in foreign direct investment[314]. What this has subsequently created is a somewhat artificial state of intellectual property reality as when the level of legislative protection for intellectual property law in the GCC states is considered, there is a body of law that meets minimum TRIPS requirements and domestic remedies available. However, as will be seen in subsequent chapters, for the GCC states to further develop their intellectual property regimes, an integrated approach to intellectual property rights is required that takes into account not only international intellectual property rights obligations but also incorporates Islamic law principles to further increase intellectual property rights protection.

There are other advantages that the US offers as part of the treaty and agreements deals. For instance, as the US has developed significant intellectual property law through its national courts and decisions with Europe, it gives the developing country a body of developed law and effectively brings states like the GCC up to speed without having to invest the centuries of time that the Americans and other developed countries have had to[315]. Here again is a systematic flaw; it is one principle to offer states access to case law and judicial decisions to a field that is new to their judiciaries and legal experts. It is another feat altogether to then be able to mirror the legal system of a country that has developed the law of intellectual property. The differences cannot simply be bridged by legislative changes alone as the US has developed intellectual property over a significantly longer period of time, with far more sophisticated institutional support, a large number of expert judges and advocates who have the capacity to apply the law and where needed interpret the law in an area that may lead to redefining intellectual property law.

It is in the area of redefining intellectual property law where developing countries lag significantly behind as developed states will take into account their own cultural and capitalist norms to pass new rulings in the intellectual property field, not those of developing states. On a surface level understanding, it would be unreasonable to expect developed states to make landmark decisions in intellectual property law that did not reflect their own territorial norms. However, in the international arena, so far, the developed states do expect developing states such as the GCC to adopt international intellectual property standards based on their protocols and practices, with minimal regard to the discrete facets of societal, cultural and religious customs[316].

The economic impact of protecting intellectual property trade, at present, outweighs the somewhat draconian measures developed countries like the US take in establishing intellectual property laws and enforcement mechanisms[317]. However, within this is another issue for international intellectual property rights and developing countries as discussed above. Developing counties can never truly mirror intellectual property laws as they lack the knowledge and expertise to apply the requisite level of judicial interpretation in complex intellectual property law cases. Take for example, *Warner Bros. Entertainment, Inc. and J. K. Rowling v. RDR Books*[318], a copyright infringement case, where Rowling argued successfully that the decision to allow a Harry Potter encyclopaedia to exist is hers alone and no other person or enterprise can use the characters in her books without her permission as this falls under her protected intellectual property rights[319]. Unlike other areas of law, where quite clear precedents can be set out and followed in an international arena[320], judicial analysis of intellectual property doctrines such as fair use, outsider works and copyrightable material can turn on the minutiae of the case[321].

Further there are cases where intellectual property law clashes with competition law and the case law in this area is equally abstruse[322]. This does lead to a very significant conundrum for developing GCC countries as they are expected to bring intellectual property legislation on a par with developed countries without fully appreciating that this branch of law is quite esoteric and constantly evolving even in countries like the US, despite their self-proclaimed intellectual property pioneer status[323].

## The US and Bilateral Agreements

Although the TRIPS Agreement was a valid vehicle through which to drive international intellectual property, US investors have continued to seek more stringent measures. Around the same time as the TRIPS Agreement was in its final stages, the US initiated a number of bilateral investment treaties with specific aims of protecting private investments, developing market-oriented policies in partner countries, promoting U.S. exports, reducing the political risk to investors' and reducing investors' exposure to uncertain business environments[324]. By guaranteeing certain standards of treatment that can be enforced through binding states to an investor-to-state dispute settlement mechanism, outside of the domestic judicial system, bilateral investment treaties offer protection beyond the realm of TRIPS.

Again, this highlights the strong consensus from the US to fiercely protect intellectual property rights in foreign states. The GCC states, while mindful of their ties with the US, must stop and consider their position before bowing down to investor-to-state dispute settlement mechanisms. The area of investor-to-state dispute settlement mechanisms is considered in more detail in Chapter 6[325].

Further, by tackling intellectual property rights through bilateral trade agreements and regional trade agreements, the US has created and secured a level of agreement to safeguard intellectual property which goes beyond TRIPS. Whereas TRIPS sets minimum standards, the US approach is in essence a to-do list, or as Pugatch describes it, a *"nanny"* approach. The US FTAs confine the ability of signatory countries to less flexible implementation time scales when compared to the TRIPS provisions in areas such as public health, compulsory licensing, extension of patent terms, parallel imports and data exclusivity rules[326]. This raises a number of concerns when considering intellectual property development from the GCC point of view. If the system of intellectual property rights protection is viewed as being "nannied" by the US, then the GCC will have an uphill struggle in increasing the level of protection it can offer intellectual property right holders, who are predominantly foreign investors, as its citizens will see the rules as foreign. What is needed is a clear breakdown of TRIPS provisions, what each provision within the TRIPS agreement means and how the provisions can be interpreted in such a way that the GCC states take ownership of the interpretation and thus create a set of intellectual property rights-based law that is in line with their own standard setting in their national governance and at a higher authoritative level within the regional GCC framework.

TRIPS standards offer developing countries flexibility in four areas: implementation, substantive standards of protection, enforcement and flexibilities in areas outside the scope of TRIPS.[327] The US approach is to erode the flexibilities afforded to developing countries in the four TRIPS flexibility areas[328]. The GCC states, as a series of emerging markets, need to be careful in writing off all the flexibilities that are available to them under TRIPS or opting out as in previous bilateral agreements.

## 6 The US and the GCC

The US already has FTAs with Bahrain and Oman. In the US-Bahrain FTA, the provisions on intellectual property go beyond TRIPS. The scope of patentability is extended by mandating that patents must be available for new uses of known products, enhancing patent protection for plants and animals, an additional three years of data exclusivity when new clinical information is established, test data exclusivity and for customs authorities to stop trade in counterfeit and pirated goods[329]. Further, in TRIPS fines are required to adequately compensate intellectual property right holders who have suffered monetary damages however the FTA stipulates an imposition of fines irrespective of the damage caused[330]. Imposing fines irrespective of the damage caused is not a method of punishment that sits nicely in existing sharia law principles as speculative risk is prohibited.

For Bahrain the FTA has, for now, lived up to its promise. Bilateral trade between the US and Bahrain has grown and the economic benefits gained from increase in trade outweigh the flexibilities lost in FTA's. Likewise for Oman, there have been similar economic benefits. Although Oman did not conclude its FTA with the US until 2009, their trade figures are on par with Bahrain. This highlights a key observation in this research. Trade takes place whether an FTA is in place or not, FTAs may have the promise of increasing trade but they should not be considered as the be all and end all to trade. States have traded based on need, FTAs aim to reduce trade barriers and thus are attractive to GCC states as there is an economic benefit to the agreement, likewise for the US, it creates more leverage to enforce their standard setting. As will be seen in Chapter 8, the role of FTAs and the process by which the GCC should modify its systems, to protect its autonomy while maintaining international development, will be a vital component of the integrated intellectual property protection framework.

For the other GCC states, the potential gain from concluding a regional agreement with the US could also lead to similar increased levels of economic benefit, above existing goods and services trade[331]. Trade figures for the GCC states have increased significantly since the GCC was established and with negotiations for a GCC-US FTA, further relations would supplement existing agreements the US has with Bahrain and Oman[332]. The US, despite having the biggest economy globally, needs to be mindful of the knock-on effect other emerging markets will have on its trade agreements with the GCC and what the implications are for TRIPS Plus provisions[333].

## 7 The EU on Intellectual Property Law

The EU has extensive legislation on intellectual property law and a body of case law to match. EU countries have for centuries tried to regulate and protect different forms of intellectual property rights[334]. As in the US, EU countries were also dealing with protecting copyright and patents from as early as the eighteenth century. Over many years intellectual property assets have become more diverse and varied, requiring discrete private laws to govern what constitutes an intellectual property asset and how it is protected beyond the realm of civil liabilities and remedies. Currently, the EU leads other political unions, in terms of quantity, as the EU has enacted 74 intellectual property laws to date[335].

The EU has specific institutions and departments designated with the task of regulating the various aspects of intellectual property law including copyright and related rights[336], protection of inventions[337], trademark law[338], community design and other intellectual property areas[339]. In terms of international treaties, the EU has supported several international negotiations most notably TRIPS provisions in the Uruguay Round of the General Agreement on Tariffs and Trade (GATT) in 1994. Other key international developments from the EU are evident in the number of WIPO treaties the EU is a signatory to[340].

From the point of view of the EU, there is a strong focus on enforcement regimes both within the EU[341] and with improving the protection and enforcement of intellectual property rights in third countries[342]. The EU and the US have established a good level of cooperation on intellectual property issues, which has facilitated a level of dialogue between the two entities to discuss common intellectual property rights enforcement challenges in third countries[343].

For the EU, intellectual property assets carry substantial economic benefits and revenue. Michel Barnier, Member of the European Commission and European commissioner in charge of the Internal Market and Services, states; "*intellectual property is the backbone of a competitive European economy, creating jobs and bringing innovative products and services to consumers and companies.*"[344] This is evident in a recent report carried out by the EPO and the OHIM, showing the intellectual property industries sector contribute 39% of total economic activities in the EU, 26% of all employment in the EU and a further 9% of jobs have been indirectly created as a result of the work of intellectual property industries[345].

## 8 The European Union's Intellectual Property Systems

Europe has two main systems in place for patent protection. These are the national patent system and the European patent system, with plans for a unitary patent by 2015[346]. The Convention on the Grant of European Patents (European Patent Convention, EPC) came into force in the late 1970s and set up two instrumental organs of the European Patent Organisation (EPOrg), the EPO and the Administrative Council[347]. The EPC has thirty-eight members making a European patent applicable over a European population of six hundred million[348]. The EU institutional framework did not initiate European intellectual property systems largely because the European Union intervenes on provisions of the European Treaty which authorise it to act[349]. The EPC has, as a result, developed its own legal institution to regulate patent protection and other similar institutions have been set up for different forms of intellectual property[350]. The provisions of the EPC are reflected in the EPO decisions[351] and aim to make decisions which are then implemented in the national courts of a contracting state;

however the system is far from water-tight and issues arise in applying EPO rulings to national courts as was seen in *Re Astron Clinica* (2008)[352]. As a general rule, national courts do aim to apply EPO decisions and European Patent Office Technical Board of Appeal decisions where it has adopted a consistent approach as seen in *Human Genome Sciences Inc. v. Eli Lilly and Company*[353].

## 9 The EU and the GCC

By the early 1980's the European Community (EC) sought to strengthen relations with the GCC and leading countries from both regions reached a framework agreement with the purpose of establishing trade relations and increasing commercial transactions between the two regions[354]. Over a number of years, as interactions between the regions increased, the scope of the framework agreement was steadily extended and bilateral relations grew between the two regions[355]. Negotiations for the establishment of a Cooperation Agreement were instigated by the GCC[356], these continued between the EC and GCC until they concluded in 1988[357]. The agreement aimed to "*promote overall cooperation between equal partners on mutually advantageous terms in all spheres between the two regions and further their economic development, taking into consideration the differences in levels of development of the parties*"[358]. This developed to the EU and GCC FTA which although initially was expected to be completed within a relatively short space of time, over 25 years have passed and it is currently ongoing and remains a work in progress. Negotiations often start and gain momentum only to be halted when the EU and GCC are unable to reach a consensus on trade provisions.

The EU and the GCC FTA, has at its roots, three main common interests; economic progress, political alliances and security issues[359]. However, in terms of trade relations, the trade between the EU and GCC has continued to grow over the years despite their differences in the FTA[360]. Therefore, although agreement cannot be reached on all components of the EU-GCC FTA, each facet of the agreement can run independently of others. There are knock on effects of the delays in concluding the EU-GCC FTA. The GCC have looked to other countries for FTAs and have completed agreements with Asian countries. For example, the GCC signed the FTA with Singapore in 2008, two years after the start of the negotiation and it took effect in September 2013[361].

## 10 Conclusion

The EU and the US have played a significant role in the development of intellectual property rights through the course of time. From its humble beginnings of two centuries ago to the modern era of intellectual property rights, the law on intellectual property has developed at a steady pace. From the birth of the internet age, protecting intellectual property rights became more cumbersome and countries have had to step up their efforts in protecting intellectual property rights of their inventors as intellectual property can no longer be confined to one territory. The advantage for both the EU and the US is that the many years it has had to develop intellectual property law has allowed the EU and the US to develop its judicial expertise and experience, its laws and regulations as well as research and development in the field.

The free trade agreements that are in negotiation with the GCC offer a sharing of knowledge and expertise to bring the GCC states a step closer to western based standard setting and intellectual property law development and protection. As the chapter demonstrates, intellectual property is not a simple field of law development, the EU and the US are often involved in high profile intellectual property law cases that involve substantial amounts of money and require a very high level of expertise by the judiciary to make a decision. The EU and the US are periodically updating legislation and adjudicating on landmark intellectual property cases which are changing the law on intellectual property law in their respective jurisdictions. Rather than play follow the leader with the EU and the US, the GCC would stand a better chance of successfully protecting intellectual property rights by taking on board their international obligations and aligning it with their own political, religious and cultural beliefs. These recommendations will be further developed in Chapters 6 to 8.

The next chapter considers the impact of TRIPS standards on the GCC states and the ramifications for the GCC states from the current emphasis on a TRIPS Plus Era. The following chapter will focus on the current international intellectual property law demands within the context of intellectual property protection and enforcement in the GCC states and answer key research objectives on; the pre TRIPS analysis of the level of intellectual property protection that existed before the GCC states began ascending to international treaties and enacting intellectual property laws, the TRIPS compliance stage that occurred at different times for all six states and will analyse the potential ramifications for the GCC states from adhering to TRIPS Plus provisions.

# 5

# Sharia and TRIPS, the Rocky Road from Pre TRIPS to TRIPS Plus in the GCC

## 1 Introduction

In order to investigate the development of intellectual property in the GCC states from pre-TRIPS, to TRIPS and subsequently TRIPS plus, this chapter will analyse intellectual property protection and enforcement on a state by state basis. The chapter will address the following research objectives; to investigate the development of intellectual property in the GCC countries from pre-TRIPS, TRIPS and TRIPS plus, the pre -TRIPS analysis on the level of intellectual property protection that existed before the GCC states began acceding to international treaties and agreements and the TRIPS compliance stage that occurred at different times for all six states. Specifically, the level of intellectual property protection that existed before the GCC states joined the WTO, the impact of the TRIPS compliance stage on each individual state and the magnitude of changes that took place from pre-TRIPS to TRIPS compliance by all states (1990 to 2010). Further, the chapter will analyse the potential ramifications for the GCC states from adhering to the TRIPS plus provisions.

The development of international standard-setting is best understood at three distinct stages; pre TRIPS, TRIPS standard and TRIPS Plus. The research objectives addressed in this chapter therefore are:

- To analyse the GCC states at a pre-TRIPS stage examine the level of intellectual property protection that existed before the GCC states began ascending to international treaties and agreements, covering a time period that runs from 1970 to 1990.
- To consider the substantive provisions of the TRIPS compliance stage as TRIPS occurred at different times for all six states covering changes that took place from 1990 to 2010[362].
- To examine TRIPS Plus provisions, to understand how they go beyond the standards set at TRIPS level and provide an overview of how TRIPS Plus

follows on from when the TRIPS agreement was complied with by the GCC states to the current state of play.

- To understand the intellectual property development of each GCC state to then be able to set out how intellectual property rights protection can be improved.

The purpose of this analysis will be to identify a series of recommendations for developing an integrated approach to intellectual property rights which takes into account the structure of the GCC states, international agreements and pressures, the international institutions, Islamic finance, and societal and religious views.

## 2 The Berne and Paris Convention

Pre-TRIPS, the main international treaties governing intellectual property protection are; the Paris Convention for the Protection of Industrial Property (1883) and the Berne Convention for the Protection of Literary and Artistic Works on Copyrights (1886). TRIPS recognised that the Berne and Paris Convention provided standards for intellectual property protection and therefore the key issue TRIPS addressed was the level of protection. TRIPS set standards by making the substantive obligations of the Paris and Berne Convention, in their most recent versions, compulsory as stated in Articles 2.1 and 9.1 of the TRIPS Agreement. The TRIPS Agreement adds a substantial number of additional obligations and the point of departure is expressed in Articles 2.1 and 9.1 obliging member states to comply with the substantive provisions of the Paris and Berne Convention[363].

The Berne Convention is the oldest international agreement in the field of copyright and was set up to create a union amongst countries who would abide by the Convention for the protection of authors literary and artistic works[364]. The Paris Convention was the first international Convention to make extensive provisions for industrial property[365]. Both the Paris and Berne Convention are overseen by WIPO which acts as an overarching, uniform standard for minimum levels of intellectual property protection[366]. The two main treaties addressed the lack of effective protection, in particular the lack of regulation of local laws that could provide protection to foreign intellectual property right holders. Especially in countries where the intellectual property laws were less developed than others[367].

Where the Paris and Berne Conventions remained inadequate was in the lack of an effective legally binding dispute settlement mechanism and detailed provisions on enforcement of intellectual property rights[368]. The Berne Convention is essentially a private international agreement that entitles private parties with rights in literary and artistic works to copyright protection[369]. TRIPS, on the other hand, extended its protection of intellectual property rights to act as a public international law instrument encompassing disputes between public entities and national states by creating mechanisms to adjudicate and settle disputes by sanctioning states for violating the TRIPS agreement[370].

The main sanctioning power of the WTO under TRIPS can be enforced where a state is seen to not meet its obligations under TRIPS and consequently face dispute settlement measures against unacceptable trade practices under Part V of the TRIPS agreement[371]. The purpose of the sanctions, to withdraw trade concessions, is to act as a deterrent and attempt to minimise intellectual property infringement. Although the numbers of litigated cases are few and far between, by including the dispute settlement mechanism in TRIPS, trade and intellectual property has conflated as intellectual property decisions are adjudicated on within the trade system[372]. This has a direct negative impact on the flexibilities afforded to developing countries as there is increasing pressure to conform to TRIPS standards at a foreign pace and not in line with local and national needs, technology and capacity[373].

## 3 The GCC at the Pre-TRIPS Stage

The Gulf region, pre-TRIPS, was mainly influenced by international intellectual property rules that began during the colonial era. As colonial powers imposed their respective legal regimes in their colonies, variations of intellectual property protection and regimes emerged in developing countries[374]. In terms of pre-TRIPS intellectual property law, there was little, if any, attention paid to the protection of intellectual property rights[375]. Influences of British India extended to Kuwait, Bahrain, Qatar, Abu Dhabi, Dubai, Sharjah, Ajman and Oman until 1947[376]; however, the main interests of Britain in the Gulf states were dictated largely by their desire to maintain the British Indian Empire in relation to commerce, strategic position, diplomacy and imperial defence[377].

From the 1970s onwards, the Gulf states were each experiencing different rates of transformation in terms of governance, independence and both national and international legislative developments[378]. This had a direct impact on intellectual property legislation development in the GCC states as in the midst of international legislative reform and international agreements, the progression from pre-TRIPS to TRIPS compliance resulted in new legislation being brought in as a somewhat rushed process[379]. It was not until the late 1990s that the GCC states started to accede to international intellectual property conventions. Therefore, whereas several developed nations have had over a century to develop extensive international intellectual property laws from their initial ratification or ascension to the Berne and Paris Convention, the GCC states introduced a suite of legislation in a few decades.

## 4 Impact of the Internet Age and Globalisation

As intellectual knowledge has become more readily available, it has, as a result, become more difficult to protect by the GCC states and by western governments[380]. This has presented both strengths and weaknesses for national and international economies. For example, the Gulf states are major exporters to China; China's subsequent exports to the US, Europe and Japan would not be possible without the plastics supplied to it by the Gulf[381]. An obvious strength of globalisation is in the escalation in investments and capital movement amongst member states and foreigners as intellectual property protection mechanisms are enhanced[382]. Certain areas of intellectual property protection can be directly linked to trade concessions, thus this highlights the benefits of better levels of protection to the GCC states. For example, improved industrial design protection has led on to concessions in textiles and likewise protection of geographical indications has led to concessions in agriculture[383]. More specifically, trade concessions have taken place individually with each GCC state as can be seen in the US -Bahrain's FTA which has granted duty free exports for most eligible exports,[384] and also the US - Oman FTA has a clause for suspension of concessions if there is non-compliance[385]. However, the global economic crisis, headed by the US financial crisis and the further debt problems of Greece and other EU countries, critically damaged the world economy, which has slowed down growth rates in developing economies[386].

## 5 The GCC at the TRIPS Compliance Stage

To present a current snapshot of the GCC at the TRIPS compliance level, the GCC is currently the European Union's (EU) fifth largest export market and the EU is GCC's second trading partner and follows the main international provisions of the General Agreement on Trade and Tariffs (GATT), WTO and TRIPS[387]. The GCC have developed national laws and regulations in intellectual property rights to bring it in on par with legislative and regulatory developments in the international arena[388]. Despite its union status, the GCC has yet to finalise uniform provisions to meet the growing challenges posed for the development and diversification of national exports and international trade[389]. For instance, in an attempt to unify legislation, the GCC states have enacted a Trademark Law; however this has not yet been put into effect. The enforcement lacunae in the GCC approach to intellectual property is a common theme; laws are set up, legislation is enacted but the implementation stage of the laws lacks effective infrastructure-related action.

Each GCC state has incorporated TRIPS into their national laws and allowed TRIPS requirements to influence policies and procedures[390]. After the Uruguay Round of trade negotiations, TRIPS was initiated as an agreement was reached between WIPO and WTO on the implementation of intellectual property worldwide[391]. TRIPS promote a free market ideology, giving intellectual property right holders a minimum level of protection in foreign territories[392]. The TRIPS agreement outlines several important trade related aspects of intellectual property. It requires signatory countries to adhere to the Paris Convention, Berne Convention and other WTO Conventions[393], giving it the alternative title of "Berne and Paris-plus" Agreement[394]. It necessitates implementation of its criteria for intellectual property protection through monopoly grants of limited duration, granting a monopoly over any type of intellectual property, enforcement provisions and dispute settlements methods. Each individual GCC state observes and strengthens their interests relating to TRIPS based on their internal development strategies, and there is considerable variation between the states[395].

To clearly understand the intellectual property development of the GCC states, each GCC state will be considered individually. As a common thread, all GCC states have intellectual property legislation; however it is their border measures which have the most significant impact on intellectual property violators. A second common thread can be seen in software piracy rates as all GCC states made significant improvements when they achieved TRIPS compliance, however they have not been able to keep their momentum going and further reduce piracy rate at the same level[396]. The pressure to incorporate TRIPS plus standards will require the states to adhere to stricter enforcement action across all areas of intellectual property protection when the example of software piracy shows they are barely managing to maintain current improvements. There is a stark contrast between the initial improvements made by the Gulf states post TRIPS compliance and the rate of improvement from 2010 onwards.

It is not in the best interests of the GCC states or the international market for that matter to continue to impose stringent laws on intellectual property protection without a deeper understanding of the individual GCC states. By understanding the intellectual property development of each GCC state, the jigsaw pieces of an integrated intellectual property approach can be put together to give a complete picture of how intellectual property rights protection can be improved. Therefore, a state-by-state analysis of intellectual property rights in the GCC will be one component of the overall set of recommendations for an integrated approach to intellectual property protection.

## 6 Saudi Arabia's Intellectual Property Development

As seen in Chapter 2, Saudi Arabia was quite slow in ascending to the WTO and updating its legislation to meet TRIPS compliance[397]. The main national laws in Saudi Arabia for intellectual property protection are in patents, copyright and trademarks[398].

The current intellectual property enforcement system is administered by the Saudi patent office at King Abdulaziz City for Science and Technology (KACST). For intellectual property violations, the Saudi patent office prefers to deal with matters mainly by arbitration and not the court process[399]. When an infringement has taken place, the council makes a decision about settlement; however, the court process tends to be used in more serious cases. As an example, the Saudi Arabia Board of Grievances imposed criminal sanctions for intellectual property violations for the first time in 2012 when the Board of Grievances sentenced a Saudi national to 10 days in jail for intellectual property violations[400].

Saudi Arabia does not have a public repository on intellectual property-based sentences; however the international intellectual property alliance (IIPA) publishes an annual special 301 report on copyright protection and enforcement where it details enforcement action taken by countries[401]. Unlike most intellectual property systems that follow two tracks for intellectual property infringement, criminal or civil, Saudi Arabia handles all piracy and counterfeiting from both criminal and civil perspectives[402]. The power lies with the Board of Grievances who can apply a broad range of punishments if intellectual property violations are found. Therefore, the level of transparency in the Saudi Arabian judicial system is insufficient and not fit for purpose as by not having two separate tracks that regulate intellectual property infringement, the judicial system lacks certainty. Consequently, one of the salient features of set an integrated approach to intellectual property rights protection will be to take into account the level of Islamic law compliance in Saudi Arabia and how the Saudi Arabian intellectual property laws can incorporate sharia principles.

## *Saudi Arabia's Copyright Law*

The Ministry of Culture and Information (MCI) is responsible for punishing copyright violations and follows the Saudi copyright system when imposing sanctions. The MCI established the Violation Review Committee (VRC) on Copyrights in order to review copyright infringement cases and it is a requirement that one member of the VRC be a sharia advisor[403]. During 2010, 483 cases were reviewed and judgments included fines, confiscations and a set number of closure days for infringing shops[404]. For example, the MCI have ordered closure of shops, between 7 days to 60 days, for copyright violations and imposed fines[405]. However, the Saudi Arabian law on copyright protection is less transparent when the case involves Saudi nationals. A state may implement laws that can be wholly or partially sharia compliant, but the acceptance and effectiveness of such laws are dependent on it being recognized by society[406]. Take for example the recent victory of Saudi author, Salwa Aededan against a renowned cleric, Sheikh Ayad al-Qarni for copyright infringement[407]. The court process took over a year with a fine as the final outcome and for the cleric's books to be removed from bookstores. What makes this case so relevant is that the cleric maintained that he had not committed intellectual property infringement and further had support from the public[408].

This case highlights the diverging opinions on intellectual property rights in the region[409]. It also adds weight to the need for a different approach to intellectual property protection. The laws enacted by any government are subject to the public acceptance of the law and the issue this case brings to the forefront is the acceptance of intellectual property right protection. For the GCC states to develop higher standards in intellectual property protection they must shake off the "foreigner rights" connotation that is associated with intellectual property rights protection[410]. This will be discussed further in Chapters 7 and 8[411].

## *Saudi Arabia's Patent Law*

The Saudi Arabia patent law grants different terms of protection for patents such as twenty years for plant varieties, ten years for industrial designs and ten years for layout designs of integrated circuits. Therefore, the protection terms are in line with TRIPS standards; however, where Saudi Arabia differs is on any inventions that violate sharia principles. The Saudi Arabian patent law, at Article 4, states that the protection shall not be granted if it is found that the commercial exploitation of the patent violates sharia law[412]. The main reasons behind the sharia law clause in the Saudi Arabian patent law are to protect against harm to life, to human, animal or plant health and the environment. The exclusion clause in the Saudi Arabian patent law shares similarities with the principle of moral rights in the Berne Convention at section 2a[413].

At present, there is no reported case law where Article 4 of the Saudi patent law has been invoked by the Saudi Arabian courts. This therefore is an area of further research, specifically the potential impact that moral rights can have in sharia compliant states and how to protect intellectual property assets in such situations[414].

## *Border Measures in Line with TRIPS*

Saudi Arabia's intellectual property enforcement is best seen in its border measures. Saudi Arabia passed new border measures in 2004 in compliance with Part III, section 4 of the TRIPS Agreement[415]. A large proportion of the customs committees' cases concern the two main areas of potential intellectual property infringement and commercial fraud. Between 2009 and 2012; out of the 1,625 cases adjudicated by the Jeddah Customs Committee (a court of first instance), 984 of these cases related to intellectual property infringement and commercial fraud[416]. The border measures are becoming more robust as the number of seizures of counterfeit goods has increased from 2011 to 2012. The number of units seized in 2012 was approximately 54.8 million units which was an increase of 13.8% when compared to 2011. The total value of the seized goods amounted to 763 million riyals[417]. However, is the increasing number of seizures a reflection of Saudi Arabia improving the level of intellectual property protection it offers or that there is a greater amount of counterfeit goods imported to Saudi Arabia than previous years?

### *Saudi Arabia Headed Back to the US Special 301 Watch List*

As noted in Chapter 2[418], Saudi Arabia was removed from the US Special 301 watch list in 2009 as it had made significant improvements to its intellectual property laws. The IIPA have recommended that Saudi Arabia be placed back on the US Special 301 watch list[419]. The main findings of the IIPA were high piracy rates, insufficient government resource allocation and market barriers such as import restrictions on many copyright products and complicated content review processes[420]. The IIPA recommendations highlight the imbalanced relationship the US and Saudi Arabia have as by placing Saudi Arabia back on the watch list, it could negate all the work carried out by the various Saudi bodies over the past ten years. Taking software piracy rates as an example, Saudi Arabia was able to make a considerable improvement from reaching TRIPS compliance and implementing new measures; however further improvements have not been apparent. Therefore, the integrated intellectual property approach for Saudi Arabia requires consideration of its sharia framework as discussed in Chapters 1 and 2 as well as its intellectual property development and make recommendations of a modified approach to amalgamate sharia law and intellectual property. As will be seen next in the case of the UAE, their intellectual property systems differ from Saudi Arabia as does their level of sharia compliance.

## 7 UAE's Intellectual Property Development

Dubai has made the most progress in intellectual property enforcement through its customs units for intellectual property rights with specialist teams in place to confiscate infringing goods. For example, Dubai Customs unit investigates goods suspected of infringing intellectual property rights. Once a complaint is filed, Dubai Customs take a sample of the suspect goods from the shipping consignment or from the free zone location where it has been confiscated and submit the sample to an official laboratory for testing to determine whether or not it is genuine[421]. Dubai Customs made 750 seizures of intellectual property-infringing goods between 2011 and 2012, with a value exceeding AED 50 million in seized goods[422]. Further, in 2008[423], the Dubai Declaration called for a new set of standards to be developed at the national and regional levels to bring in more effective remedies for both civil and criminal proceedings and enhance border measures to improve enforcement of intellectual property rights[424]. Thus, Dubai can demonstrate a real commitment to protecting intellectual property rights and taking action through its border measures to seize infringing goods.

Despite developments in the UAE, as in Saudi Arabia, the IIPA has recommended that the UAE also be put back on the US Special 301 watch list[425]. The reason for the recommendation for the UAE to be on the watch list after many years is in connection with the UAE copyright law and the IIPA requirement that the software piracy rates in the UAE are lowered. The IIPA represent the western demands on the GCC states to adhere to higher standards; however they overlook the progress and development that is being made and is for this reason that an integrated intellectual property rights protection approach is quintessential to the success of intellectual property reform in the GCC. By modifying the existing approach to take into account the nuances and differing sources of law of the GCC states, an intellectual property approach that is fit for purpose can be instigated.

## 8 Qatar's Intellectual Property Development

Qatar cites sharia law as a main source of law; it places the least importance on sharia law principles when compared to the other Gulf states[426]. It has the highest gross domestic product (GDP) per head in the GCC. It ranks 13th in the global competitiveness index and is above all the other GCC states[427]. Although intellectual property laws are relatively new in Qatar, the intellectual property legislation is the most comprehensive of all the GCC states. Qatari laws protect almost all types of intellectual property rights[428]. Further Qatar has enacted TRIPS plus provisions even though they are not mandatory as yet. TRIPS plus provisions are evident in Qatar's 2011 Law on Intellectual Property Rights Border Measures[429].

Whereas the other GCC states abide by TRIPS standards and apply Part III, Section 4 of TRIPS, Qatar goes beyond the minimum standard of protecting trademark and copyright counterfeiting to protecting any intellectual property rights[430]. As Qatar has a comprehensive set of intellectual property laws, it has not been subject to an IIPA report since 2003 and unlike Saudi Arabia and UAE, Qatar is not headed towards the US special 301 watch list any time soon. Qatar does not issue its own patents despite having a patent law. Instead, patents are issued through the GCC patent office[431].

Against the backdrop of a need for convergence between intellectual property and Islamic law is the need of both developed and developing countries to complete free trade agreements as foreign investment is more likely to take place where host countries have strong intellectual property protection[432]. The main benefit of effective intellectual property protection is a reduction in risks of infringement which then leads to an economic boost for protected products[433]. This has a positive effect on the volume of foreign direct investment (FDI) as foreign firms are able to compete compliant GCC states is a lack of ability to effectively enforce the intellectual property laws that were brought into meet TRIPS standards[434]. Also, not all the GCC states are developing their laws and systems to a uniform level[435].

## 9 Economic View on International Intellectual Property

Increasing and enhancing trade flows through liberalisation remains a priority for policymakers in developing countries[436]. A common view among economists assumes that trade liberalisation is an engine for economic development[437]. Empirical evidence to date highlights the importance of trade for economic growth in developing countries[438]. However, states with politically instability have struggled to enforce macroeconomic policies towards trade reform and the role of foreign investment is ambiguous[439]. Transparency in intellectual property development and legislation is also a contributing factor[440]. Economists argue international trade under the guise of bilateral and multilateral agreements remains unfair to developing states, given that the large proportion of benefits from trade are amassed by developed countries[441]. Therefore, consideration needs to be given to the economic impact of intellectual property to developing countries.

There is scholarly work on intellectual property in developing countries, particularly on the economic impact of intellectual property and achieving TRIPS compliance[442]. Although the general body of literature supports economic growth through stronger intellectual property laws, there is very little empirical data to measure the economic impact of intellectual property rights at varying points of time[443]. The purpose of TRIPS is to address the different ways in which intellectual property rights are protected around the world and to narrow down the deviances in protection under the umbrella of uniform international rules[444]. TRIPS established minimum levels of intellectual property protection that each WTO Member State is required to provide in order to gain membership status[445]. The TRIPS agreement sets out a *"one size fits all"* approach to international intellectual property setting[446], extending the reach of the Berne Convention. Under TRIPS, the principles of national treatment, automatic protection and independence of protection bind WTO members who are not party to the Berne Convention. In addition, the TRIPS Agreement imposes an obligation of "most-favoured-nation treatment", under which advantages conferred by a WTO Member to the nationals of any other country must also be conferred to the nationals of all WTO members[447].

For the GCC states, this was the beginning of unprecedented international pressure to develop a requisite level of intellectual property regimes that conformed to Western standards[448]. Compliance to the TRIPS Agreement can be seen in the recent proliferation of regional and bilateral free trade agreements between the GCC States and developed countries that include elements of intellectual property protection and development as defined by minimum TRIPS standards[449]. Free trade agreements are themselves multi-faceted as there are not only implications on intellectual property development in the GCC as a result of its free trade agreements with other states[450], but also where non GCC states are entering into trade agreements between themselves there is a consequential effect on GCC trade and services.

The free trade agreements between the GCC and western states are now intrusively integrating TRIPS-plus standards into a GCC region that has developed from pre-TRIPS to TRIPS standards in a very short space of time[451]. The developing GCC countries are as a result under increasing pressure to develop national intellectual property regimes, which work in line with those of developed countries[452]. Many analysts have criticised the increased pressure from developed countries on developing countries to conform to western standards as opposed to allowing progression in line with the needs of individual developing countries[453]. The crux of the dichotomy between western pressure for more stringent level of intellectual property protection and national legislative inadequacies is in what both sides perceive to be effective action[454]. For example, the statistical analysis of intellectual property infringement shows that the Gulf states have improved their intellectual property enforcement in areas such as software piracy as the rates of infringement are falling[455]. However, the pressure to incorporate TRIPS plus standard will require the GCC states to adhere to stricter enforcement action when they are barely managing to maintain previous levels of improvements[456].

## 10 What Does TRIPS Plus Really Mean?

TRIPS plus provisions are defined as *"commitments which go beyond what is already included or consolidated in the TRIPS Agreement"*[457]. The relationship between TRIPS plus regimes and international trade has become so inextricably woven by the dominant developed countries that it is difficult to see the two as separate entities[458]. For the GCC to meet its TRIPS plus requirements for both the US and the EU it is required to harmonise its current laws to that of its international counterparts[459]. The US/EU presents a resolute standing point for the Arab region of making trade liberalization and foreign investment dependent on agreement and implementation of TRIPS Plus provisions[460]. From the current EU-GCC trade agreement, it is clear the EU want more harmonisation in policies and law making, preferring to deal with regional blocs as opposed to individual states[461].

There are certain TRIPS plus requirements that set it apart from the level of TRIPS compliance which is currently in place. TRIPs plus can be seen to exert pressure for stronger obligations in intellectual property areas such as: data exclusivity, patent terms, compulsory licensing, industrial rights, trademark protection, plant and animal patents from national patent laws, copyright protection terms, membership to further international agreements, transition period privileges, dispute settlement methods, border measures and enforcement against intellectual property violation particularly criminal sanctions through court action[462].

## 11 TRIPS Plus and the GCC

Applying this to the GCC, there are certain discrete facets of the GCC states which require consideration. The oil-led growth has created weak structural foundations in Arab economies resulting in an import -dependent economy[463]. The issue of poor traditional, local knowledge development has had a negative economic impact on Arab agriculture, manufacturing and industrial production as highlighted in the Arab Human Development Report[464]. The report does highlight the real question for economic growth for the Arab world at large. As oil prices increase and developed countries look to previous unviable options for potential development[465], now is the optimum time for the Gulf States to form a strategy which seeks economic development in line with the internet age and knowledge-based assets for sustainable long term development[466]. The GCC states are aware of the benefits of a knowledge-driven economy where intangible assets are potentially becoming much more valuable than physical assets[467]. Therefore, improving intellectual property protection will not simply appease the EU and US in bringing trade agreements to a conclusion and increasing foreign direct investment, but will develop a solid foundation of legislation and policy that will enable the Gulf states and similar regions to expand their knowledge-based economies[468].

## 12 Not a Level Playing Field – Developed Countries versus the GCC

There is a stark contrast in the resources available to countries with developed intellectual property systems to those that are still at the development stage[469]. This is mainly because developed countries can utilise independent reports, legislation and case law to influence policy, whereas developing countries lack the infrastructure to effectively catch up[470]. The GCC states will want to draw on the technical expertise and experience of its international partners to advance its intellectual property agenda[471]. If the Gulf states can satisfy TRIPS plus obligations, the potential to open up new markets brings with them opportunities for economic growth[472]. However, TRIPS plus is case specific and its effect on bilateral agreements is not to the same uniform standard as standard TRIPS compliance[473]. How the TRIPS plus obligations are firstly incorporated and then implemented will be a matter of concern for the Gulf states. The TRIPS plus obligations specific to the GCC are: to move away from the flexibilities offered under TRIPS obligations, extend the definition of "data" and scope of data exclusivity, extension of patent terms, restrictions on use of compulsory licensing, increasing minimum protection for industrial rights and trademark protection, relinquish transition period privileges granted from WTO and increased enforcement against intellectual property violation through criminal proceedings and judicial decisions[474]. Out of all the TRIPS plus obligations it is the enforcement criteria which is the most complex to implement due to the lack of societal awareness/acceptance of the criminality of intellectual property infringement[475]. There isn't a substantive body of case law from the GCC states dealing with intellectual property infringement that can be referred to by the courts to aid interpretation[476]. This will be one of the main recommendations in an integrated intellectual property model as more transparency and disclosure is needed by the court system to aide legal interpretation of intellectual property and to create certainty and consistency in the law, all of which will support better intellectual property rights protection.

## 13 Customs Law in the GCC

In safeguarding against intellectual property infringement and offering better protection, Customs law has been an area of development for the Gulf region[477]. The Common Customs Law of the Cooperation Council for the Arab states of the Gulf is adhered to by all the GCC states and prohibits the admission, transit or exit of prohibited or infringing goods except with the approval of the customs authorities[478]. It also prohibits the admission into free zones of goods that infringe intellectual property rights[479]. Qatar passed the first stand-alone legislation regulating intellectual property protection in border measures with an emphasis on improving the intellectual property eco system in relation to enforcement against piracy and counterfeiting[480].

## 14 The Role of Sharia in Intellectual Property Development

Intellectual property development in the GCC is not solely dominated by the US and EU; the GCC states through increased legislative measures are emerging towards TRIPS Plus standards[481]. However, the GCC states need to avoid creating hollow intellectual property policies and pay more than lip service to the influences of sharia law on intellectual property development and enforcement[482]. Tenets of Islamic law and its underlying principles have been described as "the golden thread that binds the sharia and intellectual property protection"[483]. Before the 1980s and at the early stages of the intellectual property revolution that was to sweep the GCC States, the codification of the new laws in the GCC states and sharia were depicted as the codification of laws in the Islamic states to be an irresistible force while the sharia was an irremovable object[484]. The anomaly that existed between the two has shifted in favour of clear domination of western-based secular laws in the commercial and civil context, raising doubt as to whether sharia is an irremovable object in the enactment of intellectual property law making.

The conundrum has now shifted to being one where the position of sharia is uncertain. As the area of intellectual property law continues to develop in the GCC region, there are three possibilities for the influences of the doctrines of sharia law; whether it is to be further eroded, maintained as an underlying set of principles to uphold intellectual properly, or re-asserted to influence policy making and legislative reform. However, the Gulf states in particular are not the mere pushovers that developed countries might assume[485]. There are legislative frameworks in place which are heavily influenced by the West (for example, Bahrain, Kuwait and UAE), however given the recent Arab Spring; there is an undercurrent of political unrest that requires the GCC states to review their internal infrastructures[486].

Sharia law impacts on protection parameters in respect of copyright, patent and trademark protection. The growing influence of sharia on intellectual property is dependent on three main factors: an understanding of Islamic law to provide support for the protection of intellectual property law, provisions to protect intellectual property rights with the aim of increasing innovations and stimulate economic development and the effectiveness of any law being dependent on society both recognizing and accepting it[487].

To date, sharia law has had minimal, if any, bearing on intellectual property law development. In the UAE, the Departments of Economic Development (DED) have jurisdiction for administrative action to enforce intellectual property rights in their own emirate and Article 14 of DED states; "*Islamic law codified in the Shari'ah is applied in family courts but is less evident in the commercial sphere*".[488]

The GCC states are aware of the benefits of a knowledge driven economy where intangible assets have the potential to become much more invaluable than physical assets[489]. Intellectual property rights are the way forward for new business opportunities and as a driving force behind economic growth[490]. Therefore, for the Gulf states, intellectual property protection is a vital lever to business success. There needs to be a reinvention in how intellectual property law is projected in the public arena. The legislative changes in the region act as the foundations from which interpretation of the laws is essential to providing a working model towards TRIPS Plus standards.

The main hurdle for intellectual property enforcement in the GCC states is a lack of specialised Courts to deal with cases, making civil litigation in the region difficult. Right holders opt instead to file complaints with customs authorities where the issues are related to trade-mark and copyright infringement[491].

## 15 Conclusion

In conclusion, the GCC states are in a position to make landmark decisions in the implementation of intellectual property rights in the international arena and in respect of demonstrating Islamic approval for the enactment of more effective intellectual property laws. The Gulf states are in an enviable position; the development of international trade and services via multilateral and bilateral trade agreements allows them to act as a hub between Eastern and Western markets[492]. The GCC has an opportunity to not simply rush forward from TRIPS to TRIPS Plus standards but to take a side step and develop strategies to best implement intellectual property laws that are accepted by the public. Islamic finance could prove to be a successful vehicle to not only highlight that distinct features of sharia law can be amalgamated with western influenced products such as modern banking financial products that satisfy business growth and societal acceptance in the Muslim world, but also to promote the existence of intellectual property in Islamic finance products and beyond. Chapters 7 and 8 assess the impact of Islamic finance on intellectual property development and of Islamic finance embodying a significant role in the development of an integrated intellectual property model.

There are significant outcomes from this chapter that will influence the overall set of recommendations for an integrated intellectual property approach. The GCC states have individual nuances and traits which influence the level of sharia compliance that exists at a constitutional level, they have international agreements that they have entered into as sovereign nations and agreements they have entered into collectively. As can be seen in this chapter, Saudi Arabia has made a concerted effort to develop intellectual property protection systems in line with sharia law. For example, by stipulating that its Violation Review Committee (VRC) on Copyrights must have at least one member that is a sharia advisor, there is an attempt by Saudi Arabia to not let copyright protection act on its own volition and keep it in tandem with sharia law. A concern for Saudi Arabia will be the recommendation it be placed back on the US Special 301 Watch list as this would undermine the efforts by Saudi Arabia to implement better intellectual property strategies. There has also been a recommendation by the International Intellectual Property Alliance (IIPA) to put Dubai back on the US Special 301 Watch list and Kuwait is already still on the watch list. Therefore, an integrated intellectual property framework would be of benefit to all the GCC states as it will further enhance the protection they offer.

The next chapter considers TRIPS Plus in more detail and what the potential changes will be for the GCC states in order to increase compliance from TRIPS to TRIPS Plus with a close analysis of the economic impact of TRIPS Plus. The key question raised by this chapter is what room for manoeuvre, if any, do the GCC states have in controlling how foreign companies protect their intellectual property rights in their states.

# 6

# The International Trojan Horse: TRIPS Plus and Investor to State Dispute Settlements. Spill Over Effects on the GCC

## 1 Introduction

There are challenges facing the GCC states in stepping up from their current TRIPS compliance level of intellectual property protection to TRIPS Plus. The research carried out in this monograph up until this chapter has investigated the sharia law perspective on intellectual property law, the main sources and the justification for intellectual property. The research has also examined individual developments of the GCC states in terms of governance, intellectual property enforcement and institutional structures. The proposal of an integrated model, which is the main research aim, would not be complete without considering the impact of international trade agreements and investor to state dispute settlement mechanisms on the GCC states. Therefore the purpose of this chapter is to research international developments and the spill over effects they potentially have for the GCC states and in turn apply the findings to the overall integrated intellectual property framework. This chapter will also take into account western justifications for intellectual property rights and how the different intellectual property systems have developed over time.

Nations involved in international agreements, both bilateral and multilateral, have sought to include investor to state dispute settlements (ISDS) in the agreements as an arbitrational action. ISDS enables foreign investors to circumvent domestic legal processes and hold governments in foreign states to account in arbitration tribunals, without having to go through WTO, in effect creating a corporate sovereignty. Sovereignty is itself a contentious issue, as different states and regions have very different political structures, resulting in individual sovereignty issues. ISDS poses a series of threats to national sovereignty as it puts investors on par with nations giving them authority to seek compensation directly from states with powers such as seizing state assets[493]. Therefore, within the ambit of international intellectual property law, future GCC developments must take into account the following research objectives as outlined below.

## 2 Research Objectives

The research objectives addressed in this chapter are:

- To set out the western justifications of intellectual property rights in the differing areas of copyright, design rights, patents, confidential information and trademarks in order to inform the content of an integrated intellectual property framework.
- To carry out an in depth analysis of TRIPS Plus proposals, the significant provisions of TRIPS Plus that impact the GCC, analyse the various proposed implementation clauses in TRIPS Plus and identify what the potential ramifications for the GCC states are.
- To review the role of international organisations on law-making in GCC countries and to assess the impact of current international dispute settlement mechanisms on the GCC, outside of the WTO remit. The main mechanisms to consider are bilateral state agreements, corporate sovereignty and investor to state dispute settlements.

## 3 Justifications of Intellectual Property Rights

The justifications of intellectual property rights have evolved under three main headings of economics, labour and social benefit[494]. The majority of new intellectual property assets are drawn from an existing stock of knowledge, ideas and language, known as the common stock. If the parameters of intellectual property rights are too widely construed, the common stock will be depleted, inhibiting intellectual production and impoverishing intellectual growth. Therefore, every patent application will not be successful, nor will every copyright claim as certain criteria need to be satisfied before protection can be granted.

Intellectual property rights have established and refined functionalities in areas of; copyright, confidential information, trademark, patents and design rights. The rights were borne out of existing legal principles from contract and equity law and each individual area of intellectual property law has been developed in accordance with the specific requirements of the asset warranting protection. For example, copyright has developed under an aesthetic model, initially focused on protecting artist rights in domestic legal systems and has expanded as a set of moral, economic and social benefit principles in the TRIPS agreement and international agreements. On the other hand, unregistered design rights have followed a functional rights approach with a focus on the definition of a design, the originality of the design, the relationship between originality and the commonplace in the design and exclusions from protection.

Despite the deviances in the approach to different types of intellectual property assets, one fundamental commonality they all share is their intangible or abstract form[495]. Not all nations recognise or enforce all the doctrines of intellectual property, however due to international obligations; most nations must have minimum levels of compliance to the main types of intellectual property assets[496]. The first family of intellectual property rights to consider is the justification for copyright protection.

## *Justifications for Copyright Protection*

Copyright was initially justified as a form of protection for the creative investment of the author, with Locke's labour theory setting out the rights of an author to the fruits of her labour. In Chapter 3, Locke's labour theory was considered as a connecting factor between the sharia law principles of natural rights and western philosophy on the natural rights in intellectual property law[497]. To understand how copyright protection came into existence and has developed as an aesthetic model will impact on the recommendations for an integrated intellectual property rights approach in the GCC. Copyright has developed at a domestic level in three areas; as a natural labour right, very much in accordance with the philosophical writings of John Locke[498], as a commercial model providing an economic incentive for authors to create intangible assets[499] and as a utilitarian model which rewards the endeavours of the inventor with a perceived social benefit in mind that after a limited term of copyright, the works are freely availability in the public domain[500].

John Locke's labour theory is centred on the labour argument that each person has a property right in their own body and the subsequent labour of their own body. Property rights are then acquired when the common stock is mixed with labour to produce a new form of property which can be owned by the labourer[501]. Locke's theory had its limitations when applied to intellectual property law as the labour to property equation was restricted to two conditions; 'no spoilage' and 'enough and as good for others'[502]. The spoilage restriction of only appropriating as much as one can use before it spoils ceases to be a meaningful restriction as value can now be stored as a monetary commodity and not solely property. Secondly, the sufficiency restriction, of leaving 'enough and as good for others', also has limitations to property rights and is less applicable to intellectual property rights[503].

Given the need to balance author rights against the common stock, copyright law developed beyond the founding philosophies of Locke's labour theory and in the 1894 case of Hollinrake v Truswell, the idea of expression dichotomy was established whereby it is the expression of an idea that is protected and not the idea itself[504]. The primary focus therefore is originality in the expression of an idea, which is a different approach to other areas of intellectual property law such as the requirement of 'novelty' and 'inventive step' in patents. The TRIPS agreement enshrines the idea expression dichotomy of protecting the expression of an idea and not the idea itself as seen at Article 9.2 of the TRIPS agreement[505]. To protect the expression of an idea through copyright, the law governing copyright protection has evolved more in favour of a commercial model. The economic growth-based justification for copyright protection has had the most impact in the TRIPS agreement as investors are cautious when it comes to expanding in to foreign markets, to counteract this TRIPS allows for proprietary knowledge to be sold above its marginal cost, to offer an incentive for the production of knowledge[506].

The third area of relevance to copyright protection is the perceived social benefit doctrine and moral rights. The perceived social benefit doctrine marries well with the commercial incentive model for copyright protection as both allow for rewarding the right holder with a monopoly over the asset for a fixed term, the social benefit doctrine balances the monopoly against the eventual release of the material in the public domain whereas the economic argument is that it leads to an increase in intellectual production. Moral rights recognise the continuing interest of the author in her work, that it is treated with respect even where the copyright is transferred and the economic interest no longer lies with the original author. The TRIPS agreement excludes moral rights from the minimum level of requirements stating members do not have rights or obligations under the TRIPS Agreement in respect of the rights conferred under Article 6 relating to moral rights or of the rights derived there from[507].

## *Justifications for Design Rights*

A design right is a form of intellectual property which subsists in an original design, any aspect of the shape, configuration of the whole or any part of an article. The aesthetic model is more applicable to registered designs as an unregistered design right will not protect surface decoration. The need for unregistered design rights arose from industries such as textile and fashion that develop large numbers of designs and needed to protect the appearance of a product. The unregistered design right comes into existence automatically whenever an original design is created and it replaced the indirect protection, afforded as part of copyright law, to essentially functional designs[508].

A design can be protected as a registered design if the design is new, has individual character or constitutes a component part of a complex product[509]. Registered design rights require a formal application for registration of the design before the rights can be granted whereas copyright protection does not involve a formal registration. Design rights protection provides a course of action against someone producing the identical design or a design substantially similar to the registered design and gives the owner a monopoly in the shape, configuration, pattern and ornamentation of the design. However, copyright requires the owner to show that copying has taken place and only provides protection against somebody copying the work.

Copyright protection gave the same protection to design documents from which functional, mass produced articles were produced, as it gave to artistic works. There were therefore significant anomalies in the law relating to design rights and the aesthetic model of generic copyright protection. Aesthetics and functionality can be components of an individual design system, making it a difficult area of law to develop and distinguish from copyright protection. National laws have often had difficulty in deciding which elements belong to a design, and to what extent they should be recognised[510]. The TRIPS Agreement has set specific guidelines on the protection of industrial designs at section 4, providing protection of independently created industrial designs that are new or original for a minimum of ten years[511].

## *Justifications for Patent Protection*

Patent protection originates from three broad justifications; inventor rights, to encourage investment in innovation and to disseminate information in the public domain to encourage others to innovate[512]. The justification for inventor rights is on the premise that the labour, time and effort that are invested into creating a patentable asset require protection against economic free riders[513]. The rationalisation for patent protection is embedded in the basic principle that information, the founding basis of intangible market drivers, is expensive to create but cheap to copy[514]. Competitors can copy the information and appropriate the value of the property at a lower price, in effect reaping the benefits of someone else's invention and causing a loss to the original producers[515]. The economic free rider therefore causes several losses to the original producer namely: removes value from the product, impinges on the primary producer's ability to recoup costs, loss of revenues and incentives to invest diminish[516]. The issue is exacerbated by the fact that in some cases the value of the invention is in the information it contains and not its physical structure. Therefore patent protection requires exclusionary boundaries through secrecy, marketing skills and various types of first mover advantages[517].

A patent is an official document that confers proprietorship of an invention on the recipient, grant of a patent is preceded by examination of applications by the patenting authority. The fundamental principle behind patents is that the government awards exclusive control over an invention for a fixed number of years to the individual who first discloses the invention within its territory.

In most systems, a patent is granted to an applicant who is first to submit a detailed description of the invention, for example in the UK, the system operates on a first to file model. The TRIPS agreement sought to set international minimum standards in patent protection and at Article 27 stated the requirements for; novelty, inventiveness, industrial applicability and exclusions[518]. A successful patent application grants the inventor the right to exclude others from utilising the patented invention for a given amount of time, under the TRIPS Agreement, the monopoly right is granted for twenty years[519]. In return, the inventor is under an obligation to describe the invention in detail to give notice to the public. The counterargument to the monopoly right granted to the inventor is that monopoly is against public interest.

This is addressed through domestic patent laws and the TRIPS Agreement to provide exemptions to not let the monopoly right interfere with the public interest aspect. Articles 7 and 8 of the TRIPS Agreement include a number of flexibilities with the aim of safeguarding and protecting the public interest. This is particularly relevant to developing countries as Article 8 of the agreement makes provisions to "promote the public interest in sectors of vital importance to their socio-economic and technological development"[520]. Therefore, the public interest exception is subjective as it requires consideration of the socio-political needs of a country and gives some level of flexibility to developing countries to harmonise the inconsistencies in their public interest measures with the overall TRIPS framework.

## *Justifications for Trademark Law*

Trademark protection has traditionally followed an indicator of origin model whereby the purpose of a trademark is to be able to identify and verify the origin of the goods and services to which it attaches[521]. Trademark protection has developed to have both intrinsic functions as indicators of origin and extrinsic functions of quality and reputation[522]. Trademark law has developed in the following key areas; what constitutes a trademark, distinctiveness, scope of protection, terms of protection, absolute and relative grounds for refusal, exhaustion of rights, licensing, genuine use, cancellation and revocation[523]. The justifications for trademark protection can be distinguished from copyright and patents as the reasoning behind trademark protection is not rooted in functionality or aesthetics, it is the right of producers to identify their products. Also, a trademark may be enforceable indefinitely as long as it continues to serve to identify the origin of the goods or services, as oppose to the limited durations of protection in copyright and patents.

Existing trademark laws from EU countries and the US have in effect harmonised to create a minimum standard of trademark protection under the TRIPS Agreement. The TRIPS Agreement defines a trademark as; any sign, capable of being represented graphically and capable of distinguishing the goods or services of one undertaking from those of other undertakings[524]. Trademarks are acquired at a domestic level through registration, many countries require local use of the registered mark to maintain the registration. Therefore, whether a given mark can be registered in a particular country will depend on the law of that country. The Madrid Protocol[525], an international treaty, removes some of the difficulties for the international registration of trademarks by offering a convenient and economical means of securing trademark registration in member countries. From the GCC states, Bahrain and Oman are signatories.

## *Justifications for Confidential Information Law*

The law pertaining to confidential information can be traced back to maxims of equity and contract law. From as early as the middle of the nineteenth century, courts were able to identify an equitable jurisdiction for breach of confidentiality, as can be seen in cases such as Morison v Moat (1851)[526] and Prince Albert v Strange (1849)[527]. In both cases, as well as actions for breach of contract and trust, the courts also identified breach of confidence as a standalone cause of action[528].

Law of equity has ingrained its influence in the development of legal obligations in respect of confidential information as the law on confidential information is not contingent upon any form of contract, express or implied. Rather, it developed as an equitable doctrine of confidence, unaffected by contract and on the broad equitable principle of not taking unfair advantage of information received in confidence[529].

Confidential information is not a form of physical property; it is the right to protect the confidentiality of the information and not its physical embodiment. Unlike copyright, the law of confidence protects information that may be communicated orally and not written down or recorded in any material form. In English law there are three elements which need to be satisfied for a breach of confidence action claim to be successful which were set out in the case of Coco v AN Clark (Engineering) Ltd (1969); the information in question must have the necessary quality of confidence about it, that information must have been imparted in circumstances importing an obligation of confidence and there must be an unauthorised use of that information to the detriment of the party communicating it[530].

Countries vary on what constitutes confidential information and what the elements of a breach of confidence action entail. Countries that have acceded to the TRIPS Agreement have introduced laws on the protection of confidential information in line with TRIPS requirements which states that for information to be legally protectable: the information must be secret, as in not generally known or readily accessible to persons that normally deal with that kind of information, it must have commercial value because it is secret and the owner must have taken reasonable steps to keep it secret[531].

Article 39 of the TRIPS Agreement is the first multilateral acknowledgement of the essential role that trade secrets play in the global industry and represents the American and European notion of protecting confidential information as a means of fully protecting intellectual property rights[532]. Therefore, TRIPS standards have created minimum standards of protections in the main areas of intellectual property law based on existing national laws of EU countries and the US. Each area of intellectual property law has followed its own development line, criteria for registration, exclusions and actions for infringement. For the GCC, the existing knowledge from the TRIPS Agreement needs to be considered against increasing pressure to adopt TRIPS Plus standards.

## 4 TRIPS to TRIPS Plus – a Higher Level of Compliance

The provisions for TRIPS have been considered in detail in Chapter 5[533]. In terms of TRIPS Plus, there are three main areas of intellectual property rights that are a concern for the GCC. Firstly, under TRIPS Plus, there is a requirement for an extension of the duration of patent protection that is currently available under TRIPS. The GCC states currently adhere to TRIPS standards and offer TRIPS compliant patent protection of twenty years from the date of filing,[534] this is in compliance with the TRIPS Agreement at Article 33[535]. TRIPS Plus calls for the time period to be above twenty years, the EU and the US are in effect trying to write-off provisions of TRIPs through their FTAs and subsequently bypassing the WTO agreement. The GCC are struggling to manage at a TRIPS compliance level, increasing the standards to TRIPS Plus could bring the patent system to a halt. Oman already has TRIPS Plus in its FTA with the US, for example, at Article 15.8 of the FTA there is a provision to extend the patent term in pharmaceutical-based patents[536].

The second main TRIPS Plus provision is in the area of compulsory licensing. The scope for compulsory licensing and parallel importing is considerably narrowed in TRIPS Plus, limiting the circumstances where parties can use the measures[537]. Article 31 of TRIPS and the Doha Declaration reiterates member states' rights to compulsory licensing and government use[538]. FTA's impose TRIPS Plus restrictions such as the Article 4.20 of the US-Jordan which limits anti-competitive practice and the overall scope of compulsory licensing[539]. The benefits of compulsory licensing to developing countries cannot be understated. In 2003, Malaysia became the first Asian country to issue a government use, compulsory licence to import antiretroviral drugs. The Malaysian Minister of Domestic Trade and Consumer Affairs issued a two-year government use compulsory license to import from India[540].

Although compulsory licensing itself is sharia compliant[541], the same cannot be said for the restrictions posed by TRIPS Plus. The arguments for TRIPS Plus are spear headed by the pharmaceutical corporations who do not want drug prices reduced, however TRIPS Plus may contradict sharia principles of public interest. Therefore, there is a potential risk posed to the GCC from restrictions on compulsory licensing in pharmaceutical products[542]. Public interest aims to protect the legitimate interests of the community within the recognised sources of Islamic law and secure public welfare through promoting the benefits of a rule that is for the good of the public and has been an area of Islamic law that impacts on intellectual property protection[543]. It also creates a dichotomy between principles of riba and gharar against honouring international agreements as discussed in Chapter 3[544].

Thirdly and most pressing, is the TRIPS Plus enforcement criterion. TRIPS Plus demands stronger enforcement measures from developing countries. These include criminal sanctions, higher damages, mandatory injunctions, and transitional liability, above and beyond the TRIPS Agreement. The impacts of the enforcement criterion are potentially substantial. It is the elimination of enforcement flexibilities allowed by TRIPS that is the crux of the problem. For the GCC the problems are interwoven, there is a lack of technical expertise to incorporate and implement TRIPS Plus, coupled by an insufficient domestic research and manufacturing capacity as well as infrastructure issues.

The GCC has minimal anti-competitive practices and the TRIPS Plus enforcement criteria will necessitate higher standards. The GCC states are all developing intellectual property institutions such as the Dubai International Financial Centre (DIFC)[545], however there is less evidence of success at enforcement of intellectual property rights than there is legislative development. It is here where an integrated intellectual property approach that takes into account; the structure of the GCC states, international agreements and pressures, the international institutions, Islamic finance and both societal and religious views will have significant impact on re-evaluating intellectual property rights in the GCC.

## 5 The TRIPS Plus Increased Enforcement Criteria

The main TRIPS plus criteria that the GCC will struggle with is the increased enforcement requirements. Efforts to reduce intellectual property infringement since TRIPS have been met with lukewarm success at best as seen in areas such as software piracy which are stagnant and therefore the Gulf states need to do more than simply make legislative changes[546]. The danger for the GCC is a widening gulf between its intellectual property laws and the public acceptance of the new regimes.

These lacunae can be addressed through understanding the development and expansion of successful initiatives such as sharia compliant banking which under the heading of Islamic finance is an industry worth $2 trillion globally[547]. Islamic finance products boost the economy in the GCC and by translating the successful sharia compliant banking model to intellectual property protection there is an opportunity to fuel a knowledge driven economy that promotes intellectual property rights in conjunction with established Islamic law principles as concepts of sharia law play a significant role in Islamic finance products[548].

The rationale for riba and gharar comes from the concepts of speculative risk and unjust enrichment respectively. The argument against intellectual property protection therefore lies within the definition of unjust enrichment and links with the length of time an intellectual property right holder is awarded a monopoly right over the invention. Patents for Islamic finance products exist and are still a growth area for the Gulf states as this is an emerging market. For example, sukuk, also known as Islamic bonds, are being developed with intellectual property rights as the asset. German-based FWU group, with its subsidiary in Dubai, developed the first ever intellectual property based sukuk worth $55 million[549].

Further, there has been an increase in licensing agreements between the GCC and Malaysia as well as negotiations for a FTA. The Malaysian trade agreement is still under review however it can set the precedent for incorporating Islamic Finance in other negotiations. Islamic finance will be considered in more detail in Chapter 7.

## 6 Intellectual Property and the GCC

Intellectual property case law in the GCC is few and far between. This means doctrines such as the doctrine of legitimate expectations and minimum standard of treatment have not been put to the test. The GCC states are historically Islamic states and they have all incorporated sharia law into their constitutions[550]. There is no mention of intellectual property law in primary sharia law sources, there are however, relevant principles of sharia law that can be found in secondary sources[551]. The sharia principles on ownership of property, obligations on property right holders, remedies for property right holders and appropriation of property have been used to justify the same rights to exist in intellectual property[552]. The Islamic law principles governing contract law have been applied to intellectual property protection[553]. The exigencies of the international trade market are no longer from trading partners alone, corporations, investors and intermediaries are wanting a piece of the decision-making pie. Other areas of sharia law that have been considered namely; public interest, moral rights, financial rights, business, trade and economic gain, all play a role in creating a legal space for intellectual property to exist and develop in the GCC states[554]. Further research in the field of national heritage in the GCC states and its potential impact on intellectual property protection will be an offshoot from the current research.

In terms of sharia references to international transactions and conducting business, the Quran has clear statements regarding honouring agreements and the need for certainty whilst forbidding riba and gharar. The clearest reference can be found in Surah Al Baqarah at Verse 275[555]. Therefore, international trade agreements with intellectual property chapters are sharia compliant provided there is no breach of the Islamic doctrines of riba and gharar. Further, sources of sharia have established intellectual property as more than a standalone right. Rather, there is a public interest responsibility to the community and for financial interests to be proportionate[556].

Public acceptance of intellectual property law is the red herring the developed world has not managed to address. The speed with which the GCC adopted many new laws in the field of intellectual property could have created an unintentional side effect, the intellectual property laws can be seen as foreign and as a result seen as emasculating the GCC[557]. With the development of ISDS and corporate sovereignty, the GCC faces further challenges in upholding intellectual property rights without losing its identity. An integrated intellectual property approach that takes into account the public need for acceptance of the intellectual property protection rules and regulations, enforced at both a state and regional level in the GCC, will address the challenges the GCC states face in intellectual property rights without losing their individual and combined identity.

## 7 Impact of ISDS on Intellectual Property Rights in the GCC

The ISDS has at its core a rigid dichotomy between the critical view that investor state dispute clauses gives corporations and foreign investors corporate sovereignty against the business standpoint that the clauses are vital to protecting foreign investment, in countries where judicial systems are unpredictable. The main fear of ISDS clauses is that it could lead to governments being held to ransom by wealthy corporations, as ISDS would allow firms to sue authorities for compensation over policies that adversely affect them.

This has serious ramifications for domestic sovereignty and rule of law. In an international context, both for the contracting states and non-contracting states, the impact of ISDS on the ability of states to make laws challenges fundamental principles of constitutional law and democracy. According to Friends of the Earth investigative research findings, 127 known ISDS cases have been brought against 20 EU member states since 1994. Details of the compensation sought by foreign investors were not publicly available for all reported cases, of the 127 cases, 62 were public and the compensation sought in the 62 public cases is in excess of €30 billion[558].

The ripple effects of ISDS as a dispute settlement mechanism can be seen in the GCC as the first application for an ISDS course of action, by a GCC state, has been made by a Qatari based broadcaster known as Al Jazeera. They are relying on the investor to state dispute mechanism included in a 1999 investment treaty between Egypt and Qatar[559]. The arbitration case initiated by Al Jazeera Media Network against Egypt is based on the breach of their bilateral trade agreement by Egypt concerning the harassment and imprisonment of its journalists. This raises a key question on infrastructure limitations in the GCC. The success or failure for that matter of an ISDS process is contingent upon the expertise and experience of the judicial system that is making the decision. If there is a lack of expertise and or precedent, where is the solid foundation of knowledge from which to answer principle questions?

## 8 Lessons to Be Learnt from Eli Lilly v Canada

In relation to intellectual property, lessons can be learnt from existing intellectual property-based ISDS cases. Take for example Eli Lilly v Canada. In November 2012, Eli Lilly & Co started proceedings against the Canadian government's law on granting drug patents, claiming that the invalidation of a patent undermined the company's future profits and are asking for $500 million in compensation[560]. While the resolution of this dispute is yet to be known, it highlights three key concerns for GCC states; lack of expertise and knowledge of how to deal with ISDS's, identifying Islamic sources through which ISDS can be sharia compliant and what impact it has on the states abilities to determine their own patent standards. Foreign corporations having the same level of power as governments through ISDS clauses in trade agreements is currently a hypothetical situation in the GCC however it is only a matter of time before the hypothetical risks of investor-state claims becomes a reality. How equipped are the GCC judiciaries to deal with an ISDS claim?

## 9 Is ISDS Sharia Compliant?

ISDS has an added layer of issues with the GCC states as a question arises as to whether ISDS is compatible with sharia law. The GCC states have accepted ISDS as an acceptable dispute settlement mechanism in existing agreements[561]. Investment carries with it risk, foreign investment would in turn carry higher risks as investors would be acting in markets with different political and legal structures. If the risk is too speculative then it potentially falls under the Islamic principle of gharar[562]. The outcome of the Al Jazeera and Egypt ISDS case will set new ground for international disputes in the region as both states have sharia as part of their constitution; therefore how the arbitration process deals with principles of gharar and riba will be relevant to other countries in the Middle East region[563].

## 10 The Trojan Horse – Corporate Sovereignty Impact on the GCC

The GCC is a collection of rentier states. They have similar autocratic monarchies, political and cultural identities, which are historically rooted in Islamic beliefs[564]. Unlike other international bodies, the GCC is unique in that all its member states are Islamic states[565]. Each individual state has varying degrees of sharia law incorporated in their constitutions as discussed in Chapter 1.

The main issues with ISDS and subsequently the threat to corporate sovereignty are three fold. The first issue is the lack of clarity on arbitrator powers which in essence is because of the vague formulation of major treaty provisions. The lack of clarity on arbitrator powers has given arbitrators a pandora's box to allow a wide range of interpretations. Following on from this is the arbitration process, many are in secret therefore the risk of inconsistencies in similar cases is heightened. There is an absence of effective review for appeal processes; there is an annulment committee procedure available for arbitrations conducted by the International Centre for the Settlement of Investment Disputes[566]. However this is limited to challenging the validity of an award and whether the challenge can lead to the annulment of the award[567]. Thirdly, as a result of how ISDS is incorporated into trade agreements and is dealt with by the arbitration process, there are serious implications for national sovereignty within each GCC state, their democratic governance and the rule of law within national legal systems[568].

## 11 Conclusion

The issue remains whether the GCC states have the capacity to abide by stricter intellectual property laws and ISDS clauses. This chapter has analysed the substantive provisions of ISDS and corporate sovereignty and the analysis will inform the inform the main set of recommendations to be made to develop an integrated approach to intellectual property rights which takes into account; the structure of the GCC states, international agreements and pressures, the international institutions, Islamic finance and both societal and religious views.

An added dimension to the GCC states is they all share a common religious belief in Islam at a constitutional level. The research has shown that on the relationship between sharia law and intellectual property, the sharia sources of law and legislative decisions have favoured sharia approval for the existence and protection of intellectual property rights. However, at the heart of intellectual property protection, is acceptance by the public at large of intellectual property as predicated with Islamic law and as has been seen in earlier chapters, this is a contentious issue for the GCC states[569].

At present, laws exist without the necessary understanding or awareness for their existence. This leaves the relationship between sharia and intellectual property law at a developmental stage. The foundational stage has been met through the GCC states acceptance of the use of secondary sharia sources to permit intellectual property rights. However, the development stage requires an integrated intellectual property approach to enforcement, which is a hybrid of clear and unambiguous sharia principles, international intellectual property laws and ISDS which currently do not exist in the GCC. As the financial settlements in ISDS cases can amount to millions of pounds, how the stricter GCC states, such as Saudi Arabia, can justify ISDS clauses as sharia compliant with principles of riba and gharar will be addressed in the integrated framework for intellectual property rights in the GCC states. Therefore, the findings of this chapter will directly impact on how the GCC states can adhere to ISDS without violating principles of riba and gharar. Thus, the role of ISDS will be a component of the integrated intellectual property rights framework and will be taken into account along with the other research findings that include; the structure of the GCC states, international agreements and pressures, the international institutions and both societal and religious views.

The most concerning research finding from this chapter for the GCC states is the corporate sovereignty doctrine and how they plan to marry corporate sovereignty to their existing law-making powers. Egypt is the first Middle Eastern country to have proceedings brought against it and developments in the case are slow. As more and more ISDS cases occur, the theoretical implication of corporate sovereignty may become a reality in the near future for the GCC states and steps need to be taken to clearly define ISDS and the implications of corporate sovereignty within an Islamic context. ISDS could undermine sovereignty by exposing the policy, legislative and decisional outputs to challenges by arbitrators for whom the main focus is investment obligations and not domestic governance. The challenges of ISDS, corporate sovereignty and international intellectual property pressures have the potential to be a modern day pandora's box, sat at the centre of a mare's nest, for the GCC states.

The next chapter will complete the research findings and will meet the remaining research objectives from where the main research question will be answered, of what recommendations can be made to develop an integrated approach to intellectual property rights in the GCC taking into account the structure of the GCC states, international agreements and pressures, the relevant international institutions, Islamic finance and both societal and religious views. Chapter 7 deals with Islamic finance in detail and researches the main sharia compliant areas of; musharaka, mudaraba, murabaha, takaful, istisna, ijara, salam and sukuk to develop an understanding of sharia board governance, with particular reference to each GCC state. Further the research findings in the next chapter will identify how intellectual property development in the

GCC can be enhanced through Islamic finance and propose a more sharia complaint model for intellectual property based on Islamic finance structures. The structures and frameworks in place in the Islamic finance sector will act as a vehicle to developing a full integrated intellectual property framework.

# 7

# Islamic Finance as a Vehicle to Promote Improved Intellectual Property Rights in the GCC

## 1 Introduction

The purpose of this chapter is to assess how Islamic finance can act as a vehicle to enhance the current intellectual property rights regime in the GCC. Islamic finance has developed within the constraints of sharia law and has been a growth sector for the GCC[570]. This chapter will identify the main principles that contribute to the success of Islamic finance which can enhance intellectual property protection in the GCC. The main sharia compliant areas to be considered are musharaka, mudaraba, murabaha, takaful, istisna, ijara, salam and sukuk.

The chapter will outline the founding principles of Islamic finance, the governance of sharia boards, development of Islamic finance in the individual GCC states, different frameworks of sharia-compliant investment products and the impact of intellectual property rights on the varying Islamic finance investment tools. Further, the chapter will discuss an integrated approach to intellectual property rights which borrows from the Islamic finance sector in relation to infrastructure, regulation and sharia compliance. The lessons learnt will inform the overall framework of recommendations for an Islamic-based intellectual property model. The use of Islamic finance as a vehicle to promote better intellectual property rights in terms of defining a new intellectual property approach is novel. It is aimed at spearheading further research in this area and for the purpose of this monograph, it will form a part of the overall integrated approach proposals to intellectual property protection in the GCC.

## 2 The Research Objectives

As an overview, the objectives addressed in this chapter are:

- Clearly outline founding principles of Islamic finance and develop an understanding of sharia board governance, with particular reference to each GCC state.
- Identify how intellectual property development in the GCC can be enhanced through Islamic finance.
- Propose a more sharia compliant model for intellectual property based on Islamic finance structures.
- Make recommendations on how intellectual property rights can be better protected by avoiding the procedural flaws that exist within Islamic finance.

These objectives will inform the main recommendations for an integrated approach to intellectual property rights in the GCC in four specific areas of development to; strengthen the intellectual property market structure, improve compliance in terms of systems and controls, address issues around the efficiency of supervisory boards and generate greater public confidence in the intellectual property sector.

## 3 Background to Islamic Finance

Islamic finance is very much enshrined in ethical guidelines that are deeply rooted in the religion that it must abide by[571]. In Islamic teachings, money is a measure of value as opposed to a commodity[572]. Therefore, in line with Islamic teachings, money should be put to practical use, invested to create wealth and not be a commodity of itself[573]. It is the earning of a passive return on capital, which is identified as the backbone to the definition on the prohibition of riba[574]. In its simplest terms, sharia expressly prohibits the making of money from money[575]. It requires the creation of real value for the participants of a transaction[576]. The same prohibition of interest applies to debt whereby the risk and responsibility in the debt is shared between all contractually obligated parties[577].

Islamic finance is defined as sharia compliant financial transactions which can be used as an alternative to conventional western banking methods[578]. Islamic finance emerged in the early 1960s with the objective of providing alternative financial contracts in conformity with sharia principles as necessitated by primary and secondary sources of Islam[579]. Mit Ghamr Local Savings Bank in Egypt in 1963 is widely accepted as the first modern attempt at Islamic banking[580]. Following on from this, Dubai established the first Islamic Bank in 1975, known as the Dubai

Islamic Bank[581]. Therefore, as with the developments of intellectual property in the GCC, Islamic finance is also relatively new in the context of financial banking in the Gulf region[582]. The developments of Islamic finance in the GCC run parallel with the oil boom[583] and over the last three decades, the GCC states have heavily invested in developing sharia-compliant banking[584].

Islamic finance has developed through a series of fatwas that are passed by Islamic scholars and jurists. A fatwa is a result of human interpretation of the sharia. A fatwa can be passed based on the interpretation of texts and recordings from primary and secondary sharia sources. They are not viewed as the ordained word of Allah but rather a permissible method of analysing and or combining different sharia principles to come to a decision. Fatwas are issued by sharia boards to rule on whether a new Islamic finance product is sharia-compliant or to amend an existing fatwa. Interestingly, there is no prescribed religious hierarchy in the Quran or Sunnah, for the field of Islamic scholars who interpret the different sources of sharia law. Therefore, the decisions require enforcement by banks, legislation and financial institutions to make them binding.

As will be seen below in the founding principles of Islamic finance, the GCC states have adopted far more sophisticated and rigorous infrastructures to developing an Islamic finance market than they have in regard to intellectual property. The central findings from the Islamic finance sector of how the products are structured, the compliance mechanisms in place, the role of supervisory boards and public confidence, will be utilised to make recommendations for the intellectual property sector.

## 4 Founding Principles of Islamic Finance

*"There is nothing prohibited except that which God prohibits ... to declare something permitted prohibited is like declaring something prohibited permitted[585]."*

Islamic finance, at its core, is an ethical and equitable mode of finance, the origins of which can be traced back to sharia principles found in the Quran and Sunnah[586]. The Quran, the highest source of Islamic law, unconditionally prohibits sinful (haram) activity[587] and riba[588] in financial transactions. However, although the Quran and Sunnah are unequivocally clear on what defines haram activity, there is no unanimity about the limitations or scope of the prohibition of riba[589]. This is largely due to the interpretation of the leading Quranic verse on riba found in Surah Baqarah at verse 275 and also at eight other verses[590]. Riba and gharar are at the heart of the connection between intellectual property and Islamic finance as both sectors prohibit transactions that involve riba and gharar.

Islamic finance is not a sector that is seamless in its governance nor is it exempt from conflict. The differences in interpretation of sharia raise issues on the harmonisation of Islamic finance products. Some divergence is unavoidable given that the cultural, political, economic and social beliefs in individual countries will differ from others[591].

There are a number of sharia scholars who specialise in Islamic finance and derive the necessary Islamic jurisprudence known as fiqh[592]. Islamic jurisprudence is recognised in the Quran as a method of understanding the way of the Prophet Muhammed[593]. Based in Jeddah, Saudi Arabia, the Islamic Fiqh Academy comprises leading scholars who make decisions on permissible Islamic finance products[594]. The International Fiqh Academy, Saudi Arabia, has played a pivotal role in the development of Islamic finance. The Dow Jones Islamic Index[595] and Islamic bonds, known as sukuks, are two key changes that have been synonymous to the expansion of Islamic financial markets. The Dow Jones Islamic Index sharia board has the five most eminent sharia scholars in modern day Islamic finance, Sheikh Nizam Yaquby, Dr. Mohammed Daud Bakar, Dr. Bakar is currently a member of the Shari'ah Advisory Council of many financial institutions in Malaysia and around the world, including the Central Bank of Malaysia, Securities Commission of Malaysia, International Islamic Financial Market in Bahrain, Accounting and Auditing Organization for Islamic Financial Institutions (AAOIFI) in Bahrain and HSBC (Malaysia).Sheikh Dr. Mohamed A. Elgari, Shaykh Abdul Sattar Abu Ghuddah and Sheikh Yusuf Talal DeLorenzo. The scholars are all from different countries as a purposeful attempt to give the Dow Jones Islamic Index as wide a remit for investment as possible. Also, it needs to be noted that the scholars are from countries that are leaders in the Islamic finance market such as Malaysia, Saudi Arabia and Bahrain. The main Islamic finance products that are principal commodities in the sector are discussed below in order to then apply Islamic finance principles to developing an integrated approach to intellectual property rights in the GCC.

## 5 Islamic Finance Products

There are a number of sharia compliant frameworks that are in existence across the Islamic finance market. In relation to its impact on intellectual property, and there are a number of relevant sharia compliant practices that have overcome the inevitable dichotomy that arises when Islamic law principles are married to western concepts, something which the intellectual property sector in the GCC has not quite managed as discussed at Chapter 5[596].

In order to make recommendations on how Islamic finance can engender better compliance with intellectual property rights, the main Islamic finance products will be considered in terms of the rationale behind each product and the role of sharia boards in promulgating the sharia compliant frameworks[597]. Further, as the purpose behind analysing Islamic finance products is to identify the role Islamic finance can play in further developing intellectual property rights protection in the GCC, the areas of musharaka, mudaraba, murabaha, sukuk and takaful will be analysed to propose potential application to intellectual property.

## *Musharaka – Profit and Loss Sharing of Capital*

Musharaka is one of the most established sharia compliant products and is based on the basic tenets of Islamic finance that require financing to operate on a profit or loss sharing system as opposed to a lender borrower relationship[598]. There are different definitions of the profit or loss sharing partnership, depending upon the contribution each partner is making[599]. The most common profit or loss sharing relationship is known as musharaka where the proportion of profit to be distributed between the partners must be agreed upon when the contract is agreed. The defining feature of musharaka is that the ratio of profit for each partner must be determined in proportion to the actual profit accrued to the business, as opposed to the proportion of the capital invested by partners. Secondly, musharaka deals with the sharing of loss. Where there is a loss, musharaka stipulates a sharing of the loss in exact accordance with the capital invested by each partner. Therefore, where the profit is determined by the actual profit accrued to the business, the loss is calculated by the ratio of investment[600].

Risk-sharing partnerships based on musharaka could be a natural fit for intellectual property investment with returns flowing in from hybrid musharaka and intellectual property-based projects, licensing, royalties, subscriptions and sale of the intellectual property assets. There is a lack of understanding of intellectual property-based financing among the Islamic financial fraternity, both within the GCC and beyond, to become involved in intellectual property innovation, to fill the financial gap between ideas and the ability to commercialise them into marketable products and services[601]. As musharaka is the profit and loss sharing of capital, the sharia compliant frameworks for musharaka can be extended to intellectual property-based capital. The value of the Intellectual property asset can be the equivalent to intellectual capital invested and profit parameters can be based on agreed values.

## *Mudaraba – Profit Loss Sharing of Trade and Capital*

Another form of a profit loss sharing relationship in Islamic finance that differentiates from musharaka due to its sharing of trade and capital is known as mudaraba; it varies from musharaka as not all partners have to provide capital. Mudaraba is a special kind of partnership where some partners can provide work in trade and others can provides the capital. The partner that works in trade is known as the "mudarib" and the partner that provides the capital is known as the "rabb ul-mal."

There are three distinct differences between musharaka and mudaraba. Firstly, the investment is not the same in the two types of investment. In musharaka the investment comes from all the partners, whereas in mudaraba the investments come from the partner or partners that are investing the capital, the rabb-ul-mal. Therefore, the musharaka is a partnership where the profit and potential loss is capital, while mudaraba is a partnership in profit but not in capital. Secondly the management of the mudaraba and musharaka vary. In musharaka, the partners can determine who participates in the management of the business and to what level as well as who can work for the business. In mudaraba, the mudarib participates in the management of the business and not the rabb-ul-mal[602]. Thirdly, the sharing of loss is not the same. As not both parties provide capital in mudaraba, the loss cannot be shared based on capital invested. Instead, the party that provides capital loses capital and the party that provides the trade loses their labour[603].

From an intellectual property stance, mudaraba contracts aim to make profit by sharing trade and capital, therefore the capital need not only be in a tangible form but can also be intangible property-based capital. As a mudaraba agreement is a contract in which certain property or stock is offered by the owner or to the other party to form a joint partnership[604], there is the potential to develop intellectual property-based mudaraba agreements.

## *Murabaha – Contract of Sale*

Murabaha is a contract of sale, also known as cost plus financing and is primarily concerned with Islamic financing[605]. There are specific features of murabaha where there is a set increment on the original price, which is agreed upon by the parties from the onset. By agreeing the set increment on the original price in advance, the expected rate of return is predetermined[606]. The main purpose of this is to avoid gharar[607]. By making both the original price and profit to be made known to the buyer, the risks of usury in the dealings are limited. Along with the profit being known, all the expenses to be acquired by the seller in honouring the agreement, such as freight costs or customs duty, are included in the cost price. The mark up is then applied to the aggregate cost[608].

Murabaha has a great deal of crossover potential to intellectual property as one of the founding tenets of intellectual property protection in sharia law is found in Islamic principles of contract law as discussed in Chapter 3[609]. Intellectual property assets such as trademarks, patents and copyrights, can act as underlying assets of a murabaha contract. This is a novel approach to trademark protection in Islamic countries as it is applying risk-averse strategies that are found in Islamic finance to intellectual property rights protection and is an area of further research. For example, a murabaha mode of financing may be sought from an Islamic bank to purchase a trademark.

The Islamic bank may purchase the trademark and sell it on the basis of a murabaha agreement with a mark-up price to be paid back over an agreed time period. The Central Bank of Malaysia's sharia advisory board has considered intellectual property as the subject matter of a murabaha contract. The illustration it provides is; "*a customer seeks financing from an IFI to purchase a brand name of a distributor known as Fitforall valued at RM500,000 that will enable the customer to be part of the retail chain to sell the goods under the brand name. The brand provides product quality assurance to existing and potential brand-loyal customers, as well as an established international distribution network. The IFI may purchase the brand name and sell it to the customer at a mark-up price of RM750,000 to be paid over a period of 5 years*"[610].

## *Sukuk - Islamic Bond*

A sukuk is an Islamic bond that defines the proportionate beneficial ownership of the asset to the investor, for a specific time period[611]. A sukuk is set up in such a way that despite the sukuk investor having a common share in the ownership of the assets-based investment, it does not represent a debt owed to the issuer of the bond[612]. Whereas in conventional bonds, the capital protection is achieved through a loan agreement, sukuks are able to distinguish their structure from conventional bonds by offering an alternative to the traditional loan agreement. Instead, there is a binding agreement by the issuer to repurchase certain assets over a specified time limit[613].

Sukuks allow Islamic finance institutions to access short to long term financing against government backed bonds. For example, in Bahrain, the Central Bank of Bahrain will issue sukuks on behalf of the government[614]. Sukuks are a growing product in the Islamic finance world and cover a range of underlying assets such as a partnership bond (mudaraba sukuk), a joint venture (musharaka sukuk), leasing (ijara sukuk), purchase orders (murabaha sukuk), project finance (istisna sukuk) or a combination of assets[615]. Sukuks issue a profit rate as opposed to an interest rate that would be found under a conventional bank[616]. The profit rate is deemed sharia-compliant as it reflects the productivity of the asset[617]. Sukuks are growing at a fast pace, both within the GCC states and globally. Sukuks have been offered by the GCC and Malaysia, the traditional Islamic finance hubs, as well as Turkey, Pakistan and the United Kingdom. Most notable is the UK's bid to stamp its mark in the Islamic finance sector by issuing the first sovereign sukuk by a non-member of the Organisation of Islamic Co-operation (OIC)[618]. Other non-member countries are also considering sukuks, for example, Luxembourg, Tunisia, Kenya and South Africa[619].

Sukuks are commonly offered under ijara-based structures. Ijara translates to a lease agreement, operating as a contractual hiring agreement where a contract is entered in to where the consideration is the benefit received from an asset or a service in return for compensation. The contracting parties are defined as the lessor who is the owner of the asset and the lessee who is the beneficiary of the property. Ijara relates to the usufructs of assets and or services from the lesser to the lessee. Ijara is not a delayed sale as such as ownership remains with the lesser and the lessee has a right to the use of the asset[620]. Sukuk is an area of Islamic finance where the underlying asset of the ijara-based structure is intangible property.

The link between intellectual property and Islamic finance is only just starting to emerge. The first ever sukuk with the underlying asset a form of intellectual property right was introduced by the German-based finance company, FWU AG Group[621]. FWU AG Group issued a US $55,000,000 sukuk in 2012, making it the first sukuk of its kind that has intellectual property rights as the underlying asset in the form of a computer software programme, developed under an ijara structure[622]. This is the first time a European country has issued an intellectual property-based sukuk through the Dubai branch of its subsidiary FWU Dubai Services GmbH. The financing for the sukuk was provided by GCC-based investors[623]. Therefore, it is a hybrid of Islamic finance and intellectual property rights within a sharia compliant framework that has developed under existing compliant products of sukuk and ijara.

## *Takaful – Islamic Insurance*

Takaful is a sharia compliant form of insurance. Takaful, at its core, is founded on specific principles concerning the separation of shareholder operations from the funds. The ownership of the takaful passes to the policyholder and is based on elements of shared responsibility, joint indemnity and common interest[624]. Takaful offers insurance by setting up a contract between participants who each contribute money into a pooling system in order to guarantee each other against loss or damage. Takaful thus provides an alternative to commercial insurance which involve riba and gharar, while setting out responsibilities of each participant to cooperate and protect each other. Takaful is sharia compliant as it sets from the onset how profits from the investment are to be shared[625].

In a takaful contract, each participant is expected to make a mutual contribution, known as tabarru, which aims to limit the risk of uncertainty that typically exists in conventional insurance agreements[626]. Takaful can be combined with existing Islamic finance products such as mudaraba or a hybrid of different products[627]. In relation to intellectual property, takaful can be vital leverage in the contractual agreement as it offers security and a contingency plan to investors.

## *Other Types of Islamic Finance Products*

Other types of Islamic finance products include istisna, ijara and salam. Istisna is a contract for sale that is concerned with deferred delivery[628]. Istisna is mainly used by banks and Islamic financial institutions in housing contracts, building constructions, large scale manufacturing of goods and equipment such as aircrafts, ships and machines. Alongside this, istisna has also been applied for export financing and to meet working capital needs[629].

Salam also relates to a contract for sale; however, the difference in salam is that when the seller agrees to supply specific goods to the buyer at a future date, an exchange of an advanced price needs to be paid at the time the contract commences. Salam, as a contract of sale, generates a moral obligation on the seller to deliver the goods as per the agreement as once the agreement has been reached, the contract cannot be unilaterally cancelled[630].

What is most relevant to the development of intellectual property rights through Islamic finance is how Islamic finance is governed by the GCC states when considering the role of Islamic scholars, the structure of sharia boards and internal governance systems. Intellectual property has developed in the GCC along a very similar timeline to Islamic finance. Historically, principles of both date back to a pre-colonisation era in the GCC, however in terms of its modernisation, both intellectual property and Islamic finance have developed over the last three decades. Therefore, before Islamic finance principles can be applied to intellectual property, it is imperative to outline Islamic finance governance.Dr. Elgari is an associate professor of Islamic Economics and the director of the Center for Research in Islamic Economics at King Abdulaziz University in Saudi Arabia. He is an expert at the Islamic Jurisprudence Academy (OIC), Economics. He is also an advisor to several Islamic financial instituitons worldwide and the author of many books on Islamic banking.

## 6 Islamic Finance Scholars and Sharia Boards

Islamic scholars sit on sharia boards with the main role of acting as an independent body of specialised jurists to direct, review and supervise Islamic finance services[631]. The sharia board in an Islamic financial institution (IFI), is an integral component of corporate governance[632]. The sharia board plays a key role in endorsing the overall work of the Islamic financial institution[633]. Appointment to a sharia board is made by the board of directors of individual financial institutions and consists of a chairman, secretary and sharia advisors[634].

The sharia advisors are Islamic scholars; however, there is no centralised database of Islamic scholars. The world database for Islamic finance and banking[635] accounts for the most prominent scholars, but there is no international system of ranking scholars or rating their expertise. The sharia boards are governed by national legislation, governance frameworks and audit requirements. Standard setting in the governance of sharia boards and sharia-compliant products was introduced by the Malaysian Islamic Financial Services Board (IFSB). It was set up in 2002 to provide an international standard-setting body that regulates and supervises agencies that have a vested interest in the Islamic financial services sector[636]. The IFSB has members from all the GCC states along with Brunei, Bangladesh, Egypt, Indonesia, Iran, Jordan, Malaysia, Maldives, Mauritius, Nigeria, Pakistan, Singapore, South Africa, Sudan and Syria[637]. In relation to sharia board governance, there are five key uniform areas that all boards are required to abide by. These are confidentiality, independence, competence, consistency and disclosure[638].

As seen in Chapter 3, Islamic jurisprudence falls under four main schools of thought, Hanbali, Shafii, Maliki, and Hanafi[639]. Therefore, depending on which school of thought a particular country follows there can be some deviances in the opinions of the sharia boards. To counteract this, although sharia boards are set up by individual institutions across a number of countries, scholars from different countries sit on several boards concurrently. Inadvertently this creates a power paradigm whereby a select number of scholars sit on all the main sharia boards. For example, Mufti Muhammad Taqi Usmani, as one of the most renowned Islamic finance scholars, is in high demand and currently is chairman of eleven boards and a member of a further five boards[640].

Another example is Sheikh Dr. Mohamed Ali Elgari who also sits on a number of boards[641]. What this has led to is a significant crossover of a select few scholars who are collectively a majority of the same board members with positions on many boards[642]. There is a very direct benefit of this in terms of harmonisation of decisions across the various boards and thus providing unanimity. However, from a practical point of view, there are strategic shortcomings in the selection of board members as there are no clear regulations or protocols in place as a vetting process[643]. Nor is there any framework in place to assess how much capacity, both in time and expertise, individual scholars have to serve on so many boards[644]. Also, there are limited structures in place to ensure scrutiny, accountability for decisions and checks and balances if the same members serve on boards in conflicting capacities[645].

## 7 Main Criticisms of Sharia Boards

The main criticisms of sharia boards are in the lack of accountability of scholars, limited transparency in the decision-making processes employed by scholars and a lack of clear guidance on the minimum level of expertise required from a scholar[646]. To address the criticism, most IFIs have set up internal auditing committees and other regulatory systems such as compliance, governance ethics, periodic reviews and assurances. Auditing is the most accepted form of review as it is sharia-compliant. There are Quranic references that support the need for verification and authorisation in business. For example, in Surah al-Insyiqaq, verses 6 to 9, indicate to an auditing process as well as Surah Al-Infithar, verses 10 to 12[647].

Apart from the Islamic need for auditing and verification in the Islamic finance sector, there is a very practical and logistic need for more centralised and in-depth regulation[648]. Each GCC state has adopted their own models for auditing and monitoring the Islamic finance sector and the respective sharia boards. Consideration will be given to the sharia board governance in each GCC state, as well as highlighting the flaws in the governance structures in each individual state as to better inform the recommendations for an integrated approach to intellectual property rights protection in the GCC[649].

## 8 Sharia Board Governance in Bahrain

Bahrain has taken a leading role in the GCC to develop regulatory frameworks by passing a number of financial-based legislations[650] and setting up two key institutions: the Accounting and Auditing Organization for Islamic Financial Institution (AAOIFI)[651] and the International Islamic Financial Market (IIFM)[652]. The overarching regulatory authority is the Central Bank of Bahrain (CBB) with the sole responsibility of regulating the financial sector, thus giving Bahrain a centralised sharia governance structure[653]. The function of Bahrain's national sharia advisory board is to advise the Central Bank of Bahrain. The bank in turn implements improvements in the corporate governance framework of financial institutions, in terms of financial disclosure and transparency[654].

Bahrain's model of auditing Islamic finance, through the Accounting and Auditing Organization for Islamic Financial Institution and the International Islamic Financial Market, has allowed it to develop supervisory and control structures for fatwa accountability, sharia compliance accountability, governance for sharia auditors and procedures for internal sharia audits[655]. Bahrain has 53 Islamic finance scholars; however, it is a handful of scholars that are in high demand. Take for example, Sheikh Nizam Yaquby: he currently sits on 85 sharia boards and is highly renowned as one of the leading experts in the field[656]. However, a serious question arises as to how a scholar can fulfil duties on such a large number of boards[657].

The lack of an overarching independent Islamic finance authority leaves the industry at risk of becoming a mare's nest. There is a significant difference between international intellectual property standard setting and Islamic finance in that Islamic finance lacks an umbrella organisation that sets minimal standards for all states that offer sharia-compliant financial products. The governance system in Bahrain is limited to Bahrain, it can influence sharia board governance in other countries but cannot be binding. With growing criticism of international standard setting in Islamic finance, Bahrain is developing a central sharia board which will introduce new rules to strengthen the governance of sharia boards in the sector, both within

Bahrain and beyond[658]. Bahrain has played an instrumental role in the development of sharia compliant financial services. It was the first GCC state to introduce a sharia-compliant liquidity management service in the form of the liquidity management centre (LMC)[659]. The centre facilitates the structured investment of surplus funds of Islamic banks and Islamic financial institutions in accordance with Islamic law[660].

## 9 Sharia Board Governance in Saudi Arabia

Saudi Arabia was one of the last GCC states to formally introduce Islamic banking[661]. It does not have a centralised system for regulating Islamic finance institutions and reviewing the governance of sharia boards like Bahrain or UAE. Also, it does not have the same level of scrutiny in areas such as financial disclosures when compared to its peers[662]. Despite not having designated regulatory bodies to govern Islamic finance, Saudi Arabia has supervisory bodies in the form of the Saudi Arabia Monetary Agency (SAMA), the International Development Bank and the Ministry of Finance. The Saudi Arabia Monetary Agency performs the central banking role in Saudi Arabia and disseminates regulatory pronouncements from the Malaysia-based Islamic Financial Services Board to the financial sector[663]. This therefore offers some level of international standard setting within the Saudi Arabian Islamic finance institutions, along with the Ministry of Finance.

Saudi Arabia lacks extensive Islamic finance legislation[664] and a uniform legislative committee for Islamic finance to set checks and balances and scrutinise sharia board decisions on whether a certain financial product is sharia-compliant. Nevertheless, in spite of having weak standard setting systems, Saudi Arabia has the lion's share of the Islamic finance market as reported by the Dubai Chambers of Commerce[665]. As with Bahrain, although Saudi Arabia also has a large bank of scholars, it is still a select few Saudi Arabian scholars that have prominence. The main scholars in Saudi Arabia are Dr. Abdul Sattar Abu Ghuddah, Dr. Mohamed A. Elgari, Sheikh Al-Manea and Sheikh Al-Atram[666].

Saudi Arabia applies a more strict interpretation of riba and gharar than other states, which is in line with its overall level of sharia compliance in all aspects of governance[667]. For example, Malaysian scholars approved an Islamic credit card based on a transaction known as baya al-ina, however Arab scholars rejected the credit card as it was deemed too similar to interest-based lending[668]. The limits of Islamic finance are highlighted by the disagreement of different scholars, be it nationally or internationally, as there is no higher authority to appeal to when disagreements occur[669]. The sector lacks legally binding precedent and principles, which if enacted at a legislative level, would facilitate certainty, clarity and unequivocal rules that would add credence to decisions on sharia-compliant products.

## 10 Sharia Board Governance in the UAE

The UAE has pioneered Islamic finance development in the GCC region with its first Islamic bank, the Dubai Islamic Bank, opening in 1975. The UAE has a body of law regulating its banking and financial business[670] as well as strategic institutions to supervise sharia developments in Islamic finance[671]. The UAE Islamic banking operations are supervised by an independent sharia supervisory committee[672].

Again, the word "independent" may be treated with a pinch of salt as the three main scholars of the UAE sharia supervisory committee are the leading scholars in all the GCC states and a number of other countries, namely, Dr. Abdul Sattar Abu Ghuddah, Sheikh Nizam Yaqubi and Dr. Mohamed Ali Elgari. The UAE sharia supervisory committee derive its powers from the UAE Islamic banking legislation. The UAE has a devolved system of sharia governance whereby in accordance with Article 6 of the UAE Islamic banking law, individual Islamic financial institutions and banks must establish their own sharia supervisory committees[673].

Islamic banks are regulated under two separate entities, Emirate Islamic banks are regulated by the Central Bank of the UAE[674] and Islamic banks that fall within the Dubai International Financial Centre (DIFC)[675] are supervised by the Dubai Financial Services Authority (DFSA). To streamline sharia governance, the UAE has been developing a number of strategies for Islamic finance services. The UAE has set up a higher sharia authority under the Ministry of Justice and through the Emirates banking association, the Islamic banking committee. The purpose of the higher sharia authority and Islamic banking committee is to review the various sharia governance models and propose a standardised sharia model[676]. The UAE is following in Malaysia's footsteps by working towards a central sharia board that can impose decisions across the various sharia boards of the nation's Islamic finance institutions[677].

Further, Dubai has set up a number of research and development-based institutions in the field of Islamic finance. The centre for the development of Islamic economics was inaugurated in 2013 with the aim of promoting awareness of economic activities, both the concepts and practices of financial services with Islamic law. The GCC states as a whole are keen to become the Islamic finance hub in an international context. Dubai is a driving force behind the desire to lead on Islamic finance with its sights on being the global capital in the Islamic financial sector[678].

## 11 Sharia Board Governance in Kuwait

Kuwait is similar to Bahrain in that it has specific provisions on what constitutes a sharia advisory board and that sharia boards are answerable to the Central Bank of Kuwait as predicated by legislation[679]. However, there is no higher sharia advisory authority at the Central Bank of Kuwait nor does Kuwait have specific primary legislation on the governance of Islamic finance sharia boards. As there is no specific legislation on sharia board governance, there is no limitation on the number of sharia boards a scholar can sit on.

Given that Kuwait has 2 Islamic banks and 31 Islamic finance institutions, it is clear that there will at times be a difference of opinion between institutions. Although it is not compulsory, where such a conflict arises amongst sharia advisors, there is recourse for the board of directors of the designated institutions. They can refer the matter to the Ministry of Awqaf and Islamic Affairs Fatwa Board[680]. The Fatwa Board sits as an external entity to the Central Bank of Kuwait in order to maintain independence and has the authority to make a final decision on a given matter. Nevertheless, there is no legal restriction on a sharia advisor that sits on the fatwa board also having a board seat on a number of other Islamic financial institutions.

Therefore, questions arise as to how fit for purpose a fatwa board can be when its members may very well come from the same institutional boards for whom the decision is being made. This is a common theme among fatwa boards and is not confined only to Kuwait. To increase transparency and levels of scrutiny and accountability, fatwa board members need to be expressly prohibited from taking advisory positions as board members of other Islamic finance institutions where there is a potential for conflict of interests as this defeats the very objective the sharia boards were set up to address.

## 12 Sharia Board Governance in Oman

Oman has been a relatively late comer to Islamic finance[681]. It has two main pieces of legislation that make provisions for Islamic finance within its existing banking system; the Central Bank of Oman Banking Law promulgated by Royal Decree 55/90 and Money Laundering Law promulgated by Royal Decree 34/2002[682]. Up until 2012, conventional banking had Islamic units as there were no designated stand-alone Islamic banks. From a royal decree in 2012, that amended the banking law in Oman, two new Islamic banks were launched, Bank Nizwa[683] and Al Izz Islamic Bank[684]. Given its late start to taking the Islamic finance market seriously, Oman has been very proactive in evolving its Islamic finance sector. For example, in 2014, the Sultanate of Oman announced a centralised system for sharia board governance, in the form of a Central bank of Oman sharia supervisory board[685]. Further, unlike the other GCC states, Oman has sought to implement rigorous standards for regulating sharia boards and Islamic finance scholars. It is currently the only GCC state that has imposed limitations on sharia board and scholar activity in the form of an Islamic finance regulatory framework that deals with maximum length of service, minimum level of qualifications required, mandatory years of experience required, maximum number of Islamic finance institutions a scholar can serve on, performance reviews and a minimum of 75% attendance for board meetings[686].

Oman has in effect addressed a number of criticisms pertaining to sharia boards. The most crucial of these has to be the restriction on scholars from serving on two competing Islamic financial institutions, thus removing the likelihood of a conflict of interest and making the role of sharia scholars more fit for purpose[687]. Nonetheless, Oman has considerable work to do in ensuring the workings of the Islamic finance institutions and banks are both transparent and demonstrating the requisite level of disclosure[688].

## 13 Sharia Board Governance in Qatar

As in Kuwait and Bahrain, Qatar also has a self-regulation model for sharia boards whereby Islamic financial institutions appoint their own sharia boards. Another similarity to the other GCC states is that there is no limit on the number of boards a scholar can be a member of. The central bank of Qatar does not have a higher sharia authority, instead the central bank of Qatar appoints scholars on a case by case basis[689]. Also, the Ministry of Awqaf has a national sharia board known as the Supreme Council[690].

Qatar has four Islamic banks that specialise in sharia-compliant financing. The first Islamic bank, Qatar Islamic Bank, opened in 1982. From 2011, Qatar brought an end to Islamic units in the conventional banking system[691], making a clear distinction between conventional banking and Islamic banking[692]. Qatar has adopted practices from Malaysia by separating its Islamic banking from conventional banking[693]. It has also kept abreast of innovation and development through three key institutions coming together to enhance Qatar's risk stratification framework, namely the Qatar Central Bank, the Qatar Financial Markets Authority and the Qatar Financial Centre Regulatory Authority[694].

## 14 International Standard Setting in Islamic Finance

Despite the various anomalies in the level of sharia compliance by each GCC state and in the interpretation of Islamic finance by different Islamic finance institutions, Islamic finance is a growing industry in the GCC[695]. All the states have varying levels of sharia compliance as seen above, yet despite this they are able to offer a range of products that are accepted by the public. This is a key feature of the success of Islamic finance that the intellectual property sector has not managed to address. If

Islamic finance can continue to grow within the GCC and despite the varying levels of sharia compliance in each individual state, then there are grounds for developing similar Islamic based intellectual property structures that can be adopted across the GCC states.

The crux of the success of Islamic finance is in its sharia boards, prominent scholars who are well respected and the decisions of whom are accepted. Although serving on several sharia boards consecutively has been criticised as discussed earlier in this chapter, it can also be said to be a vital lever for success in the industry. By having sharia scholars from different states serve together on a given board, it gives the decisions unilateral appeal and as a result, more weight. This is mainly due to the fact that the decision is consequently not seen as the decision of one nation or one particular school of thought, but rather as a sharia compliant decision that appears to transcend cultural and political differences. The intellectual property sector in the GCC does not have the same level of emphasis on sharia boards and this is where both developed countries and Islamic countries as a whole are missing an opportunity in gaining public acceptance of the intellectual property sector.

## 15 The Role of Islamic Finance in Intellectual Property

The potential role of Islamic finance in the development of an integrated approach to intellectual property protection in the GCC has not yet been fully considered. The first ever intellectual property-based sukuk within an ijara structure was introduced by the German based finance company, FWU AG Group[696]. The intellectual property based sukuk introduced by FWU AG Group demonstrates how intellectual property-based assets can be a viable option in Islamic finance services and structures. Consequently, Islamic intellectual property financing will not only protect the intellectual property rights in the underlying asset, but promote intellectual property rights as sharia-compliant and therefore stemming from Islamic, rather than western roots.

The link between Islamic finance and intellectual property is only just starting to emerge with the global Islamic finance market closely following FWU's intellectual property based sukuk. Many other countries are now developing Islamic finance-based products and it is only a matter of time before intellectual property as an asset permeates the Islamic finance sector. This is why an integrated approach to intellectual property rights through the medium of Islamic finance will prove crucial to not only the GCC states, but across all international regions.

## 16 Islamic Finance as a Vehicle to Drive Intellectual Property in the GCC

Overall, there are four main components of Islamic finance regulation that need to be re-enforced in intellectual property protection. All the GCC states have developed some form of a financial market infrastructure, they have improved consumer and investor protection, promoted regulatory cooperation, have built and continue to build human capital. Therefore, rather than treating intellectual property as standalone rights, the systems and regulations in Islamic finance can be applied to intellectual property protection.

By placing emphasis on more effective co-ordination between the GCC states, there is an opportunity to improve enforcement and public acceptance of intellectual property law. Intellectual property protection needs to be developed under five main strands; consistent regulation of intellectual property rights demonstrating consistency with sharia law, strengthening the intellectual property market structure, improving compliance in terms of systems and controls, addressing issues around the efficiency of supervisory procedures and most importantly, engendering greater public confidence in the intellectual property sector.

## 17 Intellectual Property-Based Sharia Boards

The first area of Islamic finance that would make a significant change to the governance of intellectual property in the GCC is an intellectual property rights equivalent to Islamic finance sharia boards. As seen in Chapter 3, although there is a general acceptance of intellectual property rights in the GCC and each GCC state is TRIPS compliant[697], internal frameworks for exhibiting a level of sharia compliance that is both transparent and publicly accepted are not yet in place. The first recommendation, from the analysis of Islamic finance, is to address the shortfall in the somewhat minimalistic approach to intellectual property protection through the introduction of intellectual property-based sharia boards. The recommendation is twofold, firstly to adopt the successful principles of Islamic finance and secondly to overcome the shortcomings in Islamic finance from the onset[698].

Each GCC state has a dedicated institution to intellectual property protection as seen in Chapter 2[699]. As can be seen from the research, these institutions are heavily influenced by international pressures to conform to higher standards of TRIPS without addressing the reasons behind why the GCC are struggling to maintain TRIPS compliance, let alone accelerating to TRIPS Plus. Therefore, there are two levels of intellectual property sharia boards that are required.

An overarching regional board that is represented by each GCC state and comprises a GCC state level intellectual property board would act as a higher authority for internal disputes and appeals. The regional board would have clear criteria for what constitutes an Islamic intellectual property scholar. Oman, as the latecomer to Islamic finance had an opportunity to not only reinvent the wheel with Islamic finance in the GCC, it reflected on the shortcomings of the sharia boards in other states to give Islamic finance the best start possible. It is the same logic that needs to be applied to intellectual property, as this is an opportunity for the GCC to mitigate ahead of the changes in the international market. The overarching GCC intellectual property board can set limitations on how many boards an Islamic intellectual property advisor can be a member of, the maximum tenures, the level of commitment needed from each board member and their key duties.

The intellectual property system in the GCC is missing an "Islamisation" of the rights that the GCC states are obliged to protect, both from national legislative commitments and international agreements. By Islamisation, the meaning is to add a bridge between international standards on intellectual property and national laws. By investing in intellectual property sharia boards which are composed of well-respected scholars who can create sharia compliant frameworks that specify how intellectual property rights are compliant, the GCC states can develop from a TRIPS compliance level to an integrated approach to potential higher standards. It requires taking a step back from the current approach to intellectual property and re-evaluating the approach through a different lens, through Islamic finance. The regional Islamic intellectual property sharia board can act as a higher authority and the sharia scholars that sit on the regional board should not sit at a national level board to avoid potential conflict of interests.

National level intellectual property-based sharia boards will add an extra tier to the integration of intellectual property in the GCC as from Chapter 3, it is clear that not all the GCC states adhere to sharia law at the same constitutional level[700]. By creating national level boards, each GCC state can safeguard its autonomy and create a stronger and more efficient sharia compliance framework for intellectual property in line with its own legislation and governance. As discussed earlier in this chapter, not all the Islamic finance sharia boards follow a centralised system, although they are able to govern Islamic finance successfully.

Therefore, the practices national Islamic intellectual property-based sharia boards can adopt from Islamic finance sharia boards are to set standards for what qualifications an Islamic intellectual property sharia scholar should have, minimum and maximum terms of appointment, minimum attendance requirements and sub divisions based on individual areas of expertise in intellectual property.

# 18 Strengthening the Intellectual Property Market Structure

The intellectual property market structure in the GCC as researched in earlier chapters highlights pertinent structural and operational flaws in the current intellectual property system[701]. As a synopsis, the structure of intellectual property protection in the GCC is regionally led through the GCC patent office, as well as national provisions such as domestic patent offices and intellectual property rights protection and enforcement institutions[702]. The GCC patent office is ill-equipped to cope with the sheer number of patents filed with the number of applications in progress in excess of 15,000[703].

Therefore, in order to strengthen the intellectual property market structure, lessons can be learnt from Islamic finance. The three main recommendations are to adopt regulation and auditing frameworks for Islamic finance sharia boards, have a sharia compliant structure in place for each type of intellectual property right and develop intellectual property based assets within an Islamic finance structure[704].

Islamic finance sharia boards are subject to scrutiny and review, there are national level issues as not all GCC states adopt a centralised model nor do they impose limitations on sharia scholar commitments, however each GCC state offers structural parameters which are not so apparent in intellectual property. By implementing national and regional level structures there is more co-ordination of intellectual property as a holistic approach to development as currently there are ad hoc powers delegated to state institutions without the necessary harmonisation of structural frameworks.

Fundamental to the success of Islamic finance is that it has created sharia-compliant alternatives to conventional financial products. The intellectual property field has not done this and as a result intellectual property rights have failed to shake off their "foreigner rights" image[705]. There are legislation and rules in place to prohibit riba and gharar in intellectual property, however Islamic finance has gone one step further and developed an Islamic version of conventional financial products. To succeed in developing an integrated approach to intellectual property, the GCC states need to develop alternative sharia-compliant structures to existing intellectual property concepts.

Thirdly, the GCC states, in their bid to be market leaders for Islamic finance, need to invest in research and development structures that build on the work of FWU AG group and incorporate intellectual property-based assets in existing Islamic finance products. By developing intellectual property-based assets through Islamic finance, the assets are better protected as in the eyes of the public they have a seal of approval by sharia scholars.

The shortcomings identified in the Islamic finance structure which should be addressed in the integrated approach to intellectual property rights are the lack of a centralised database of scholars, continued professional development of scholars, adopting a fit for purpose approach and addressing transparency issues.

## 19 Improving Compliance in Terms of Systems and Controls

Systems and controls already exist in intellectual property protection in the GCC. Chapter 4 analysed compliance measures and to date, the customs authorities have been the most prominent in restricting trade in counterfeit and pirated goods[706]. This epitomises the GCC approach to intellectual property compliance as it is a very top-heavy approach. As seen in Chapter 5[707], the GCC states do not have access to the level of resources available to countries with developed intellectual property systems, in terms of; infrastructure, legislation, case law, technical expertise and independent reports[708]. Therefore, there are specific development needs in relation to the systems and controls that are currently in operation.

In order to improve existing systems and controls in intellectual property, the GCC states need to take a step back from the front-line issue and reassess their compliance procedures to be able to take a holistic approach to intellectual property rights protection. A potential avenue through which to improve existing systems and controls in intellectual property is to learn from the shortcomings in Islamic finance in this regard by setting up internal auditing committees, introducing governance ethics, initiating periodic reviews and assurances for intellectual property rights.

## 20 Addressing Issues Around the Efficiency of Supervisory Procedures

There are practices from Islamic finance that can have a positive influence on how the GCC states supervisory procedures operate in the field of intellectual property. There are issues around transparency and disclosures in intellectual property law which could be addressed by setting up case specific supervisory boards. There is no accessible database or bank of information on case law or judicial decisions. Further, there is a lack of access to cases that have been settled out of court, to information on judicial experience or expertise or alternative dispute settle mechanisms[709]. Therefore, taking heed from Islamic finance, more transparency is required at government and regional levels to integrate intellectual property as a sharia-compliant industry[710].

## 21 Greater Public Confidence in the Intellectual Property Sector

Islamic finance has secured public confidence in its established products. There is conflict between different scholars on the Islamic legalities of a product and this is a flaw within the Islamic finance sector that needs to be addressed as the public will accept a principle that is a unanimous decision but will be less receptive to a product that has scholars at loggerheads. Intellectual property has never truly won the Islamic world. El Bialy's and Gouda's empirical research showed Islamic developing countries had a high level of IPR piracy as well as a high level of religiosity to Islam[711]. In contrast, Islamic finance is not only well received; it is an industry that is growing despite almost a decade of global financial woes.

Public confidence is difficult to quantify as it is very subjective. Lessons need to be learnt from the Islamic finance sector in the GCC states as how Islamic finance has been introduced, the indexes and financial institutions set up and the regulatory frameworks all demonstrate a level of ownership of Islamic finance. The GCC states need to similarly demonstrate ownership of the intellectual property rights they seek to protect, be they as they may from predominantly foreign investors.

## 22 Conclusion

Islamic finance has achieved success as a sharia-compliant alternative to conventional banking. The industry is growing, with the market expanding beyond the Organisation of Islamic Co-operation and non-member countries weighing in with their own Islamic finance products and services. The approach taken by the GCC in developing Islamic finance is not uniform across all the GCC states, a similarity it shares with intellectual property development. Another similarity is that there is no overarching supervisory body that acts as a higher authority, where the decision would bind ratified states, at a regional level in the GCC. The timeframe in which Islamic finance has developed also runs parallel with intellectual property development amongst the GCC states.

However, the purpose of this chapter was to identify the sharia-compliant structures that exist within the GCC states and identify how the successes of Islamic finance can be a vehicle for promoting better intellectual property rights protection in the GCC. There are five key recommendations from the analysis of Islamic finance which have been outlined in this chapter that can be applied to an integrated Islamic based intellectually property-based model. The recommendations are: Islamic based intellectual property sharia boards, strengthened intellectual property market structures, improved compliance to increase transparency through systems and controls, increased efficiency of supervisory procedures and greater public confidence in the intellectual property sector.

The findings from Islamic finance and its sharia-compliant models are a springboard to creating a successful sharia-compliant intellectual property rights protection approach. The next chapter will build on the findings of this chapter and earlier chapters and incorporate the research findings on the structure of the GCC states, international agreements and pressures, the international institutions and sharia law to propose a series of recommendations to develop an integrated approach to intellectual property rights protection.

# 8

# Recommendations to Develop an Integrated Approach to Intellectual Property

## 1 Introduction

This work set out to examine the intellectual property regimes in the Gulf Co-operation Council (GCC) states. The main aim was to answer the key question of what recommendations could be made to develop an integrated approach to intellectual property rights protection in the GCC and its potential impact on intellectual property protection in the region. The integrated intellectual property rights approach has taken into account the structure of the GCC states, international agreements and pressures, the international institutions, Islamic finance and both societal and religious views.

The monograph examined current intellectual property laws in the GCC states and considered the protection of intellectual property from two perspectives, international demand for higher standards of intellectual property protection in the GCC states[712] and defining the relationship between intellectual property and sharia law[713]. The monograph aimed to contribute to the existing research in the field as previous research has investigated intellectual property development under one of the two perspectives but not both. Thirdly, the theoretical analysis of Islamic finance structures as a vehicle for promoting better intellectual property rights is a novel contribution to the field and will lead on to further research.

The GCC share certain commonalities which make developments in the region relevant to many other countries who share similarities in religious influence, societal and cultural norms, economic progression and development. The monograph has contributed to an important area of study as the developing GCC states are struggling with meeting international standards and a successful integrated framework will impact on how the GCC states move forward with intellectual property rights protection within their constitutional religious obligations. Further, the proposed integrated approach to intellectual property rights protection will impact on other Islamic states and as a result lead to more informed negotiation in trade agreements with developed states. Also, it will meet the overall objective of developing a framework within which Islamic states can improve the level of intellectual property rights protection offered without alienating their own distinct sharia-based constitutional obligations.

The research has argued that there are systematic flaws in the GCC states adopting intellectual property laws which have been nothing short of a complete overhaul of domestic laws, modified to reflect foreign laws from colonial occupation or laws taken from donor countries. As can be seen from the research, each GCC state has differing levels of national sharia compliance, intellectual property laws and international agreements. There is a strong dichotomy that exists between the religious characteristics of each GCC state, the intellectual property laws that exist under western legal principles and therefore the foreign laws, as they stand, are unsuitable for the GCC states and require modification. There is a significant paucity of research in developing an integrated approach to intellectual property rights in the GCC and therefore the one of the fundamental aims of this research is to act as a catalyst for further research in this area.

## 2 The Research Questions

The integrated intellectual property rights protection framework addresses the following key research questions:

- How can the GCC states satisfy international demands for better intellectual property protection without compromising their Islamic values and traditions?
- Do the GCC states have the necessary capacity both in their legal structure and internal institutions to increase their levels of intellectual property rights protection?
- What recommendations can be made to develop an Islamic law-based integrated approach to intellectual property rights in the GCC, taking into account the structure of the GCC states, international agreements and pressures, the relevant international institutions, Islamic finance and both societal and religious views?

The recommendations for an integrated approach to intellectual property rights protection in the GCC are three-fold; firstly they centre on embedding existing sharia principles of property law, contract law, ijaza and public interest to intellectual property laws, secondly they are focused at a GCC level and at a national level with specific recommendations for each GCC state and thirdly they assess the impact of Islamic law, the US and the EU, TRIPS standards, international trade and Islamic finance.

## 3 First Area of Recommendations: Embedding Sharia Principles to Intellectual Property Law

### *Embedding Sharia Principles of Property Law*

Key recommendations:

- balance the rights of the inventor in line with how sharia law protects the rights of property right holders against the prohibition of excessive wealth;
- quantify the non-tangible asset and the consequential loss and
- create sharia compliant punishments for intellectual property infringement.

Proprietary rights have been established by Quranic verses that make specific references to proprietary interests[714]. Therefore, there is a strong foundational base of proprietary rights-based knowledge within the primary sources of sharia law that can be embedded into an integrated intellectual property framework in order to create a stronger link to Islamic law[715]. There needs to be an intellectual property doctrine that reflects the proprietary principle of Istikhlaf as discussed in Chapter 3[716].

Established practices in the GCC states accept that all property belongs to God, allowing the exercise of a right to ownership subject to the public interest of society. Where the interpretation of Islamic proprietary rights to intellectual property rights has fallen short in the past is in the quantification of the asset. Under sharia law, property law dictates on the ownership of property, the right to possess and enjoy wealth through lawful means[717], theft of property[718] and the doctrine of mutual consent[719]. For an integrated intellectual property framework to have an impact on intellectual property protection, the quantification of the asset and the consequential loss necessitates compliance within set parameters in the way that Islamic finance has sought to limit speculative loss, and intellectual property law can develop sharia-compliant remedies which can implement control measures that would allow intellectual property rights protection to be more fit for purpose in the GCC.

Theft of property is also referenced in the Quran[720] and punishments are set in line with Islamic teaching; however there is no crossover principle to intellectual property theft in the primary sharia sources of the Quran or the Sunnah. The Quran is very detailed on criminal law and the application of tangible property theft to intangible assets requires a formal analysis of intellectual property theft and corresponding Islamic principles of theft.

The recommendation is to balance the rights of the inventor, in line with how sharia law protects the rights of tangible asset holders, against the prohibition of excessive wealth and to create sharia-compliant punishments for intellectual property infringement. The main counterarguments to this recommendation are two-fold: how can sharia compliant punishments for intellectual property infringement be aligned with the one size fits all TRIPS approach to intellectual property rights protection and secondly as profit is based on market value, how can a prohibition apply when markets are inherently uncertain?

In response to the one size fits all TRIPS approach, the GCC states need to consider a modified approach to TRIPS and especially TRIPS Plus whereby they can be granted some level of flexibility to develop an intellectual property model which addresses the lack of certainty in profit driven markets as this will satisfy the doctrines of riba and gharar while providing safeguards for intellectual property right holders[721]. Further, there is a lack of legislative reform to resolve the issue of economic free riders in the GCC states. This can be addressed through the implementation of an Islamic doctrine in establishing an Islamic-based principle to deal with economic free riders[722].

## *Embedding Sharia Principles of Contract Law*

Key recommendations:

- develop intellectual property rights through incorporating sharia compliant doctrines of contract law;
- incorporate principles of mutual consent and gainful exchange to the protection of knowledge-based assets and
- promulgate Islamic-based contractual law ethics to intellectual property rights protection.

Islamic principles of contract law can be integrated into intellectual property rights protection by developing recognised sharia-compliant doctrines of contract law to create more sophisticated Islamic-based intellectual property rights[723]. Mutual consent and gainful exchange are two key doctrines of contract law that are evident in the Quran at Surah An-Nisā', Verse 4[724]. These principles of contract law need to be applied beyond a justification for intellectual property rights and develop elements of Islamic law-based theory of intellectual property rights protection. It puts emphasis on the role of sharia scholars to evolve from reaching a consensus on whether intellectual property rights are compliant with sharia law, to developing sharia compliant intellectual property rules and regulations. Islamic approval of intellectual property rights protection is not a contentious issue, it is how Islamic law can uphold the doctrines of intellectual property law and develop sharia-compliant frameworks for improved levels of intellectual property protection.

The recommendation is to apply contract law principles at two levels. First, to incorporate contract law principles that are underpinned by sharia law in existing GCC practices of regulating contractual agreements and for providing sharia-compliant remedies for where agreements have been breached. The Islamic doctrines of contract law are needed to strengthen the argument for an Islamic-based approach to intellectual property rights protection as contractual agreements to license the use of assets can spearhead Islamic doctrines for granting knowledge-based asset owners monopoly rights for a given time period.

Second, the GCC states would benefit from applying primary sharia references in respect to international transactions[725], economic gain[726], moral rights[727], financial rights and conducting ethical contractual law-based business to intellectual property rights protection[728]. The Quran and Sunnah have clear statements regarding honouring international agreements, economic gain and the rights of each party while balancing the need for certainty against the prohibition of riba and gharar[729]. Therefore, these statements can be utilised to develop an integrated Islamic-based intellectual property framework without violating the doctrines of riba and gharar.

## *Embedding Sharia Principles of Ijaza*

Key recommendations:

- develop the doctrine of ijaza to offer a sharia compliant authentication process for intellectual property rights protection;
- utilise the doctrine of ijaza to highlight the protection of moral rights from an Islamic perspective and
- apply Islamic law-based protection for intellectual property rights as an acknowledgment for the time, labour and efforts of the inventor.

The sharia principle of ijaza, as discussed in Chapters 3 and 7, is a principle that needs to be brought to the forefront of intellectual property protection. In ancient Islamic customs there was a system of knowledge acknowledgement by way of a certificate, known as ijaza[730]. The doctrine of ijaza protects the moral rights of an author to a certain degree as it is believed that the knowledge itself belongs to God, not to any individual. By applying inferential reasoning, if the moral rights of the author are protected, within limitations, then as a result, ijaza can be interpreted and developed by sharia scholars to offer an authentication process for intellectual property rights protection.

The developmental stage of intellectual property rights protection in the GCC requires more than legislative changes, it require an Islamic law-based protection process for intellectual property rights as an acknowledgment for the time, labour and efforts of the inventor as established in the doctrine of ijaza. This will have a positive impact on public acceptance of intellectual property rights as if the protection of the time, labour and efforts of the inventor are seen to have a connection to Islamic principles, then intellectual property rights are less likely to be considered as a "foreigner right".

## *Embedding Sharia Principles of Public Interest*

Key recommendations:

- modify intellectual property rights protection to have a greater appreciation of ethical business;
- give more weight to the doctrine of public interest when balancing the rights of the inventor against the potential harm to public welfare and
- develop from identifying the primary sharia sources on public interest that can justify intellectual property rights protection to a more stringent and rigorous application of public interest.

The impact of public interest in the development of intellectual property rights protection is interwoven into all aspects of sharia law. There are primary source sharia references which state the need for a moral and ethical code to be adopted in conducting daily tasks and activities[731]. The Sunnah references identified in Chapter 3 have been found to specifically weigh the importance of moral and financial rights, placing the development of intellectual property protection within the ambit of ethical business[732]. Public interest in sharia law aims to protect and progress the legitimate interests of the community within the recognised sources primary and secondary sharia sources in order to secure public welfare through promoting the benefits of a rule or protecting against harm[733].

Intellectual property development in the GCC states has overlooked the importance of public interest principles as it requires a modification of western laws as opposed to directly adopting western laws into domestic legal structures. Intellectual property legislation in all the GCC states accounts for prohibitions on haram activity, riba and gharar. However, what the research highlights is that the level of protection offered to prevent breaching sharia law are just scratching the surface of sharia law and by delving deeper into existing Islamic doctrines, intellectual property protection can exist under more stringent and rigorous sharia principles.

The counter argument to broadening the public interest doctrine is that there is a potential negative impact on the level of protection available to inventors while narrowing the public interest could have a detrimental effect on public welfare[734]. The role of public interest in the protection of intellectual property rights on the GCC and neighbouring states will be an area of further research as from the proposals in TRIPS plus it is evident that the public interest doctrine is being strait-jacketed and with the development of investor to state dispute mechanisms and corporate sovereignty, grounds for public interest are facing further restrictions.

## 4 Second Area of Recommendations: Proposals for the GCC and Each Individual GCC State

### *Assessing the Capacity of the GCC States to Increase Intellectual Property Rights Protection*

As outlined in the research, the GCC states not only place differing levels of importance on sharia law at a constitutional level, they also differ on the level of intellectual property rights protection available domestically[735]. In order to assess the capacity of the GCC states, both in their legal structure and internal institutions, to increase their levels of intellectual property rights protection, international intellectual property rights standard setting was considered.

The research was concerned with national intellectual property structures within the GCC states, the viewpoints of the US and the EU on international intellectual property rights standard setting, the impact international trade, TRIPS agreement and pending trade agreements had on the GCC states, as well as the influence of corporate sovereignty and ISDS.

### *The Current Intellectual Property Structures in the GCC*

- Each GCC state has its own set of domestic intellectual property legislation and institutions with an overarching GCC patent office based in Saudi Arabia;
- All the GCC states abide by minimum TRIPS standards and display a set of intellectual property laws that are largely compliant with TRIPS and
- The GCC states have intellectual property legislation which legislates on both criminal prosecutions and civil sanctions.

Each GCC state has its own set of domestic intellectual property legislation and institutions set up to regulate intellectual property rights protection with an overall regional patent office based in Saudi Arabia. The GCC patent office has the authority to grant a regional community patent that is valid in all the GCC states[736]. The Gulf states all abide by minimum TRIPS standards and display a set of intellectual property laws that are largely compliant with TRIPS. The GCC states have intellectual property legislation which legislates on both criminal prosecutions and civil sanctions available to intellectual property right holders where their rights have been infringed. The capacity of the GCC states to raise existing levels of TRIPS compliance to TRIPS Plus standards has been a key research question.

In order to assess whether the GCC states have enough scope in their current laws to comply with TRIPS plus provisions, each GCC state has been considered in turn to outline how effective their current measures are and what recommendations can be made to improve the current model of intellectual property rights protection by the GCC states. Thus, each GCC state is summarised individually to examine their current intellectual property rights protection and signpost areas for improvement.

## 5 Improving Intellectual Property Rights Development

### *Improving Intellectual Property Rights Development in Saudi Arabia*

Key recommendations:

- lead on integrating intellectual property rights with sharia principles at both a regional and national level with representation from sharia scholars who have expertise in sharia law and intellectual property law;
- modify its approach to intellectual property rights protection by instigating an intellectual property rights system which does more than comply with sharia law; it can prompt the development of sharia-compliant intellectual property frameworks and
- develop an integrated intellectual property rights approach that can offer uniform guidance on how sharia-compliant intellectual property rights can be identified and implemented.

Saudi Arabia remains an absolute monarchy with Article 1 of its Basic Law of Government stating the Holy Quran is the constitution and state governance must abide by sharia law[737]. From the research it was found that Saudi Arabia operates a judicial system that is the most reliant on sharia principles[738]. Sharia law has formed the basis of all decision-making in the criminal and civil courts and is given a higher level of importance in the law-making process as compared to the other GCC states.

Saudi Arabia has a number of laws pertaining to intellectual property rights protection with a total of 21 pieces of legislation[739]. Internationally, Saudi Arabia is a signatory to four international agreements[740]. Intellectual property rights protection is administered by the Saudi patent office at the King Abdulaziz City for Science and Technology (KACST). For intellectual property violations, the Saudi patent office prefers to deal with matters mainly by arbitration and not the court process[741]. Saudi

Arabia is the only GCC state that does not follow a two track approach to intellectual property infringement in that whether the infringement is seen a criminal or civil, Saudi Arabia handles all piracy and counterfeiting from both criminal and civil perspectives[742]. The power lies with the Board of Grievances who can apply a broad range of punishments if intellectual property violations are found.

The Ministry of Culture and Information (MCI) is responsible for punishing copyright violations and follows the Saudi copyright system when imposing sanctions. The Ministry of Culture and Information established the Violation Review Committee (VRC) on copyrights in order to review copyright infringement cases and it is a requirement that one member of the committee be a sharia advisor[743]. Therefore, rather than set up independent sharia boards for intellectual property rights protection, Saudi Arabia has sought to include sharia advisors to existing intellectual property-related committees and boards.

Thus, Saudi Arabia has the necessary legislation to protect intellectual property rights and provide remedies for when infringement takes place. From an internal institution perspective, Saudi Arabia has boards and committees set up to review and regulate intellectual property rights protection. This has been most apparent when consideration was given to Saudi Arabia's intellectual property enforcement through more stringent border measures[744].

To better integrate intellectual property rights into the Saudi Arabian legal system, the existing infrastructure needs enhancement by way of independent sharia boards. Saudi Arabia has taken a lead within the GCC union and is also the most sharia-compliant of the GCC states. As the regional patent office is in Saudi Arabia, it can lead on integrating intellectual property rights with sharia principles at both a regional and national level. A regional intellectual sharia board can be set up with representation from sharia scholars who have expertise in sharia law and intellectual property law. In conjunction with a regional sharia board, Saudi Arabia can take a lead in proposing national level intellectual property-based sharia boards.

By modifying its approach to intellectual property rights protection, Saudi Arabia can instigate an intellectual property rights system which does more than comply with sharia law; it can prompt the development of sharia-compliant intellectual property frameworks. There are further ramifications of such an approach on the international intellectual property standards setting arena. By developing an integrated intellectual property rights approach that can offer uniform guidance on how sharia-compliant intellectual property rights can be identified and implemented, there are crossover benefits of such an approach to other Islamic countries and the relationship between developed western states and Islamic states.

## Improving Intellectual Property Rights Development in Bahrain

Key recommendations:

- given Bahrain already accedes to TRIPS Plus clauses in their free trade agreement with the US, it is recommended Bahrain take a lead on developing sharia-compliant frameworks for intellectual property;
- address the lack of a positive correlation between extensive legislative measures and enforcement and
- replicate the progress it has made in the Islamic finance industry for a modified approach that further incorporates Islamic law with the intellectual property sector.

Bahrain has a hereditary constitutional monarchy with a bicameral parliament[745]. The legal system of Bahrain is based on several sources, including customary law, Islamic law and civil law[746]. Sharia law is a principal source of legislation[747]. In terms of intellectual property legislation, Bahrain is the most progressive of the GCC states with 16 national laws[748] and 11 international treaties[749], most notably it was the first of the GCC states to agree a bilateral trade agreement with the US[750].The bilateral agreement with the US enforced TRIPS Plus measures such as investor to state dispute settlement mechanisms, ratification to further international treaties and longer durations for patent terms[751]. However, Bahrain has not had to deal with an investor to state dispute proceeding or breach of TRIPS Plus measures, therefore the impact of TRIPS Plus has not yet been tested in court proceedings.

Bahrain does not have the same level of oil reserves as its neighbours[752] and as such has developed in other areas, with intellectual property being one of them. Bahrain has been the most proactive of all the GCC states in relation to its intellectual property-based legislative reforms, however this does not equate to Bahrain being the most successful at protecting intellectual property rights. The Business Software Alliance study places Bahrain second highest out of the GCC states on piracy rates, only offering better protection than Kuwait. This further supports the need for an integrated approach to intellectual property rights protection both in Bahrain and in the GCC collectively. It may be well and good to satisfy international agreement obligations by acceding to higher standards of intellectual property law, however, in order to see the obligations through, more needs to be done.

As Bahrain is one of only two GCC states to have TRIPS Plus clauses in their FTAs with the US, the recommendation is for Bahrain to take a lead on developing sharia-compliant frameworks for intellectual property within its extensive intellectual property law provisions. Bahrain can replicate the progress it has made in the Islamic finance industry for developing its intellectual property sector. As a latecomer to Islamic finance, Bahrain has made the most significant improvements in the field as will be summarised later in this Chapter (11) and it needs to invest a similar level of commitment to the intellectual property sector. Further, by taking a lead in developing sharia-compliant intellectual property rights while taking into account international agreements and pressures, Bahrain can demonstrate how sharia law can be utilised to create Islamic-based intellectual property rights. This in turn will impact on the agreements being negotiated by the GCC Union with other countries and unions as well as the international agreements being considered by the other GCC states individually.

## *Improving Intellectual Property Rights Development in the UAE*

Key recommendations:

- to focus the intellectual property research in the UAE to incorporate Islamic law principles into developing improved intellectual property systems;
- the UAE has invested in innovation and human capital and this can be an avenue through which to reassess the role of Islamic law in creating intellectual property rights that are more balanced in terms of traditional western rights and sharia principles.

The UAE stands out for its commitment to improving intellectual property rights development. It has a body of national legislation in many areas of intellectual property including copyright[753], trademarks[754], industrial designs[755] and other areas[756]. The UAE patent system has been operating under two systems; the Patent Cooperation Treaty (PCT) system for domestic patents and the GCC Patent system for regional patent applications[757]. As seen in Chapter 2[758], the UAE is signatory to several international treaties which has put it on a par with Qatar's international obligations but below Oman and Bahrain[759].

Dubai has made the most progress in intellectual property enforcement through its customs intellectual property rights units[760]. Further, through the Dubai Declaration to set new standards for developing intellectual property based civil and criminal proceedings at national and regional levels, Dubai has introduced more effective remedies in intellectual property rights protection[761]. However, on the one hand, the UAE can be seen to be progressive in developing its knowledge-based economy, but on the other, the western pressure to satisfy higher standards of intellectual property rights protection is at odds with the development.

The UAE, along with the remaining GCC states, has been stagnant in its ability to further reduce piracy rates as seen in Chapter 5. Thus, by initiating an integrated approach to intellectual property rights protection in the UAE, the

Emirate state can capitalise on its investment in innovation by committing to a modified approach to intellectual property law. An approach which incorporates the human capital into intellectual property research and development through an amalgamation of sharia law principles, western laws, international agreements and international intellectual property law standard settings, will have a more significant impact on intellectual property protection than simply, albeit with some success, trying to follow western laws.

## *Improving Intellectual Property Rights Development in Qatar*

Key recommendations:

- Qatar, as the least sharia-compliant state, does not have the most successful intellectual property protection system in the GCC; therefore the argument is that deviating away from sharia law is not the answer to improving intellectual property protection;
- Stronger national infrastructure as to issue its own patents and
- Make a concerted effort to bring Islamic-based intellectual property research on a par with its TRIPS plus commitments.

Qatar, as a legislative authority, has developed towards a more semi-democratic model with sharia law as a main source of law[762]. Consequently, Qatar places the least importance on sharia law as a source of law when compared to the other GCC states. This indirectly supports the recommendation for a more sharia-compliant intellectual property framework as if Qatar was the best performing GCC state in intellectual property rights protection then there would be a strong counterargument against embedding sharia-compliant frameworks into intellectual property rights protection. Qatar does not have the lowest piracy rates in the GCC; therefore, Qatar is further evidence that deviating away from sharia law is not the key to better intellectual property rights as legislative changes alone can only make improvements to a certain point.

Qatar has been very active in developing its intellectual property law in line with TRIPS and international agreements. Qatar has set up internal infrastructures to regulate intellectual property rights protection through the Centre for the Protection of Intellectual Property Rights. Also, Qatar's intellectual property laws are controlled by the Ministry of Justice with the justice minister having the authority to appoint independent experts to help the centre carry out its functions[763].

Chapter 2[764] highlighted how the Qatari intellectual property legislation is the most comprehensive of all the GCC states as Qatari laws protect a vast array of intellectual property rights[765]. Further, the analysis of Qatar's legislative developments showed that Qatar has enacted TRIPS plus provisions despite the fact that the minimum requirement is TRIPS compliance and not TRIPS plus. TRIPS plus provisions have been evident in Qatar's 2011 Law on Intellectual Property Rights Border Measures as discussed in Chapter 5[766], where Qatar has gone beyond the minimum standard of protecting trademark and copyright counterfeiting, as specified in the TRIPS standards at Part III, Section 4 of TRIPS, to protecting any intellectual property rights[767].

As Qatar does not issue its own patents, an integrated sharia-compliant intellectual property approach would require a regional sharia board which can streamline the approach to intellectual property rights protection to be more fit for purpose by setting up accountability and scrutiny measures as well as checks and balances. The recommendation of a regional office is based on the lessons learnt from the Islamic finance industry where the lack of an overarching higher authority was identified as a shortcoming in the sector and can be avoided in an integrated approach to intellectual property rights protection. The lessons learnt from the Islamic finance sector will be discussed in more detail further in this chapter (11).

## *Improving Intellectual Property Rights Development in Oman*

Key recommendations:

- Oman needs to take advantage of on its position of adhering to TRIPS plus standards and having sharia law as its constitution to draw the two divergent areas together for an integrated approach and
- to improve innovation by introducing effective measures that can strike a balance between enforcement mechanisms and sharia law.

Oman is the second of the GCC states to have a bilateral agreement with the US. The Oman and US FTA which entered into force in 2009, is built on previous ties to promote economic reform and as in Bahrain, included an intellectual property chapter to increase the existing levels of intellectual property rights protection and enforcement[768]. Therefore, as a result of bilateral treaties, Bahrain and Oman have both acceded to TRIPS Plus intellectual property provisions and agreed to ratify further international treaties[769].

Further, as inBahrain, Oman's intellectual property based legislative progress does not run parallel with placing Oman at the pinnacle of intellectual property success. It has one of the highest software piracy rates, second only to Kuwait. Thus, the lack of effective measures to further reduce software piracy rates in Oman highlights a common theme in intellectual property rights protection in the GCC states. The common theme reflected by Oman is that the initial improvements made from the advent of TRIPS are barely maintainable by the GCC states and a modified approach is needed to make a positive impact on intellectual property regimes.

Oman is quite the anomaly state as it is the only GCC state to share its importance to sharia law as a source of law with the most compliant of the GCC states with sharia law, Saudi Arabia, whilst also sharing its level of intellectual property law compliance with Qatar, the least sharia-compliant state at a constitutional level. It is similar to Saudi Arabia in that it states in its constitution very clearly that the basis of law is sharia law at Article 2 of the Omani constitution[770]. However, Oman has developed its intellectual property laws more in line with Qatar than Saudi Arabia with a number of Acts enacted in intellectual property law[771].

Thus, Oman could play an important role in the development of an integrated approach to intellectual property rights protection as it can act as a bridge from Saudi Arabia, the most compliant state to sharia law to Qatar which is the least. Oman shares its religiosity with Saudi Arabia and intellectual property law progress with Qatar and could play a key role in developing sharia-compliant frameworks that strike a balance between sharia law and international intellectual property rights standards settings. To date, the intellectual property system in the GCC states has developed with minimal sharia law involvement with sharia law acting only as a conduit to justifying intellectual property rights protection. What an integrated intellectual property rights approach can achieve is more conductive harmonisation between sharia law and intellectual property law.

## *Improving Intellectual Property Rights Development in Kuwait*

Key recommendations:

- address inadequacies in its intellectual property laws, mainly: its lack of progress on enforcement efforts against piracy and counterfeiting, failure of the judiciary to enforce penalties severe enough to act as a deterrent to intellectual property infringement and the lack of legislative reform in Kuwaiti copyright law;
- improve its intellectual property rights protection to a level that would bring it on a par with the remaining GCC states and
- take advantage of the freedom it has to develop sharia-compliant intellectual property based frameworks and enact legislation in accordance with an integrated model structure, given its lack of intellectual property legislative reform.

Kuwait is a fully sovereign state with sharia as a main source of legislation[772]. It was the first of the GCC states to have a constitution[773] and formed a precedent for other

Gulf states[774]. It seeks to have a partly democratic composition in Parliament, similar to Qatar, as its Parliament consists of elected representatives and members appointed by the Emir[775]. The Kuwait legal system is based on civil law jurisdiction and does not refer to intellectual property in its constitution[776]. The research has shown that intellectual property development in Kuwait lags behind the other GCC states with Kuwait currently having four statutes dealing with intellectual property[777].

Kuwait is the only GCC state that remains on the US Special 301 Report Watch List for its lack of progress on enforcement efforts against piracy and counterfeiting, failure of the judiciary to enforce penalties severe enough to act as a deterrent to intellectual property infringement and the lack of legislative reform in Kuwaiti copyright law[778]. Kuwait ranks the lowest of all the GCC states in its ability to protect intellectual property rights and innovation.

Kuwait has not managed to improve its intellectual property rights protection to a level that would bring it on a par with the remaining GCC states. However, Kuwait can take heed from states such as Bahrain and Oman who have legislated extensively in the intellectual property field yet still have hit a glass ceiling in their attempts to further improve. Given that Kuwait has minimal intellectual property legislation, it has more room for manoeuvre in developing an integrated approach to intellectual property rights protection.

Whereas other GCC states will need to reassess their existing agreements and legislations, Kuwait has more freedom to develop sharia-compliant intellectual property-based frameworks and enact legislation in accordance with an integrated model structure. Thus, before concluding on the mechanics of an integrated intellectual property rights-based model, the western standards on intellectual property rights will be summarised next.

## 6 Third Area of Recommendations: Assess the Impact of Islamic Law, the US and the EU, TRIPS Standards, International Trade and Islamic Finance

### *Improved Intellectual Property Protection in the GCC through Islamic Law*

The GCC states can satisfy international demands for better intellectual property protection without compromising their Islamic values and traditions by reassessing the role sharia law can play in intellectual property rights protection. In areas such as ijaza, property law, contract law and public interest, where primary sharia law sources have been interpreted to develop more established and sophisticated legal structures in the GCC, similar infrastructures are needed for intellectual property rights protection. Therefore, the main recommendations on how the GCC states can improve the level of intellectual property rights protection through sharia law and advance the GCC states from a foundational stage of intellectual property protection to a development stage are:

- Develop intellectual property focused sharia law principles that can embed existing sharia law principles in ijaza, property law, contract law and public interest to intellectual property rights protection.
- Create Islamic law-based doctrines that derive authenticity from primary and secondary sources of Islamic law to establish sharia-compliant intellectual property products. Therefore, rather than adopting international rules and regulations on intellectual property products, derive Islamic equivalents to the products which can then be better protected and relied upon by inventors and companies as they enshrine sharia law.
- Develop clear and transparent sharia-compliant frameworks for intellectual property rights protection that balance the rights of the intellectual property right holder whilst safeguarding prohibitions on established principles of riba (interest), gharar (speculative risk) and forbidden activity (haram activity).

## 7 Intellectual Property and Islamic Law

The Quran and the Sunnah, as primary sources of sharia law, make no direct reference to intellectual property rights, no provisions as to how intangible assets should be protected or any guidelines regarding remedial action for infringement of intangible assets. Therefore, no Islamic law-based legal provisions exists, at a primary source level, in how intellectual property law should be regulated by Islamic states. As a result, intellectual property has developed as a new area of law, derived from secondary sources of sharia law. There is an inherent weakness in producing new laws in areas where there are no Quranic or Sunnah references and this weakness has been the stumbling block for improvements in intellectual property protection[779].

Secondary sources of sharia law have been interpreted to provide justification for the protection of intellectual property rights. As the number of extensive legal references in the Quran and the Sunnah are limited, secondary sources of sharia law are accepted as an interpretive tool where the primary sources are silent or ambiguous. The secondary sources, qiyas and ijma, follow strict guidelines on how new principles can be founded as discussed in Chapter 3[780]. Secondary sources of sharia law have been applied to infer Islamic reasoning from existing areas such as property law, contract law and public interest. Secondary sources have formed the basis of sharia approval for intellectual property protection[781]. However, whereas the

Islamic law systems in relation to protecting rights and providing remedies against infringement for property law, contract law and public interest are well established, intellectual property law protection has not managed to cement its foundations in Islamic law[782].

The research has shown that although the GCC states have enacted a number of intellectual property-related laws, the acceptance by the general GCC public of intellectual property laws having an Islamic foundation has not transferred across the vertical axis of institutions of state and individual. This was quantitatively analysed in a religious loyalty index by El Bialy and Gouda where their empirical research found that Muslim citizens of developing Islamic countries have a high level of both intellectual property piracy as well as a high level of religiosity to Islam[783]. What this highlights is that intellectual property protection has not truly solemnised its union with Islamic law as the research has shown that there is Islamic jurisprudence which supports the existence of intellectual property rights, however it falls short of setting parameters within which intellectual property rights can develop from an Islamic law perspective[784]. Legislative success in reaching minimal international intellectual property standards is not the same as having the necessary understanding of informal moral beliefs, cultural norms and ethical structures.

## 8 The Islamic Law-Based Approach to an Integrated Intellectual Property Model

Key recommendations:

- develop intellectual property-focused sharia law principles through the established areas of ijaza, property law, contract law and public interest to develop the protection of intellectual property rights further from the justification that intellectual property rights exist in Islam;
- propose an integrated intellectual property rights approach with the aim of reducing intellectual property infringement and promote an approach that is a hybrid of clear and unambiguous sharia principles and international intellectual property laws and
- through an Islamic-based approach shake off the foreign rights connotations attached to intellectual property rights as well as stimulating intellectual property growth in the region.

The Islamic law-based approach has informed the development of an integrated approach to intellectual property rights by making recommendations to spotlight what influence sharia law can have for the betterment of intellectual property protection[785].

The examination of Islamic law sources and their application to intellectual property law highlighted that at a foundational level, the GCC states have accepted intellectual property rights protection as sharia-compliant through the use of secondary sharia sources to permit intellectual property rights protection.

However, in the development stage of intellectual property rights, sharia law was silent and all the GCC states adopted minimum TRIPS standards in their legislative institutions. What is needed is an integrated intellectual property rights approach to essentially reduce intellectual property infringement and promote an approach that is a hybrid of clear and unambiguous sharia principles and international intellectual property laws. Clear and unambiguous principles of sharia law that directly justify the tenets of intellectual property law will have a profound impact on improvement measures in the GCC as it will help shake off the foreign rights connotations attached to intellectual property rights and also has the potential to stimulate intellectual property growth in the region[786].

This can be achieved by developing sharia-compliant intellectual property rights; therefore the GCC states need to do more than simply accept intellectual property rights as designed by western states and demonstrate how sharia-compliant intellectual property rights work. Therefore, the recommendation is to develop intellectual property-focused sharia law principles through the established areas of ijaza, property law, contract law and public interest. Overarching the Islamic law presence on developing an integrated intellectual property protection framework is that the supreme source of sharia law is God, as stated in the Quran; "Legislation is not but for Allah"[787].

## 9 The US and the EU on International Intellectual Property Rights Protection

Key recommendations:

- to share knowledge and expertise to improve intellectual property law development in the GCC states with the overall aim of protecting international intellectual property rights;
- for the US and the EU to reassess their bilateral and free trade agreements to allow the GCC states to develop an integrated approach to intellectual property protection without risking trade sanctions and
- a willingness from both the western states setting the international intellectual property agenda and the GCC states to want to modify the intellectual property systems.

The US and the EU have sought to protect intellectual property rights internationally for their inventors in the form of international agreements[788] and treaty memberships[789]. Over the years the US, in its trade agreements, has incorporated a number of intellectual property provisions with many countries[790]. In respect of bilateral investment treaties, the US has thirty-nine agreements in force[791]. The US has bilateral agreements in force with Bahrain and Oman. It is in trade talks with the remaining GCC states and the GCC Union[792]. The main benefit of the bilateral agreements is the enforcement of intellectual property rights as it has proven to be a more effective method of raising international intellectual property standards than pursuing intellectual property rights as a standalone agreement.

The US international intellectual property strategy has been to safeguard intellectual property rights of international US corporations through the special 301 program, which allows the USTR to monitor a watch-list of countries that are violating intellectual property rights. The main power of the USTR is to assess the violations of intellectual property rights and where necessary impose trade sanctions against countries with high levels of infringement.

The EU does not have an equivalent to the USTR although it does have very robust infrastructures and designated departments tasked with intellectual property regulations in copyright and related rights[793], protection of inventions[794], trademark law, community design and other intellectual property areas[795].

The EU is still negotiating its FTA with the GCC. The EU has a strong focus on intellectual property enforcement regimes both within the EU[796] and with improving the protection and enforcement of intellectual property rights in third countries[797]. Both the EU and the US have free trade agreements that are in negotiation with the GCC and an integral part of the agreements is to share knowledge and expertise to bring the GCC states a step closer to western-based standard setting and intellectual property law development and protection.

Therefore, the GCC states require a meeting of minds with the EU and the US whereby the knowledge and expertise of western based standard setting can be utilised for the development of an integrated approach to intellectual property rights protection which also takes into account the idiosyncrasies of the GCC states. Further it requires a willingness from both the western states setting the international intellectual property agenda and the GCC states to want to modify the intellectual property systems currently in place to foster innovation and protect investor rights from a different approach.

## 10 Impact of International Trade on the GCC

Key recommendations:

- for the GCC to take a step back and reassess its intellectual property agenda and
- to develop the requisite knowledge and expertise in ISDS and corporate sovereignty by setting clear parameters for both in respect to riba and gharar, challenges to fundamental principles of constitutional law and domestic sovereignty.

International trade agreements have brought into play investor to state dispute settlement mechanisms (ISDS) and corporate sovereignty. The GCC states need to develop the requisite knowledge and expertise in ISDS and corporate sovereignty by developing clear parameters for both in respect to riba and gharar. ISDS has serious ramifications for domestic sovereignty and rule of law as it impacts on the ability of states to make laws challenging fundamental principles of constitutional law and democracy. To date, the GCC states have not had to deal with ISDS proceeding from the EU or the US.

Nonetheless, the GCC states will struggle to justify the compensatory remedies of ISDS proceedings as compliant with sharia law as there are no frameworks or internal infrastructures in place to control the level of damages that can be sought. The first application of ISDS by a GCC state, made by the Qatari based broadcaster, Al Jazeera, was discussed in Chapter 6[798]. Qatar is relying on the ISDS included in their 1999 investment treaty between Egypt and Qatar[799]. Qatar is arguing Egypt has breached their bilateral trade agreement and the outcome of the proceedings will be relevant to the remaining GCC states and the international application of ISDS. What the case spotlights is that there are issues with judicial expertise, arbitration court structures and transparency in ISDS proceedings in the GCC and neighbouring states such as Egypt where new areas of law are being developed. The remainder of this chapter will consider the impact of TRIPS Plus and will be dedicated to the two differing intellectual property standard setting models, the western standard setting approach to intellectual property rights and the novel integrated Islamic based model.

## 11 Impact of TRIPS Plus on the GCC

Key recommendations:

- to not rush to implementing TRIPS plus standards of extending the duration of patent protection, narrowing the scope of compulsory licensing and parallel imports and more stringent enforcement mechanisms;
- the detrimental effect of patent term extensions on the sharia principle of public interest;
- to not blindly narrow the scope of compulsory licensing without taking into account public interest and
- to approach the demands for higher standards of enforcement through an integrated approach to intellectual property rights protection.

The GCC states are TRIPS-compliant and their international trade agreements are imposing TRIPS plus provisions as discussed in Chapters 5 and 6. The three main TRIPS plus provisions that will impact on the GCC are extending the duration of patent protection, narrowing the scope of compulsory licensing and parallel imports and more stringent enforcement mechanisms[800]. The GCC states can demonstrate TRIPS-compliant patent protection; however TRIPS plus calls for the time-period of patent protection to be above twenty years. As Oman already has TRIPS plus in its FTA with the US in relation to extending the patent term in pharmaceutical based patents[801], the issue arises as to the detrimental effect of such an extension on the sharia principle of public interest.

The second main TRIPS plus provision which increases the level of compliance from the TRIPS agreement, is in the changes to compulsory licensing. The scope for compulsory licensing and parallel importing is much narrower in TRIPS plus as the new provisions limit the circumstances in which parties can use the measures[802]. Therefore, there is a risk posed to the GCC from restrictions on compulsory licensing in pharmaceutical products[803]. Again, the issue arises as to how sharia-compliant the restrictions of TRIPS plus are as by limiting compulsory licensing there is a risk of conflicting with the sharia principles on public interest. Public interest aims to protect the legitimate interests of the community within the sources of Islamic law and is interpreted to find a balance between public interest and a competing area of law. Imposing further limitations on compulsory licensing in intellectual property protection requires careful consideration as creating sharia-compliant intellectual property frameworks that take into account public interest will have more longevity than passing legislation which circumvents the public interest doctrine[804].

The third area of TRIPS plus is the escalation of enforcement measures. TRIPS plus demands stronger enforcement for criminal sanctions, higher damages, mandatory injunctions, and transitional liability. The criticism of increasing enforcement measures is that it is not the solution to deterring intellectual property infringement. TRIPS allows flexibility in developing enforcement measures which the GCC states need in order to develop technical expertise, stronger institutional infrastructures, research and development. The GCC states need to develop anti-competitive practices and approach the demands for higher standards of enforcement through an integrated approach to intellectual property rights protection.

There is a real risk that the GCC states are widening the gulf between their intellectual property laws and the public acceptance of the new regimes. Rather than simply accept the provisions on TRIPS plus, the GCC states can aim to understand the progress and expansion of successful initiatives such as sharia-compliant banking and apply the methodology of Islamic finance development to intellectual property rights protection. Islamic finance is considered next.

## 12 Islamic Finance as a Catalyst for a Modified Intellectual Property Rights Approach

Key recommendations:

- to not rush ahead with TRIPS plus provisions without analysing alternative methods for improving intellectual property rights protection, similarly to how Islamic finance provides an alternative to western banking;
- develop intellectual property-focused independent sharia boards;
- improve consumer and investor protection through mirroring ethical banking principles to intellectual property;
- promote regulatory cooperation through setting up internal auditing committees, introducing governance ethics, initiating periodic reviews and assurances for intellectual property rights and
- build human capital by investing in research and development.

Islamic finance has coincidentally developed in the GCC over the same time period as intellectual property; however there are significant differences in how the two sectors have evolved over three decades. Islamic finance is an area where the GCC states have made significant progress in the evolution of the industry and lead on the initiation of a number of sharia-compliant financial products. The GCC states have not been as dominant in the intellectual property field, choosing to apply sharia law solely for the purposes of justifying intellectual property law within the ambit of Islamic jurisprudence. The integrated intellectual property rights approach recommends a modified approach to intellectual property rights protection. The recommendation is to not rush ahead with TRIPS plus provisions without considering alternative methods to improving intellectual property rights protection.

Chapter 7 identified the main principles of Islamic finance and applied lessons learnt from Islamic finance success to intellectual property rights protection. The main Islamic finance principles identified were the founding principles of Islamic finance, the governance of sharia boards, the development of Islamic finance in the individual GCC states, different frameworks of sharia-compliant investment products and the impact of intellectual property rights on the varying Islamic finance investment tools.

Islamic finance has achieved success as a financial institution with ethical guidelines that abide by Islamic law and consequently operate without contravening the doctrines of riba and gharar[805]. Islamic finance products have been established through fatwas that are passed by Islamic scholars that sit on sharia boards to rule on whether a new Islamic finance product is sharia-compliant or not. Where the Islamic finance sector and intellectual property differ is that Islamic finance can trace its roots back to primary sources of sharia law as the Quran and the Sunnah prohibit sinful (haram) activity[806] and riba[807]. It is the financial sources of sharia law that have been used to infer sharia compliance of intellectual property rights, but Islamic finance has not been utilised to develop an integrated intellectual property rights protection framework.

Islamic finance has managed to grow as an industry despite not all Islamic countries adhering to sharia at the same constitutional level. Applying this to the GCC states, each state has its own Islamic finance institutions with Islamic scholars that sit on sharia boards with the main role of acting as an independent body of specialised jurists to direct, review and supervise Islamic finance products[808]. The GCC states are paving the way with recognizing the relationship between Islamic finance and intellectual property rights. The first ever sukuk with intellectual property rights as the underlying asset was introduced in the form of a computer software programme by the German-based finance company, FWU AG Group[809], developed under an ijara structure[810]and financed through the Dubai branch of FWU AG Group.

There are four main Islamic finance structures that can be translated to an integrated intellectual property rights protection approach. These are to develop sharia board based market infrastructures, improve consumer and investor protection, promote regulatory cooperation and build human capital[811]. By developing intellectual property-based sharia board-based market infrastructures, the GCC will start to take control over the intellectual property sector and promote fit for purpose control mechanisms through setting up internal auditing committees, introducing governance ethics, initiating periodic reviews and assurances for intellectual property rights.

The premise behind adopting Islamic finance structures to promote better intellectual property rights protection is twofold; it is based on learning the role of sharia law in taking ownership of the Islamic finance sector and secondly addressing the shortcomings in Islamic finance in order to overcome these in the integrated intellectual property rights approach. There are aspects of Islamic finance products that can form the basis of an intellectual property framework such as risk-sharing partnerships known as musharaka and could be translated to intellectual property investment with returns flowing in from hybrid musharaka and intellectual property based projects, licensing, royalties, subscriptions and sale of the intellectual property assets[812].

Islamic finance is not without its faults, but rather than reject Islamic finance because of its shortcomings such as lack of transparency, the level of independence observed by sharia boards and accountability measures, the GCC have an opportunity to learn from both the strengths and weaknesses of the Islamic finance sector to pioneer an integrated approach to intellectual property rights for Muslim countries.

## 13 Further Research

The work of this monograph is foundational in nature, with the aim of laying down the fundamentals of an Islamic-based intellectual property model that incorporates the key research objectives to act as a springboard for further research in this area. Although the monograph is non-empirical, there was a clear intention from the onset to further develop the findings through empirical research. Further research is crucial to the implementation of a more effective intellectual property framework and the following areas are at the forefront:

- intellectual property law and Islamic law,
- entrenching higher standards in TRIPS plus and international agreements for minimum intellectual property standards,
- analysing the potential risks attached to investor to state dispute settlement mechanisms and corporate sovereignty,
- implications of protecting national heritage and folklore expressions to provide fit for purpose intellectual property protection,
- the role Islamic finance and sharia-compliant frameworks can play in intellectual property protection in Islamic states and
- the impact of intermediary vehicles for intellectual property rights protection in the GCC such as public interest, moral rights and Islamic finance from a sharia perspective.

# Notes

## Chapter 1

1 Hussain, A. (2012), So History Doesn't Forget: Alliances Behaviour in Foreign Policy of the Kingdom of Saudi Arabia, 1979-1990, AuthorHouse and Patrick, N. (2011), The GCC: Gulf state integration or leadership cooperation? Kuwait Programme on Development, Governance and Globalisation in the Gulf States.

2 Reasons include the facts that Yemen is no longer an autocratic monarchy and not as wealthy. For a detailed analysis see Caton, S. (2013), Yemen, Middle East in Focus, page 20.

3 See Chapter 5 (5)-(13). See also Price, D. (2009), The Development of Intellectual Property Regimes in the Arabian Gulf States Infidels at the Gates, Chapter 1, Wiley & Sons Limited.

4 See Chapter 2 (7)-(10), Chapter 4 (6), Chapter 5 (9)-(11), Chapter 6 (10)-(15). See also Ulrichsen, K. (2011), Knowledge Economies in the GCC States, The Political Economy of the Gulf, Summary Report, Center for International and Regional Studies Georgetown University School of Foreign Service in Qatar, Thirwall, A. (2000), Trade, Trade Liberalisation and Economic Growth: Theory and Evidence. Economic Research Papers, The African Development Bank, Number 63 and Berg, H. (2007), International trade and economic growth, M.E. Sharpe Incorporated.

5 Price, D. (2007), The Dynamics Of Intellectual Property Protection In The Arab Gulf States, International Review of Business Research Papers, Volume 3, pages 147-161.

6 El-Bialy, N. (2011), Can Shari'a be a Deterrent for Intellectual Property Piracy in Islamic Countries? The Journal of World Intellectual Property, Volume 14, pages 441-466.

7 Khoury, A. (2007), Trademark Policy: The case of Arab Countries, pages 299-333, Oxford University Press and Price, D. (2009), The Development of Intellectual Property Regimes in the Arabian Gulf States Infidels at the Gates, Chapter 1, page 6, Wiley & Sons Limited.

8 See Chapter 2 (3), Table 1.

9 See Chapter 1 (4).

10 Corbin, J. & Strauss, A. (2007), Basics of qualitative research: Techniques and procedures for developing grounded theory, Third Edition, Thousand Oaks, CA: Sage Publications.

11 Hart. S. (2001), Doing a Literature Search: A Comprehensive Guide for the Social Sciences, Sage Publications. Hart provides insight in to qualitative writing in social sciences and humanities and offers a practical and comprehensive guide to carrying out literature searches.

12 Corbin, J. & Strauss, A. (2007), Basics of qualitative research: Techniques and procedures for developing grounded theory, Third Edition, Thousand Oaks, CA: Sage Publications. Corbin and Strauss have written a number of books in the qualitative research field with the first edition in 1990, then followed up in 1998 and the most recent version in 2007. The text is written with social sciences in mind and has crossover application to the current research as there are three distinct strands of; sharia law, intellectual property law and Islamic finance to be qualitatively analysed to provide an integrated model for intellectual property rights protection in the GCC.

13 Braithwate, J. (2000), Global Business Regulation, Cambridge University Press.

14 Strauss, A. & Corbin, J. (1998), Basics of qualitative research: Grounded theory procedures and techniques. Thousand Oaks, CA: Sage Publications.

15 Glaser, B. & Strauss, A. (1967), The discovery of grounded theory: Strategies for qualitative research. Chicago: Aldine.
16 Sahih International, (1997), The Quran: Arabic Text with Corresponding English Meanings, Almunatada Alislami, Abul Qasim Publishing House.
17 Khan, M. (1996), The Noble Quran in the English Language, King Fahd Printing Complex, Madinah, Saudi Arabia.
18 Pickthall, M. (1997), The Meaning of the Glorious Koran, Reprinted by Plume.
19 Yusuf Ali, (2001), The Holy Quran: Translation and Commentary, Reprinted by Islamic Vision.
20 Shakir, M. (1999), The Holy Quran Translated, Published by Tahrike Tarsile Quran.
21 Ghali, M. (2001), Towards Understanding the Ever-glorious Qur'an, Cairo Publishing House for Universities.
22 The book of hadith is available online at www.sunnah.com
23 Hibberd, F. (2006), Unfolding Social Constructionism, Springer Science and Business Media, Chapter 7, page 171.
24 Gergen, K. (1995), Relational theory and discourses of power in Gergen, J. (1995), Management and Organization: Relational Alternatives To Indivdualism, Aldershot Avebury.
25 Burr, V. (2002), An Introduction to Social Constructionism, Taylor & Francis.

## Chapter 2

26 Hussain, A. (2012), So History Doesn't Forget: Alliances Behaviour in Foreign Policy of the Kingdom of Saudi Arabia, 1979-1990, AuthorHouse and Patrick, N. (2011), The GCC: Gulf state integration or leadership cooperation? Kuwait Programme on Development, Governance and Globalisation in the Gulf States.
27 Matthiesen, T. (2014), The Other Saudis, Shiisms, Descent and Sectarianism, page 118, Cambridge University Press, Gorodetsky, G. (2014), Soviet Foreign Policy, 1917-1991: A Retrospective, page 206, Routledge and Joyce, M. (2012), Bahrain from the Twentieth Century to the Arab Spring, Palgrave McMillan.
28 Shaked, H. (1986), Middle East Contemporary Survey, Volume 8, 1983-84, The Moshe Dayan Center.
29 Partington, D. (1982), The Middle East Annual, Issues and Events, volume 2, page 178, G. K. Hall & Company.
30 BP Statistical Review of World Energy 2021. Available at Oil – Statistical Review of World Energy 2021 (bp.com)
31 Hvidt, M. (2013), Economic diversification in GCC countries: Past record and future trends, Kuwait Programme on Development, Governance and Globalisation in the Gulf States.
32 The GCC Charter Preamble. Available at الأمانة العامة لمجلس التعاون لدول الخليج العربية (gcc-sg.org).
33 The GCC Charter, Article 4. Available at Charter of the Gulf Cooperation Council (GCC) (ethz.ch)
34 GCC Charter Article 6 states, "*Organization of the Cooperation Council - The Cooperation Council shall have the following main organizations: 1. The Supreme Council to which shall be attached the Commission for Settlement of Disputes. 2. The Ministerial Council. 3. The Secretariat General*" Each of these organizations establish sub-agencies as may be necessary.
35 Article 7 states " *Supreme Council - The Cooperation Council shall be formed of the six states that participated in the Foreign Ministers' meeting held in Riyadh on 4 February 1981. The Supreme Council is the highest authority of the Cooperation Council and shall be formed of heads of member states. Its presidency shall be rotatory based on the alphabetical order of the names of the member states. The Supreme Council shall hold one regular session*

*every year. Extraordinary sessions may be convened at the request of any member seconded by another member. The Supreme Council shall hold its sessions in the territories of member* states. *A Supreme Council's meeting shall be considered valid if attend by two-thirds of the member states".*

36 GCC Charter Articles 11 to 13.
37 GCC Charter Articles 14 to 16.
38 The Patent Office of the Gulf Cooperation Council (GCC Patent Office)stopped accepting new patent applications on January 6, 2021 | Global law firm | Norton Rose Fulbright
39 Further details can be found on the WIPO Directory. Available at http://www.wipo.int/directory/en/urls.jsp.
40 For Saudi Arabia see Table 1 and Chapter 2 (6), Oman at (7), Bahrain at (8), Qatar at (9), the UAE at (10) and Kuwait at (11).
41 GCC: Council Approves the Trademark Law - Saba & Co. Intellectual Property (sabaip.com)
42 Shuai, A. (2013), Coming Together, Afridi and Angell Company, page 18.
43 Others include; Australia-Gulf Cooperation Council Free Trade Agreement negotiations, New Zealand-Gulf Cooperation Council (GCC) Free Trade Agreement, Singapore and the Gulf Cooperation Council, India and GCC, Asean and GCC FTA. Other countries include; Turkey, South Korea, Iran, Seoul, China and Pakistan.
44 Delegation of the European Union to Bahrain, Kuwait, Oman, Qatar and Saudi Arabia. Available at http://www.eeas.europa.eu/delegations/gulf_countries/eu_gulf_countries/trade_relation/index_en.htm.
45 The Economic Agreement between the GCC States Adopted by the GCC Supreme Council (22nd Session; 31 December 2001).
46 All information available at World Intellectual Property Office at http://www.wipo.int/portal/en/index.html.
47 Commins, P. (2012), The Gulf States – A modern history, I.B. Tauris, page 103.
48 Hvidt, M. (2013), Economic diversification in GCC countries: Past record and future trends, Kuwait Programme on Development, Governance and Globalisation in the Gulf States at pages 5 and 6.
49 Beblawi, H. (1987), The Rentier State in the Arab World, New York Croom Helm. There are four main criterions to a rentier state: first, the rent belongs to the owners of all natural resources and the rent is prevailing, second, there is a weak domestic productive sector, third, there is a limited part of the population involved in the generation of rent and fourth, the state is the biggest recipient of the rent.
50 See Chapter 3 (1).
51 See Chapter 3, Table 1.
52 Price, D. (2007), The Dynamics of Intellectual Property Protection in the Arab Gulf States, International Review of Business Research Papers, Volume 3, pages 147 to 161, Routledge.
53 See Chapter 2 (6)-(11).
54 See Chapter 2 (6)-(11).
55 OECD Benchmark Definition of Foreign Direct Investment, (2008), Fourth Edition. Available at https://www.lb.lt/n22873/benchmark_fdi_4-en.pdf.
56 The Economic Agreement Between the GCC States, (2001), Article 2, International Economic Relations. Available at www.gcc-sg.org.
57 Carlos, A. (1998), The Relationship Between Intellectual Property Rights and Foreign Direct Investment, Duke Journal of Comparative and International Law, Volume 9, pages 163 to 187.
58 Javorcik, B. (2003), Does Foreign Direct Investment Increase the Productivity of Domestic Firms? In Search of Spillovers Through Backward Linkages, The American Economic Review, Elsevier, Volume 48, pages 39 to 62.

59 Saudi Arabia Basic Law of Government Article 1 states "*The Kingdom of Saudi Arabia is a sovereign Arab Islamic State. Its religion is Islam. Its constitution is Almighty God's Book, The Holy Qur'an, and the Sunna (Traditions) of the Prophet (PBUH)*".

60 Khan, A. (2000-2001), Islam as Intellectual Property My Lord! Increase Me in Knowledge, Cumberland Law Review Volume 31, Pages 1-46, Gattje, H. (1997), The Qur'an and its exegesis, [English trans. & ed. Alford T. Welch], Oxford Oneworld and Price, D. (2012), The Development of Intellectual Property Regimes in the Arabian Gulf States: Infidels at the Gates, Routledge.

61 Saudi Arabia Basic Law of Government Article 46 states *"the judiciary is an independent authority. There is no control over judges in the dispensation of their judgments except in the case of the Islamic Shari'ah"*.

62 Wahabbism is a conservative interpretation of Sunni Islam. Please see Commins, D. (2006), The Wahhabi Mission and Saudi Arabia, I.B.Tauris Publishers.

63 Lapidus, I. (2002), A History of Islamic Societies, Cambridge University Press, page 157.

64 Oxford Business Group, The Report: Saudi Arabia 2008, page 202.

65 The Basic Law of Governance, Saudi Arabia, Article 44 states: *"The Authorities of the State consist of: the Judicial Authority, the Executive Authority and the Regulatory Authority. These Authorities will cooperate in the performance of their functions, according to this Law or other laws. The King is the ultimate arbiter for these Authorities"*. Also Article 55 states *"The King shall rule the nation according to the Sharia. He shall also supervise the implementation of the Sharia, the general policy of the State, and the defense and protection of the country"*. Also see Ansary, A. (2008), A Brief Overview of the Saudi Arabian Legal System, Hauser Global Law School Program, New York University School of Law.

66 Fox, J. (2006), Globalization and the Gulf, Chapter 9, Saudi Arabia's role in the global economy, page 172, Routledge.

67 The World Trade Organisation. Available at http://www.wto.org/english/thewto_e/countries_e/saudi_arabia_e.htm.

68 Price, D. (2009), The Development of Intellectual Property Regimes in the Arabian Gulf States Infidels at the Gates Chapter 4, Routledge Cavendish research in intellectual property.

69 Legislation includes; Law Of Trade Names (2010), Law of Patents, Layout-Designs of Integrated Circuits, Plant Varieties, and Industrial Designs (2004), Copyright Law (2003), Law of Trademarks (2002), Commercial Register Law and its Explanatory Memorandum and Implementing Regulations (2011), Electronic Transactions Protection Law (2007), Regime of E-Transactions (2007), GCC Common Law on Anti-dumping and Countervailing Measures and Safeguards (2006), Retail Business Regime (2005), Competition Law (2004), Law Against Dissimulations (2004), Law of Commercial Data (2002), Law on Trade in Agricultural Fertilizers (2002), Law on Private Laboratories (2002), Law of Criminal Procedure (2001), Telecommunication Law (2001), Printing and Publishing Law (2000), Chartered Accountants Law (1991), Law against Commercial Fraud (1984), Arbitration Law (1983) and Saudi Arabia's Regime of commercial agencies (1962)

70 Ministry of Information, Sultanate of Oman.

71 Omani Constitution Article 2 reads, "*The State's religion is Islam and Islamic Sharia is the basis for legislation*".

72 International Religious Freedom Report for 2021, United States Department of State, Bureau of Democracy, Human Rights and Labor.

73 The Shura Council is an elected representative council whose members, including women, are chosen directly by the citizens in the governorates of Oman.

74 Omani Constitution Article 58 reads, *"The Oman Council shall consist of: 1 - The Shura Council and 2 - The State Council the Law shall specify the jurisdiction of each, its term, sessions, and rules of procedure. Also the Law shall determine the number of its members, the conditions*

*they should satisfy, the way they are selected or appointed, the reasons for their dismissal and other regulatory provisions."*

75 Hassanien, M. (2008), Bilateral WTO-plus free trade agreements in the Middle East: A case study of OFTA in the post-TRIPS era, Intellectual Property Law Journal, pages 161 to 197.

76 Al-Haj, A. (1996), The Politics of Participation in the Gulf Cooperation Council States: The Omani Consultative Council., Middle East Journal, Volume 50, Number 4, Middle East Institute.

77 Referred to as "*the Majlis Oman*".

78 Referred to as "*Majlis al-Dawla*".

79 Referred to as "*Majlis al-Shura*".

80 Bayliss Associates Pty Limited, (2008), Business Guides to the Arab Gulf - The Sultanate of Oman, Council for Australian-Arab Relations (CAAR) and Australia Arab Chamber of Commerce and Industry (AACCI).

81 Omani Royal Decree No: 74/96. Also see WIPO at http://www.wipo.int/treaties/en/ShowResults.jsp?treaty_id=1&country_id=135C. Oman acceded to WIPO in November 1996 and it came into force in February 1997.

82 United States Trade Representative Office. Available at http://www.ustr.gov/trade-agreements/free-trade-agreements/oman-fta.

83 Byrnes, A. (2013), International Law in the New Age of Globalization, Page 413, Brill Publications.

84 Price, D. (2011), The Development of Intellectual Property Regimes in the Arabian Gulf States Infidels at the Gates, Chapter 2, page 137, Routledge.

85 Omani Royal Decree No. 65/2008 promulgating the Law on Copyright and Related Rights (2008).

86 Omani Industrial Property Rights and their Enforcement for the Sultanate of Oman (Royal Decree No. 67/2008) (2008).

87 OmaniRoyal Decree No. 49/2009 promulgating the Law on the Protection of Breeders' Rights in New Varieties of Plants (2010).

88 Omani Royal Decree No. 81/2002 promulgating the Law on Consumer Protection (2002).

89 Omani Royal Decree No.29/2002 promulgating the Law on Civil and commercial procedure (2002).

90 Omani Royal Decree No. 6/80 promulgating the Law on the Protection of National Heritage (1980).

91 See Chapter 2 (3), Table 1.

92 United States Trade Representative Office.Available at http://www.ustr.gov/trade-agreements/free-trade-agreements/oman-fta.Accessed on 02.02.2015.

93 The Report: Emerging Bahrain, (2007), page 30, Oxford Business Group.

94 Price, D. (2012), The Development of Intellectual Property Regimes in the Arabian Gulf States: Infidels at the Gates, Chapter 2, page 14.

95 Cordesman, A. (2004), The Military Balance In The Middle East, page 339, Praeger Publishers.

96 Looney, R. (2009), The Omani and Bahraini Paths to Development, World Institute for Development Economic Research.

97 Power, G. (2012),The difficult development of parliamentary politics in the Gulf - Parliaments and the process of managed reform in Kuwait, Bahrain and Oman.

98 Constitution of the Kingdom of Bahrain (2002).

99 Chapter 1, Article 1 (b), Constitution of the Kingdom of Bahrain (2002).

100 Peck, M. (2008), The A to Z of the Gulf Arab States, Scarecrow Press Incorporated, page 40.

101 Katzman, K. (2013), Bahrain: Reform, Security, and U.S. Policy, Page 6, Congressional Research Service.

102 World Intellectual Property Organisation, Constitution of the Kingdom of Bahrain. Available at WIPO Lex, Bahrain, Constitution of the Kingdom of Bahrain.

103 Constitution of the Kingdom of Bahrain, Part 1, Article 2 states *"The Islamic Sharia is a principle source for legislation"*. Available at WIPO Lex, Bahrain, Constitution of the Kingdom of Bahrain.

104 Bahrain Economic Development Board, (2013), Bahrain Transparency, page 3.

105 Act No. 22 of the Year 2006 relating to the Protection of Copyright and Neighbouring Rights (2006), Act No. 12 of 2006 amending some provisions of Law No. 7 of 2003 pertaining to Trade Secrets (2006), Act No. 14 of 2006 amending some provisions of Law No. 1 of 2004 in respect of Patents and Utility Models (2006), Act No. 5 of 2006 on Designs of Integrated Circuits (2006), Act No. 6 of 2006 on Industrial Designs and Models (2006), Act No. 16 of 2006 amending Law No. 16 of 2004 on the protection of Geographical Indications (2006), Act No. 35 of 2005 pertaining amendment of Article No. 5 of Law No. 7 of 2003 on Trade Secrets (2005), Act No. 16 of the Year 2004 relating to the Protection of Geographical Indications (2004), Act No. 1 of 2004 on Patents And Utility Models (2004), Act No. 7 of 2003 on The Trade Secrets (2003), Law No. 12 for the Year 2006 Amending Law No 7 for the year 2003 Pertaining to Trade Secrets, Law No. 16 for the year 2006 Amending Law No 16 for the year 2004 On the Protection of Geographical Indications, Law No. 35 For the year 2005 Amending Law No. 7 for the year 2003 on Trade Secrets, Law No. 35 For the year 2005 Amending Law No. 7 for the year 2003 on Trade Secrets, Law No. 5 for the Year 2006 On Designs of Integrated Circuits, Law No. 5 for the Year 2006 On Designs of Integrated Circuits, Law No.7 for the Year 2003 On The Trade Secrets, Law No.7 for the Year 2003 On The Trade Secrets, Law no 14 2002 The Law of the Shura Council and the Parliament, Legislative Decree No. 10 of 1991 with respect to Trade Marks (Arabic), Legislative decree No. 1 of 2004 with respect to Patent and Utility Models, Legislative decree No. 1 of 2004 with respect to Patent and Utility Models, Legislative Decree No. 10 of June 7, 1993 with respect to Copyright Law, Legislative decree No. 11 of 2006 with respect to Trade Marks, Legislative decree No. 11 of 2006 with respect to Trade Marks, Legislative decree No. 14 of 2006 amending certain provisions of Decree No.1 of 2004, Legislative decree No. 14 of 2006 amending certain provisions of Decree No.1 of 2004, Legislative decree No. 6 of 2006 with respect to Industrial Designs and Legislative decree No. 6 of 2006 with respect to Industrial Designs.

106 See Chapter 2 (3), Table 1.

107 United States Trade Representative Office. Available at http://www.ustr.gov/trade-agreements/free-trade-agreements/bahrain-fta.

108 Bahrain approves property law amendments, (2013), Trade Arabia, Business News Information. Available at http://www.tradearabia.com/news/LAW_232499.html.

109 Patrick, N. (2011), The GCC: Gulf state integration or leadership cooperation? Number 19, Kuwait Programme on Development, Governance and Globalisation in the Gulf States.

110 Cavendish, M. (2006), World and Its Peoples, Arabian Peninsula Bahrain, Oman, Qatar, Saudi Arabia, UAE, Yemen, Marshall Cavendish.

111 See Chapter 2 (4), Table 1.

112 Price, D. (2012), The Development of Intellectual Property Regimes in the Arabian Gulf States: Infidels at the Gates, Chapter 2, page18, Routledge.

113 Constitution of Qatar, 2004, Part 1, Article 1. The Qatari constitution has been amended and what is significant for the purposes of this research, sharia has been downgraded from the principal source of law to a main source of law. See further at Chapter 3 (1).

114 The committee, named the Permanent Constitution Drafting Committee, was formed, with a membership of a chairman, a deputy chairman and 30 members.

115 World Intellectual Property Organisation, Constitution of Qatar, Part 1, Article 77. Available at http://www.wipo.int/wipolex/en/text.jsp?code=QA.

116 World Intellectual Property Organisation, Constitution of Qatar. Available at http://www.wipo.int/wipolex/en/text.jsp?code=QA.

117 Decree Law No. 16 of 2010 on the Promulgation of the Electronic Commerce and Transactions Law (2010), Law No.21 of 2009 issuing the Income Tax Law (2010), Emiri Decree No. 53 of 2009 establishing the Center for the Protection of Intellectual Property Rights (2009), Law No. 8 of 2008 on Consumer Protection (2008), Commercial Law No. 27 of 2006 (2007), Decree Law No. 30 for the year 2006 To Issue Patents Law (2006), Law No. 19 of 2006 on the Protection of Competition and Prevent Monopolistic Practices (2006), Law No. 25 of 2005 on Commercial Register (2005), Law No. 5 of the year 2005 on Protection of Secrets of Trade (2005), Law No. 6 of the year 2005 on Protection of Layout Designs of Integrated Circuits (2005), Law No. 27 of 2004 on the Protection of the Signs, Slogans, Works and Related Rights of the Fifteenth Asian Games - Doha 2006 (2004), Law No. (11) of 2004 promulgating the Penal code (2004), Law No. 11 of 2003 on the State Merit Awards and Encouragement of Science, Arts and Letters (2003), Customs Law No. 40 of 2002 (2002), Law No. 9 of 2002 on Trademarks, Trade Names, Geographical Indications and Industrial Designs (2002), Law No. 7 of 2002 on the Protection of Copyright and Related Rights (2002), Law No. 5 of 2002 Issuing the Commercial Companies Law (2002), Decree Law No.14 of 1982 concerning the Deposit of Works in the National Library (1982), Law No. 2 of 1980 on the Antiquities (1980) and Law No. 8 of 1979 on the Press and Publication (1979).

118 The seven monarchies are: Abu Dhabi, Ajman, Dubai, Fujairah, Ras Al-Khaimah, Sharjah, and Umm al-Qaiwain.

119 The World Intellectual Property Office. Available at http://www.wipo.int/wipolex/en/details.jsp?id=10673.

120 UAE Constitution, Part 1, Article 7 states "*Islam is the official religion of the Union. The Islamic Tiara's shall be a main source of legislation in the Union*".

121 The UAE constitution, Chapter 1, Article 49 states "*Supreme Council on substantive matters shall be by a majority of five of its members provided that this majority includes the votes of the Emirates of Abu Dhabi and Dubai. The minority shall be bound by the view of the said majority*".

122 Permanent Mission of the United Arab Emirates to the United Nations.

123 UAE Constitution, Chapter 1, Article 46.

124 Benson-Colpi, M. The Report: Abu Dhabi (2010), Oxford Business Group, page 221.

125 Federal Law No. 7 of the Year 2002 Concerning Copyrights and Neighbouring Rights (2002).

126 Federal Law No. 37 of 1992 on Trademarks amended by Law No. 19 of 2000 and Law No. 8 of 2002 (1992).

127 Federal Law No. 31 for the Year 2006 Pertaining to the Industrial Regulation and Protection of Patents, Industrial Drawings, and Designs (2002).

128 Federal Law No. 17 of 2009 on the Protection of New Plant Varieties (2010), Federal Law No. 6 of 2008 on establishing a national council for tourism and Antiquities (2008), Federal Decree No.85 of 2007 on The Common Customs Law for the Arab States of the Gulf (2007), Federal Law No. 24 of 2006 Concerning Consumer Protection (2006), Law No. 1 Of 1992 Of the Emirate of Sharjah On Antiquities (1992), Federal Law No. 15 of 1980 on the Press and Publication (1980), Federal Law No. 8 of 1980, on Regulation of Labour Relation (1980) and Law No. 5 of 1973 on Commercial Register (1973).

129 Latham and Watkins LLP, 2013, Doing Business in the United Arab Emirates, Middle East and Africa Technology, IP and Sourcing Focus.

130 See Chapter 2 (3), Table 1.

131 Expo 2020 Dubai, United Arab Emirates. Available at http://expo2020dubai.ae/en/world_expos.

132 Please see further at Chapter 7 (14)-(20).

133 Al Sabah family have ruled State of Kuwait since 1756. Full details of the rulers can be found at http://www.e.gov.kw/sites/kgoenglish/Portal/Pages/Visitors/AboutKuwait/GoverningBody_KuwaitGoverners.aspxx

134 Kuwaiti Constitution, Part 1, Article 2 states "*The religion of the State is Islam, and the Islamic Shari'a shall be a main source of legislation*".

135 Kuwait gained independence from Britain in 1961 and approved its first constitution in 1962.

136 Price, D. (2012), The Development of Intellectual Property Regimes in the Arabian Gulf States Infidels at the Gates, Chapter 2, page 30.

137 Power, G. (2012), The difficult development of parliamentary politics in the Gulf - Parliaments and the process of managed reform in Kuwait, Bahrain and Oman. The Kuwait Programme on Development, Governance and Globalisation in the Gulf States.

138 The World Intellectual Property Office. Available at http://www.wipo.int/wipolex/en/details.jsp?id=6148.

139 Kuwaiti Constitution, Part IV, Powers, Chapter I, Article 50, Separation and Constitutionality of Powers.

140 Kuwaiti Constitution, Part II, Article 18, Private Property, Inheritance states "*private property is inviolable. No one shall be prevented from disposing of his property except within the limits of the law. No property shall be expropriated except for the public benefit under the circumstances and in the manner specified by law, and on condition that just compensation is paid*".

141 Decree-Law No. 68 of 1980 on Trademarks, as amended by Decree-Law No. 10 of 1987 and Law No. 1 of 2001 (2001), Law No. 4 of 1962 relating to Patents, Designs and Industrial Models as amended by Law No. 3 of 2001 (2001), Law No. 64 of 1999 concerning Intellectual Property Rights including Explanatory Memorandum (1999) and Law No. 56 of 1996 promulgating the Industrial Law (1996).

142 International Monetary Fund, 2012, Economic Prospects and Policy Challenges for the GCC Countries.

143 Al-Hajeri, M. (2006), The Gulf Cooperation Council (GCC) patent office. World Patent Information, Volume 28, pages 14 to 19 at page 14.

## Chapter 3

144 See Chapter 2 (4)-(9).

145 Saudi Arabia gives the Quran the highest importance in its law making as at Saudi Arabia Basic Law of Government Article 1 which states: "*the Kingdom of Saudi Arabia is a sovereign Arab Islamic State. Its religion is Islam. Its constitution is Almighty God's Book, the Holy Qur'an, and the Sunna (Traditions) of the Prophet (PBUH)*". Available at http://www.saudiembassy.net/about/country-information/laws/The_Basic_Law_Of_Governance.aspx.

146 Oman has sharia as the basis for legislation at Omani Constitution Article 2.

147 Qatar has sharia as a main source of law at Constitution of Qatar, 2004, Part 1, Article 1. Also, UAE has sharia as a main source of law at UAE Constitution, Part 1, Article 7 and Kuwait at Kuwaiti Constitution, Part 1, Article 2.

148 Bahrain has sharia as a principal source of law at Constitution of the Kingdom of Bahrain, Part 1, Article 2.

149 All six GCC states have achieved minimum TRIPS compliance and have membership to WIPO since national intellectual property legislation has been put in place.

150 Matulionyte, R. (2013), Iran: in search of a balanced approach to copyright, Intellectual Property Quarterly, page 2.

151 Hassanein, M. (2008), Bilateral WTO-Plus Free Trade Agreements In the Middle East: A Case Study of OFTA In The Post-Trips Era. Wake Forest Intellectual Property Law Journal Volume 8, pages 161 to 197 and Raslan, H. (2007), *Sharī'a* and the Protection of Intellectual Property: The Example of Egypt, The Intellectual Property Law Review, pages 497 to 559.

152 Malmvig, H. (2006), An unlikely match or a marriage in the making? EU-GG relations in a changing security environment, Danish Institute for International Studies, pages 1 to 15.
153 The relevance of considering cultural norms in assessing intellectual property social and economic development on intellectual property protection is considered by Margaret Chon, see Chon, M. (2006), Intellectual Property and the Development Divide, Seattle University School of Law, Cardozo Law Review, Volume 27, pages 2821 to 2912.
154AbdulHamid, A. (1987), The Islamic Theory of International Relations: New Directions for Islamic Methodology and Thought, The International Institute for Islamic Thought, Islamization of Knowledge (Series 1). See page 58.
155 Price, D. (2009), The Development of Intellectual Property Regimes in the Arabian Gulf States: Infidels at the Gates, Routledge Research in Intellectual Property, Routledge.
156 Zimowski, S. (2013), Consequences of the Arab Spring: How Shari'ah Law and the Egyptian Revolution Will Impact IP Protection and Enforcement, Penn State Journal of Law and International Affairs, Volume 2, Issue 1.
157 Alghamdy, N. (2005), Protection of Intellectual Property in Islamic Jurisprudence and Its Economic Consequences (in Arabic), presented at the third international conference for Islamic economics, Umm al-Qura University, Mecca.
158 See Chapter 5 (14) and Chapter 6 (11)-(15).
159 See Chapter 6 (3), (5) and (10). Also see Chapter 7 (20).
160 Al-Fadhli, S. (2009), The Ethical Dilemma of Software Piracy in Islamic Societies: The Case of Kuwait, The Electronic Journal of Information Systems in Developing Countries, Volume 39.
161 Haleem, M. (2010), The Qur'an: English translation with parallel Arabic text, Oxford University Press. See Introduction, The Life of Muhammed and Historical background Page 4. Also see Ali, A. and Razwy, S. (2009), The Qur'an: A Translation, Mass Market Paperback for general principles on Quran structure and formation. The Quran can be accessed on www.quran.com.
162 The Quran, across its chapters, has established jurisprudence on; financial matters, marriage and family life, property, contract law, morality and moral values, welfare, economics, trade, environmental matters, gender, and inheritance.
163 Rahman describes the Quran as *"it works by its own laws and is autonomous; but not autocratic, for, in itself, it has no warrant for its own existence and it cannot explain itself."* See Rahman, F. (2009), Major Themes of the Qur'an, University Of Chicago Press, page 3.
164 Coulson, N. (1978), A History of Islamic Law, The Scholar Press Limited, page 5.
165 The Quran was recited by the Prophet off by heart; the Prophet's followers would also recite the Quran by heart until it was written down after which it is believed to have been rewritten without alteration.
166 Khan, A. (2001), Islam As Intellectual Property My Lord! Increase Me In Knowledge, Cumberland Law Review, Ray Rushton Distinguished Lecturer Series.
167 See the Quran at 12:40. The full translation of the verse is; *"You worship not besides Him except [mere] names you have named them, you and your fathers, for which Allah has sent down no authority. Legislation is not but for Allah. He has commanded that you worship not except Him. That is the correct religion, but most of the people do not know"*. Available at http://quran.com/12.
168 El-Bialy, N. (2011), Can Shari'a be a Deterrent for Intellectual Property Piracy in Islamic Countries? The Journal of World Intellectual Property Volume 14, pages 441-466. At page 12, the use of ijma is for when there is no direct Quran and Sunnah reference for a topic of law, *"then if a certain point in history can be found when all Muslim legal scholars agreed upon a particular interpretation of a certain Islamic text, then in this case, their consensus may be relied upon as a valid source of Islamic legal traditions"*.
169 Adigun, T. (2005), The Relevance of Qiyas as a source of Islamic Law in Contemporary Times, page 8.

170 Ramadan, H. (2006), Toward honest and principled Islamic Law scholarship, Michigan State Law Review, pages 1573 to 1606.

171 See the Quran at 3:130. Other references to support ijma from the Quran can be found at 4:59, 4:115, 18:29 and 42:14. All available at www.quran.com.

172 Brown, D. (2009), A New Introduction to Islam, Wiley-Blackwell, page 157.

173 Hukm, Far and Illah are discussed at Page 20 by Kamali, H. (1989), Principles of Islamic Jurisprudence, Khalifa Books. Asl is explained further at page 19. Qiyas operate by identifying an original case known as Asr and relating it to a new case, Far, through an effective cause known as Illah. The effective cause therefore triggers the new law that leads to a ruling, the Hukm.

174 See the Quran at www.quran.com. Dr Ghalil interpretation at 5:90. Accessed on 27.03.2015.

175 Jamar, S. (1992), The protection of intellectual property under Islamic law, Capital University Law Review, page 2. Vikor, K. (2006), Between God and the Sultan, A History of Islamic Law, Oxford University Press.

176 See Chapter 5 (11)-(14) and Chapter 7 (13)-(21).

177 The four main schools are followed by Sunni Muslim as the law making power in the GCC States rests with Sunni Muslims and not Shia Muslims. Islamic jurisprudence from Shia scholars has not been considered in this research and is beyond the scope of the research.

178 Zimowski, S. (2013), Consequences of the Arab Spring: How Shari'ah Law and the Egyptian Revolution Will Impact IP Protection and Enforcement, Penn State Journal of Law and International Affairs, Volume 2, Issue 1.

179 Abdal-Haqq, I. (2002), Islamic Law: An Overview of Its Origin and Elements, Journal of Islamic Law and Culture at pages 1 to 61.

180 Carroll, J. (2001), Intellectual Property Rights in the Middle East: A Cultural Perspective, Fordham Intellectual Property, Media and Entertainment Law Journal Volume 11, Issue 3.

181 Khan, A. (2000), Islam as Intellectual Property My Lord! Increase Me in Knowledge, Cumberland Law Review, Volume 31, at page 361.

182 Raslan, H. (2007), *Sharī'a* and the Protection of Intellectual Property: The Example of Egypt, The Intellectual Property Law Review, page 498.

183 Cullen, C. (2010), Can TRIPS Live In Harmony With Islamic Law: An Investigation Of The Relationship Between Intellectual Property And Islamic Law? Page 13.

184 Nabil, S. (1989), The Law Governing Contracts in Arabia, International and Comparative Law Quarterly Review, pages 761 to 781; Gamal, M. (1978), Islamic Law: Its Reaction to Other Legal Systems, 26 American Journal of Comparative Law, pages 187 to 189 and Jamar, S. (1992), The protection of intellectual property under Islamic law, Capital University Law Review, pages 1 to 26 at page 2 and Vikor, K. (2005), Between God and the Sultan, C Hurst and Co Publishers.

185 Zimowski, S. (2013), Consequences of the Arab Spring: How Shari'ah Law and the Egyptian Revolution Will Impact IP Protection and Enforcement, Penn State Journal of Law and International Affairs, Volume 2, Issue 1.

186 See Jamar, S. (1992), The protection of intellectual property under Islamic law, Capital University Law Review, pages 1 to 26, Raslan, H. (2007), *Sharī'a* and the Protection of Intellectual Property: The Example of Egypt, The Intellectual property Law Review, page 497, Beltrametti, S. (2010), The Legality of Intellectual Property Rights under Islamic Law, The Prague Yearbook of Comparative Law, pages 55 to 94 and Carroll, J. (2001), Intellectual Property Rights in the Middle East: A Cultural Perspective, Fordham Intellectual Property, Media and Entertainment Law Journal Volume 11, Issue 3.

187 Cullen, C. (2010), Can TRIPS Live in Harmony with Islamic Law: An Investigation of the Relationship between Intellectual Property and Islamic Law? Page 13.

188 See Shaykhul-Hadeeth Maulana Zakariyya Kandhalwi (RA) published by Muhammad Shahid Saharunpuri entitled, "Kutub-e-Fadhail Par Ashkalat Aur Unkay Jawabaat" and Shaykhul (Mufti) Rasheed Ahmed Gangohi(RA) from Fatawa e Rashidiya.

189 See the Quran at 4:23 Available at www.quran.com.

190 Jamar, S. (1992), The Protection of Intellectual Property under Islamic Law, Capital University Law Review, Adigun, T. (2005), The Relevance of Qiyas as a source of Islamic Law in Contemporary Times, Page 8, *"Qiyas therefore is a mode of reasoning to legislate for novel questions, to reveal the divine rule of law and to harmonize between divine legislation and human interests"*, the point made here at page 72 is relevant; *"classes of prohibited women are mentioned. Although father's aunt were not included in the verse, but father and mother's aunt are prohibited by jurist based on analogy of father's sisters and mother's sister, because of close blood relationship"*, Kamali, M. (1998), Principles of Islamic Jurisprudence, 2nd Edition Kuala Lumpur, Ilmiah Publishers, page 267, Zaidan, A. (1994). Al-Wajiz fi Usul Fiqh, Beirut: Muassasah Risalah. Pages 236 to 244, Arafa, A. (2012), Corruption and bribery in Islamic law: are Islamic ideals being met in practice? Available at http://papers.ssrn.com/sol3/papers.cfm?abstract_id=2149982. Cullen, C. (2010), Can TRIPS Live in Harmony with Islamic Law: An Investigation of the Relationship between Intellectual Property and Islamic Law? El-Bialy, N. (2011), Can Shari'a be a Deterrent for Intellectual Property Piracy in Islamic Countries? The Journal of World Intellectual Property Volume 14, pages 441 to 466 and Beltrametti, S. (2010), The Legality of Intellectual Property Rights under Islamic Law, The Prague Yearbook of Comparative Law, pages 55 to 94.

191 Hallaq W. (2009), An Introduction to Islamic Law, Cambridge University Press pages 22 to 25, Jamar, S. (1992), The Protection of Intellectual Property under Islamic Law, Capital University Law Review and Beltrametti, S. (2010), The Legality of Intellectual Property Rights under Islamic Law, The Prague Yearbook of Comparative Law, pages 55 to 94.

192 Jamar, S. (1992), The Protection of Intellectual Property under Islamic Law. Capital University Law Review and Beltrametti, S. (2010), The Legality of Intellectual Property Rights under Islamic Law. The Prague Yearbook of Comparative Law, pages 55 to 94.

193 Hettinger, E. (1989), Justifying Intellectual Property, Philosophy and Public Affairs, Volume 18, Number 1, Blackwell Publishing, pages 31 to 52.

194 Philosophers have written on property rights from Plato and Aristotle to Locke, Kant and Marx.

195 Merges, R. (2011), Justifying Intellectual Property, Chapter Ten, Harvard University Press Cambridge, Massachusetts London, England.

196 Locke, J. (1690), Second Treatise on Civil Government, Chapter 5, Section 28.

197 For further analysis of John Locke's philosophy on copyright protection, see Chapter 6 (3).

198 See The Book of Paradise, its Description, its Bounties and its Inhabitants, Chapter 53, section 16 which states *"The property which I have conferred upon them is lawful for them"*.

199 Narrated by Muaz bn Jabal Al-Wahbah Al-Zuahaily, Figh Al-Islam Wa Adillahtuh, Volume V, (Damascus, Darul Fikr), (Arabic Text), (1989), page 561. See Quran at 4:29 for the reference.

200 Gulaid, M. (1991), Land Ownership in Islam (A Survey), Research Paper Number 14, Islamic Research & Training Institute, Islamic Development Bank, Jeddah, page 45.

201 Claypool, J. (2007), Islamic Law and Modern Patent Law, Center for Advanced Study & Research on Intellectual Property.

202 Price, D. (2009), The Development of Intellectual Property Regimes in the Arabian Gulf States: Infidels at the Gates, Chapter 2, page 29, Routledge Research in Intellectual Property.

203 See the Quran for example at; 2:188, 2:220, 2:275, 2:278-279, 4:2, 4:5-6, 4:95, 4:161, 6:152, 9:41, 9:88, 49:15 and 61:11. Available at www.quran.com.

204 Vaughan, R. (1996), Defining Terms in the Intellectual Property Protection Debate: Are the North and South Arguing Past Each Other When We Say "Property"? A Lockean, Confucian, and Islamic Comparison, International and Comparative Law, pages 354–59 and Pilvar, R. (2012), Theory of labor as justification of ownership in Islam and philosophy of John Locke, The Journal of Studies in Islamic Law & Jurisprudence, Volume 3, pages 63-85 and Cullen, C. (2010), Can TRIPS Live in Harmony with Islamic Law: An Investigation of the Relationship between Intellectual Property and Islamic Law?

205 See the Quran 3:77. Available at www.quran.com.

206 See the Quran at 53:39 Sahih International Translation. Available at www.quran.com.

207 See the Quran at 2:195, 2:254, 2:267 and 9:103. Available at www.quran.com.

208 The Hedaya, Or Guide: a Commentary on the Mussulman Laws: Translated by Charles Hamilton, Volume 1-4, London, T. Bensley 1791 Book VIII, page 92.

209 See Oxford v. Moss (1979) 68 Cr App Rep 183 which highlighted the exact same principal, albeit minus the threat of amputation, where the case is an example that intellectual property is intangible as the thief never intended to steal the paper and therefore there was no theft of a tangible property.

210 There is an equity parallel here and a state, king and/or god rationale. See Hallaq, W. (2009), An Introduction to Islamic Law, Cambridge University Press.

211 See the Quran at 57:7. Available at www.quran.com. Kamali, M. (2002), Principles of Islamic Jurisprudence, Ilmiah Publishers, page 44.

212 Scholarly writers include; Ebrahim, M. (1995), Behavioral norms in the Islamic doctrine of economics: A comment, Journal of Elsevier, Journal of Economic Behavior and Organization, Volume 27, pages 151 to 157, Kuran, T. (1986), The economic system in Contemporary Islamic thought: interpretation and assessment, International Journal of Middle East Volume 18, pages 135-164, Khan, S. (2004), Intellectual property law and globalization, Elsaman, R. and Eldakak, A. (2012), Is the Middle East moving toward Islamism after the Arab spring? The case study of the Egyptian Commercial and Financial Laws, Richmond Journal of Global Law and Business and Hassanein, M. (2008), Bilateral WTO-Plus Free Trade Agreements In the Middle East: A Case Study of OFTA In The Post-Trips Era. Wake Forest Intellectual Property Law Journal Volume 8, pages 161 to 197.

213 Azhar, R. (2010) Economics of An Islamic Economy, Chapter 7, page 232, Brill. Khan, M. (1994), An Introduction to Islamic Economics, Chapter 6, International Institute of Islamic Thought and Institute of Policy Studies. Khoury, A. (2009), Dubai's New Intellectual Property-Based Economy: Prospects for Development Without Dependency, Marshall Review Intellectual Property Law.

214 Adam, M. (2005), Remarks about the TRIPS Agreement with Particular Reference to Compulsory Licensing.

215 See Quran at 59:7. Available at www.quran.com. See Usmani, M. (2009), Present Financial Crisis Causes And Remedies From Islamic Perspective. Available at http://www.muftitaqiusmani.com/index.php?option=com_content&view=article&id=41:present-financial-crisis-causes-and-remedies-from-islamic-perspective-&catid=12:economics&Itemid=15. Also see Chaudhry, M. (2003), Islam And Other Economic Systems, Chapter 20. The interplay between intellectual property rights and the Quranic references against excessive wealth is considered in the following articles; Beltrametti, S. (2010), The Legality of Intellectual Property Rights under Islamic Law. The Prague Yearbook of Comparative Law and Jamar, S. (1992), The Protection of Intellectual Property under Islamic Law, Capital University Law Review.

216 See for example the UAE Federal Law No (3) of 1987 on Issuance of The Penal Code in regard to punishments for theft which can be anywhere from a nominal term to 15 years as opposed to intellectual property infringement which carries a maximum 5 year term. The

UAE Federal Law No (3) of 1987 on Issuance of The Penal Code. Articles 378 and 379 of the UAE Federal Law No (3) of 1987 on Issuance of The Penal Code relates to data privacy with a maximum 5 year prison term.

217 Malkawi, B. (2013), The Alliance Between Islamic Law And Intellectual Property: Structure And Practice, University of St. Thomas Law Journal, Volume 10, Issue 3.

218 See the Quran at 5:1, Sahih International Translation. Available at www.quran.com.

219 See the Quran at 2:282, Sahih International Translation reads, *"O you who have believed, when you contract a debt for a specified term, write it down. And let a scribe write [it] between you in justice. Let no scribe refuse to write as Allah has taught him. So let him write and let the one who has the obligation dictate. And let him fear Allah, his Lord, and not leave anything out of it. But if the one who has the obligation is of limited understanding or weak or unable to dictate himself, then let his guardian dictate in justice. And bring to witness two witnesses from among your men. And if there are not two men [available], then a man and two women from those whom you accept as witnesses - so that if one of the women errs, then the other can remind her. And let not the witnesses refuse when they are called upon. And do not be [too] weary to write it, whether it is small or large, for its [specified] term. That is more just in the sight of Allah and stronger as evidence and more likely to prevent doubt between you, except when it is an immediate transaction which you conduct among yourselves. For [then] there is no blame upon you if you do not write it. And take witnesses when you conclude a contract. Let no scribe be harmed or any witness. For if you do so, indeed, it is [grave] disobedience in you".* Available at www.quran.com. Also see Quran at 2:177, 4;12, 4:33, 5:89, 9:1, 9:111, 17:34 and 23:8.

220 See the Quran at 2:219, 5:3, 5:90, 5:91 and 5:92. Available at www.quran.com. The link between intellectual property and gambling comes from the potential for royalties to be deemed so uncertain as to be like gambling and therefore further research in the relationship between intellectual property and gambling within an Islamic context will shed light on how a potential reward for risk can exist. See Jamar, S. (1992), The protection of intellectual property under Islamic law, Capital University Law Review.

221 See the Quran at 2:219, 5:3, 5:90, 5:91, 5:92 and 16:67. Available at www.quran.com.

222 See the Quran at 2:259,, 5:3, 6:121, 6:145, 16:14, 22:37. Available at www.quran.com.

223 Fisho-Oridedi, A. (2009), The prohibition of riba under Islamic law: what are the implications for international contracts? See Quran 4:161 *"And [for] their taking of usury while they had been forbidden from it, and their consuming of the people's wealth unjustly. And we have prepared for the disbelievers among them a painful punishment".*

224 Al Satti, A. (2003), The Permissible Gharar (Risk) in Classical Islamic Jurisprudence, Islamic Economy, Volume 16, No 2, Pages 3 to 19. See page 3.

225 Wilson, R. (2009), The development of Islamic finance in the GCC Working Paper, Kuwait Programme on Development, Governance and Globalisation in the Gulf States at page 27.

226 See the Quran at 4:29. Available at www.quran.com.

227 Sahih Bukhari Chapter Number 34, Hadith number 327.

228 Fisho-Oridedi, A. (2009), The prohibition of riba under islamic law: what are the implications for international contracts?

229 See Chapter 7.

230 See the Quran at 2:275, 3:130, 4:29, 4:161, 5:1, 5:62, 5:90, 9:4-12, 13:20 and 30:39. Available at www.quran.com.

231 See the Quran at 2:275. Available at www.quran.com.

232 Carlos, A. Braga, P. and Fink, C. (1998), The Relationship between Intellectual Property Rights and Foreign Direct Investment, Duke Journal of Comparative and International Law, Volume 9, pages 163-188 and Javorcik, B. (2004), Does Foreign Direct Investment Increase the Productivity of Domestic Firms? In Search of Spillovers Through Backward Linkages, The American Economic Review, Volume 94, Number 3. Available at http://spot.colorado.edu/~utar/javorcik.pdf.

233 Drahos, P. (2003), When the Weak Bargain win the Strong, Kluwer Law, pages 79 to 109.
234 Penubarti, M. and Maskus, K. (1995), How trade-related are intellectual property rights? Journal of International Economics, Volume 39, Issues 3-4, pages 227 to 248.
235 See the Quran at 9:1, 9:4, 9:7, 9:8, 9:10, 9:12 and 13:20. Available at www.quran.com. Also see Beltrametti, S. (2010), The Legality of Intellectual Property Rights under Islamic Law. The Prague Yearbook of Comparative Law, pages 55 to 94.
236 In relation to intellectual property, see for example, the Berne Convention and Paris Convention.
237 Khoury A. (2003), Ancient and Islamic Source of Intellectual Property protection in the Middle East: A focus on Trademarks, Volume 43, Number 2, IDEA: The Journal of Law and Technology, Franklin Pierce Law Center, pages 151 to 206.
238 Kamali, M. (1998), Principles of Islamic Jurisprudence, 2nd Edition, Kuala Lumpur, Ilmiah Publishers, page 267. See also Zaidan, A. (1994), Al-Wajiz fi Usul Fiqh, Beirut, Muassasah Risalah, pages 236 to 244.
239 Kamali, M. (1989), Principles of Islamic Jurisprudence, 1-2 Pelanduk Publications and Raslan, H. (2007), *Sharī'a* and the Protection of Intellectual Property: The Example of Egypt, The Intellectual property Law Review, page 497.
240 Hasan, Z. (2007), Islamic perspective on the competition law and policy in issues in law and syariah, Islamic Science University of Malaysia, pages 61 to 76.
241 Jamar, S. (1992), The Protection of Intellectual Property under Islamic Law, Capital University Law Review and Beltrametti, S. (2010), The Legality of Intellectual Property Rights under Islamic Law, The Prague Yearbook of Comparative Law 2009, pages 55-94. Also public interest plays a significant role in patents associated with medicines, see the Doha Declaration on the TRIPS Agreement and Public Health.
242 See Chapter 6 (11)-(15).
243 Khalid, M. (2001), Muslim Jurist's Quests for the Normative Basis of Shariah, ISIM Newsletter, Leiden, page 13.
244 See Chapter 7.
245 Olwan, R. (2013), Intellectual Property and Development: Theory and Practice, Springer Publishing.
246 See the Quran at 11:15 stating; "*we fully repay them for their deeds therein, and they therein will not be deprived*".
247 Delong-Bas, N. (2010), The Five Pillars of Islam: Oxford Bibliographies Online Research Guide, Oxford University Press.
248 Zakat is mentioned at several points in the Quran; 2:3, 2:43, 2:83, 2:177, 2:267, 2:277, 3:17, 3:180, 4:77, 4:162, 5:12, 5:55, 6:141, 7:156, 9:5, 9:11 and 9:18. Available at www.quran.com.
249 See Chapter 2 (11).
250 See the Quran at 46:4 stating, "*Show me what they have created of the earth; or did they have partnership in [creation of] the heavens? Bring me a scripture [revealed] before this or a [remaining] trace of knowledge, if you should be truthful*".
251 See the Quran at 16:90 states; "*Indeed, Allah orders justice and good conduct and giving to relatives and forbids immorality and bad conduct and oppression. He admonishes you that perhaps you will be reminded.*" Available at www.quran.com.
252 The Book of Virtue, Good Manners and Joining of the Ties of Relationship (Kitab Al-Birr was-Salat-I-wa'l-Adab) Translation of Sahih Muslim, Book 32 at Chapter 27.
253 Jamar, S. (1992), The Protection of Intellectual Property under Islamic Law. Capital University Law Review, Khoury A. (2003), Ancient and Islamic Source of Intellectual Property protection in the Middle East: A focus on Trademarks, The Journal of Law and Technology at 153 and 154, Raslan H.(2009), Shari'a And The Protection Of Intellectual Property—The Example Of Egypt, The Intellectual Property Law Review 47(4), pages 497-559, Mahafzah Q.(2009), The Perspective of Moral and Financial Rights of Intellectual Property in Islam, Arab Law Quarterly, Volume 23, Issue 4, pages 457 to 468, Loutfi, M.

(2003), The Protection of Intellectual Property Rights: The views of the Pharos, Islamic Jurisprudence and Masters of Poetry and Literature, pages 232 to 233, Cullen, C. (2010), Can TRIPS Live in Harmony with Islamic Law: An Investigation of the Relationship between Intellectual Property and Islamic Law? and Beltrametti , S. (2010), The Legality of Intellectual Property Rights under Islamic Law. The Prague Yearbook of Comparative Law, pages 55 to 94.

254 Hassanein, M.(2008),Bilateral WTO-Plus Free Trade Agreements In The Middle East: A Case Study Of OFTA In The Post-Trips Era, Wake Forest Intellectual Property Law Journal, Volume 8, pages 161 to 197, Said, E. (2007), The European Trips Plus Model and the Arab World, Liverpool Law Review, Said, E. (2005), The Road from TRIPS-Minus, to TRIPS, to TRIPS-Plus Implications of IPRs for the Arab World, Tamimi, E. (1999), Current U.A.E. Copyright Law and how it Compares and Contrasts with WTO's Trips-Agreement and the Berne Convention, The Journal of World Intellectual Property, Volume 2, pages 371 to 391, Price, D. (2011), Politics, Piracy and Punishment: Copyright Protection in the Arabian Gulf, Journal of World IP Volume 14, Numbers 3-4, pages 276 to 300 and Deere, C. (2009), The implementation game: the TRIPS agreement and the global politics of intellectual property reform in developing countries.

255 Al 'Afghani, M. (2005), Islam in IP, Commons Law, Beaver Group.

256 See Chapter 2.

257 Khoury, A. (2003), Ancient and Islamic Source of Intellectual Property protection in the Middle East: A focus on Trademarks, The Journal of Law and Technology, Raslan, H. (2009), Shari'a And The Protection Of Intellectual Property—The Example Of Egypt, The Intellectual Property Law Review, Volume 47, pages 497 to 559, Mahafzah Q. (2009), The Perspective of Moral and Financial Rights of Intellectual Property in Islam, Arab Law Quarterly, Volume 23, Issue 4, pages 457 to 468, Loutfi, M. (2003), The Protection of Intellectual Property Rights: The views of the Pharos, Islamic Jurisprudence and Masters of Poetry and Literature, pages 232–233, Beltrametti, S. (2010), The Legality of Intellectual Property Rights under Islamic Law. The Prague Yearbook of Comparative Law and Jamar, S. (1992), The Protection of Intellectual Property under Islamic Law, Capital University Law Review.

258 Price, D. (2012) The Development of Intellectual Property Regimes in the Arabian Gulf States, Infidels at the Gates, Routledge Research in Intellectual Property, Chapter 2, Beltrametti, S. (2010), The Legality of Intellectual Property Rights under Islamic Law, The Prague Yearbook of Comparative Law, see pages 55 to 94, Cullen, C. (2010), Can TRIPS Live in Harmony with Islamic Law: An Investigation of the Relationship between Intellectual Property and Islamic Law?, Raslan H. (2009), Shari'a And The Protection Of Intellectual Property—The Example Of Egypt, The Intellectual Property Law Review, Volume 47, pages 497 to 559, Mahafzah, Q. (2009), The Perspective of Moral and Financial Rights of Intellectual Property in Islam, Arab Law Quarterly, Volume 23. Issue 4, pages 457 to 468 and Loutfi, M. (2003), The Protection of Intellectual Property Rights: The views of the Pharos, Islamic Jurisprudence and Masters of Poetry and Literature, pages 232 to 233.

259 Price, D. (2009), The Development of Intellectual Property Regimes in the Arabian Gulf States: Infidels at the Gates, Routledge Research in Intellectual Property.

260 Beltrametti, S. (2010), The Legality of Intellectual Property Rights under Islamic Law. In: The Prague Yearbook of Comparative Law states; "*At the end of the day the effectiveness of a law is ultimately dependent on it being recognized by society. A state may implement laws that can be wholly or partially Sharī'a compliant, but the ultimate judge on the acceptance and effectiveness of such laws is the public at large.*"

261 See Chapter 6 (11)-(16) and Chapter 7 (14)-(21).

262 The religious loyalty index is based on the adherence of followers to their religion and the research of El Bialy and Gouda found that Muslims have the highest level of religiosity

as seen in El Bialy, N. and Gouda, M. (2011), Can Shari'a be a Deterrent for Intellectual Property Piracy in Islamic Countries?, The Journal of World Intellectual Property, Volume 14, pages 441 to 466.

263 El-Bialy, N. and Gouda, M. (2011), Enforcing IPR Through Informal Institutions: The Possible Role of Religion in Fighting Software Piracy, Joint Discussion Paper Series in Economics, by the Universities of Aachen, Gießen, Göttingen, Kassel, Marburg and Siegen.

264 Abu-Ghazaleh, T. (2001), Challenges to Arab Industries in Acquiring and Selling Appropriate Technologies, Beltrametti, S. (2009), The Legality of Intellectual Property Rights under Islamic Law. In: The Prague Yearbook of Comparative Law and Jamar, S. (1992), The Protection of Intellectual Property under Islamic Law, Capital University Law Review, Carroll, J. (2001), Intellectual Property Rights in the Middle East: A Cultural Perspective, Fordham Intellectual Property, Media and Entertainment Law Journal Volume 11, Issue 3 and Cullen, C. (2010), Can TRIPS Live in Harmony with Islamic Law: An Investigation of the Relationship between Intellectual Property and Islamic Law?

265 El-Bialy, N and Gouda, M. (2011), Enforcing IPR Through Informal Institutions: The Possible Role of Religion in Fighting Software Piracy, Joint Discussion Paper Series in Economics by the Universities of Aachen, Gieben, Gottingen, Kasel, Marburg and Siegen, page 26.

266 See Chapter 4 (6) and (10), Chapter 5 (6)-(14), Chapter 6 (3) and (10)-(16).

267 See Chapter 3 (6)-(7).

268 See Chapter 3 (8) "Defining Intellectual Property Infringement".

269 See Chapter 3 (9)-(10).

270 See Khan, A.(2001), Islam as Intellectual Property My Lord! Increase Me In Knowledge, Cumberland Law Review, Volume 31, Part 3, pages 631-684.

271 See Chapter 7.

## Chapter 4

272 Frontier Economics, Estimating the Global Economic and Social Impacts of Counterfeiting and Piracy, February 2011.

273 Business Action To Stop Counterfeiting And Piracy (BASCAP) (2011), Estimating The Global Economic And Social Impacts of Counterfeiting And Piracy, Frontier Economics.

274 For the purpose of this research, the GCC' s free trade agreements, both concluded and pending, with other countries is outside the scope of this research but will be a topic for further research.

275 For full details on the working of the EU see http://europa.eu/about-eu/index_en.htm.

276 U.S.-GCC Framework Agreement for Trade, Economic, Investment and Technical Cooperation, (2012). Available at https://ustr.gov/sites/default/files/uploads/agreements/Trade%20Investment/U.S.-GCC%20TIFA%20Final%20Text%20--%20English%209-25-12.pdf.

277 Ayadi, R. (2013), EU-GCC Trade and Investment Relations: What Prospect of an FTA between the Two Regions?, Sharaka Enhancing Understanding and Cooperation in EU-GCC Relations, Number 4. Kostadinova, V. (2013), What is the Status of the EU-GCC Relationship?, Gulf Research Center Papers.

278 The first patent was signed by President George Washington on July 31, 1790 and has been archived at the Chicago Historical Society.

279 US Constitution, 1787, Article 1, Section 8, Part 8.

280 Copyright Act of 1790.

281 Friedman, D. (1994), Standards As Intellectual Property: An Economic Approach, University of Dayton Law Review, Volume 19, Number 3, pages 1109 to 1129.

282 Example US cases include; A&M Records, Inc. v. Napster, Inc. 239 F.3d 1004 (9th Cir. 2001), MGM Studios, Inc. v. Grokster, Ltd., 545 U.S. 913 (2005) and Evenson, E. (1928), The Telephone Patent Conspiracy of 1876: The Elisha Gray-Alexander Bell Controversy and Its Many Players. Other inventors contested Bell's patents and founding principles of first to file and originality in patent law were established in the Bell case.

283 In 1898, when the US took over the governance of the Philippines, any patent applications made in the Philippines went to the US Patent and Trademark Office and were considered under US law. For more information see Drahos, P. (2002), Developing Countries and International Intellectual Property Standard-Setting, The Journal of World Intellectual Property.

284 The trademark laws in the US are extensive and the most recent are; U. S. Trademark Law, 15 U.S.C. §§ 1051 et seq. (as amended in 2013), U.S. Trademark Law, Rules of Practice, 37 C.F.R. 2 et seq. & Federal Statues, 15 U.S.C. § 1051 et seq. and 35. U.S.C. 1 (2012) and Trademark Technical and Conforming Amendment Act of 2010 (Pub. Law No. 111-146, 124 Stat. 66, 2010).

285 The most recent update on the US Copyright Act was in 2009; U.S. Copyright Act of 1976, 17. U.S.C. §§ 101 et seq. (2009).

286 The US Patent law was amended in 2013; U.S. Patent Law, 35 U.S.C. §§ 1 et seq. (2013).

287 Uniform Trade Secrets Act With 1985 Amendments, drafted by the National Conference Of Commissioners on Uniform State Laws.

288 Sherman Anti-Trust Act of 1890, codified at 15 U.S.C. 1-7; Clayton Act of 1914, codified at 15 U.S.C. 12-27, 29 U.S.C. 52-53; The Federal Trade Commission Act of 1914, 38 Stat. 717 (Sept. 26, 1914), codified at 15 U.S.C. 41 et seq.

289 Detailed information on USPTO and all aspects of its work and protection of intellectual property rights for US citizens can be found at http://www.uspto.gov/index.jsp.

290 The US Office of Policy and International Affairs in Trade produce an annual Special 301 report and Special Out-of-Cycle Reviews (OCRs) which was established through the Trade Act 1998. With the Special 301 provisions, the USTR can, under the amendments made to the Trade Act of 1974, identify foreign countries that deny US intellectual property right holders the level of intellectual property protection required to give right holders a fair and equitable market access.

291 Pugatch, M. (2007) A Transatlantic Divide? The US and EU's Approach to the International Regulation of Intellectual Property Trade-Related Agreements, ECIPE Working Papers.

292 See for example the Madrid Protocol which allows a trademark right holder to file for trademark registration in several countries. By filing one trademark registration application with USPTO, US applicants can be granted protection for their intellectual property asset in as many as 84 countries.

293 The US has many bilateral agreements in place with several countries around the globe including; Jamaica, Mongolia, Panama, Columbia, Korea, Peru, Oman, Uruguay, Bahrain, Morocco, Mozambique, Australia, Singapore, Chile, Jordan, Vietnam, Lithuania, Azerbaijan, Croatia, Bolivia, Korea, Bulgaria, Grenada, Cameroon, Bangladesh, Zaire, Poland, Congo, Ukraine, Trinidad and Tobago, Czech, Slovakia, Argentina, Hungary, Cambodia, Turkey, Sri Lanka, Albania, Ecuador, Kyrgyzstan, Tunisia, Kazakhstan, Armenia, Egypt, and Senegal. Each agreement can be found at http://www.wipo.int/wipolex/en/profile.jsp?code=US. Accessed on 04.03.2015.

294 Patent Law Treaty, Beijing Treaty on Audio-visual Performances , Marrakesh Treaty to Facilitate Access to Published Works for Persons Who Are Blind, Visually Impaired or Otherwise Print Disabled, Singapore Treaty on the Law of Trademarks, Protocol Relating to the Madrid Agreement Concerning the International Registration of Marks, WIPO Performances and Phonograms Treaty, WIPO Copyright Treaty, Trademark Law Treaty, Berne Convention for the Protection of Literary and Artistic Works, Brussels Convention Relating to the Distribution of Programme-Carrying Signals Transmitted by Satellite,

Budapest Treaty on the International Recognition of the Deposit of Micro-organisms for the Purposes of Patent Procedures, Patent Cooperation Treaty, Strasbourg Agreement Concerning the International Patent Classification, Convention for the Protection of Producers of Phonograms Against Unauthorized Duplication of Their Phonograms, Nice Agreement Concerning the International Classification of Goods and Services for the Purposes of the Registration of Marks, Convention Establishing the World Intellectual Property Organization and Paris Convention for the Protection of Industrial Property. Available at http://www.wipo.int/wipolex/en/profile.jsp?code=US.

295 Kaminski, M. (2014), The Capture Of International Intellectual Property Law Through The U.S. Trade Regime, Southern California Law Review.

296 See http://tcc.export.gov/Trade_Agreements/Bilateral_Investment_Treaties/index.asp for each individual bilateral investment treaty.

297 Chapter 15(2) US-Oman FTA Available at http://www.ustr.gov/sites/default/files/uploads/agreements/fta/oman/asset_upload_file715_8809.pdf. Accessed on 16.01.2015.

298 The committee originally consisted of twelve multinational US organisations including; Pfizer, IBM, Bristol-Myers, CBS; Hewlett-Packard, Monsanto, Du Pont, General Electric, General Motors, Johnson & Johnson and Merck. For the US IPC, its main commonality among its members was that they all lost millions in revenues from intellectual property infringement and there was a consensus amongst the member organisations to compel the US government to steer changes in the international trade arena.

299 Sell, S. (2003), Private Power, Public Law, the Globalization of Intellectual Property Rights, Cambridge Studies in International Relations, Pugatch, M. (2004), The International Political Economy of Intellectual Property Rights, Edward Elgar Publishing, page 209 and Drahos, P. (2002), Developing Countries and International Intellectual Property Standard-setting. Report commissioned by IPR Commission.

300 Mirza, B. (2006), A Dilemma of Intellectual Property Rights For Developing Countries? Economics of Technological Innovation.

301 Drahos, P. and Braithwaite, J. (2002) Information Feudalism: Who Owns the Knowledge Economy? Earthscan Publications Limited and the original article by Pfizer is; MacTaggart, B. (1982), Stealing from the Mind, New York. Times and can be found at http://fabien.benetou.fr/Archives/StealingFromTheMind. The article criticised a number of countries for developing laws that allowed them to legally use US intellectual property assets and also criticised WIPO. See extract; "*Through political and legal dealings, many governments, including Brazil, Canada, Mexico, India, Taiwan, South Korea, Italy and Spain, to name a few, have provided their domestic companies with ways to make and sell products that under proper enforcement and honourable treatment of patents would be considered the property of the inventors. And now, the United Nations, through its World Intellectual Property Organization, is trying to grab high technology inventions for underdeveloped countries*".

302 Morin, J. (2009), Multilateralizing TRIPs-Plus Agreements: Is the US Strategy a Failure? The Journal of World Intellectual Property, pages 175 to 197.

303 Braithwaite, J. and Drahos, P. (2000), Global Business Regulation, Cambridge, Cambridge University Press.

304Tellez, V. (2009), The changing global governance of intellectual property enforcement: a new challenge for developing countries, Chapter 1 and Editors, Li, X. and Correa, C. (2009), Intellectual Property Enforcement: International Perspectives, Edward Elgar Publishing.

305 The Uruguay Round took seven years to reach conclusion in 1993 with 123 countries agreeing to the agenda. The agenda is still to date the largest trade negotiation to reach completion, it covered fifteen subjects; tariffs, non-tariff barriers, natural resource products, textiles and clothing, agriculture, tropical products, GATT articles, Tokyo Round codes, Anti-dumping, subsidies, intellectual property, investment measures, dispute settlement, the

GATT system and services. Available at http://www.wto.org/english/thewto_e/whatis_e/tif_e/fact5_e.htm.

306 The General Agreement on Tariffs and Trade came into force in 1948 and was applied provisionally by all contracting parties. The full agreement is available at http://www.wto.org/english/docs_e/legal_e/gatt47_e.pdf and covered; agriculture, health regulations for farm products, textiles and clothing, product standards, investment measures, anti-dumping measures, customs valuation methods, pre shipment inspection, rules of origin, import licensing, subsidies and counter-measures, safeguards, movement of natural persons, air transport, financial services, shipping and telecommunications. What the GATT agreement did not cover was intellectual property rights and the Uruguay Round addressed the lack of intellectual property protection along with creating the WTO to address the failings of GATT in sustaining an international trade organisation.

307 Pratt, E. (1998), Intellectual Property Rights and International Trade, Pfizer Incorporated, Available at http://www.iatp.org/files/Intellectual_Property_Rights_and_International.htm. To strengthen the impact of the US IPC, the USTR advised the committee to forge links and join forces with its equivalent European counterpart, namely the Union of Industrial and Employers Confederations of Europe and also the Japan business federation group, Keidanren.

308 Drahos, P. and Braithwaite, J. (2003), Three tests of US trade policy on intellectual property rights, Nth Position, Ilias, S. and Ferguson, I. (2011) Intellectual Property Rights and International Trade, Congressional Research Service and Sell, S. (2003), Private Power, Public Law, the Globalization of Intellectual Property Rights, Cambridge Studies in International Relations.

309 Ramachandran, A. (1977), Self-Reliance in Technology and the Patent System in WIPO, World Symposium on the Importance of the Patent System to Developing Countries, page 304.

310 UNCTAD acts as a forum for where member states can engage in dialogue and discuss ways to establish a better balance in the global economy. It offers technical assistance to developing countries and countries with economies in transition, in order to build capacities in developing countries to become more integrated into the global economy. UNCTAD holds a ministerial-level meeting every four years to discuss major global economic issues and every two years, UNCTAD organizes the World Investment Forum. The Forum brings together the international investment community to discuss challenges and opportunities and to promote investment policies and partnerships for sustainable development and equitable growth. Available at http://unctad.org/en/Pages/AboutUs.aspx.

311 United Nations, (2006), Investment Provisions In Economic Integration Agreements, United Nations Conference On Trade and Development, United Nations Publication.

312 Qaqaya, H. And Lipimile, G. (2008), The Effects Of Anti-Competitive Business Practices On Developing Countries and Their Development Prospects, United Nations Papers Publication. Available at http://unctad.org/en/docs/ditcclp20082_en.pdf. United Nations, (2013), Investment Policy Monitor a Periodic Report by the UNCTAD Secretariat, United Nations Conference On Trade And Development, Number 11. Available at http://unctad.org/en/PublicationsLibrary/webdiaepcb2013d11_en.pdf.

313 Sell, S. (2011), Everything Old Is New Again: The Development Agenda Then and Now, WIPO Journal, Issue 1, Thomson Reuters (Professional) UK Limited and Contributors.

314 Neumayer, E. and Spess, L. (2005), Do bilateral investment treaties increase foreign direct investment to developing countries? [online] London: LSE Research Online. Available at http://eprints.lse.ac.uk/archive/00000627.

315 See for example US cases on the idea-expression dichotomy in copyright law that have developed over a number of years; Baker v. Seldon 1879 101 U.S. 99, Mazer v. Stein 1954 347 U.S. 201, Sid & Marty Krofft Television Productions, Inc. v. McDonald's Corporation

9th Cir. 1977 562 F.2d 1157, Durham Industries, Inc. v. Tomy Corporation 2d Cir. 1980 630 F.2d 905 and Apple Computer, Inc. v. Franklin Computer Corporation 3d Cir. 1983 714 F.2d 1240.

316 Davis, N. (2012), The GCC Countries and the World: Scenarios to 2025, Chapter 3. European Parliament, (2010), Report on European Union relations with the Gulf Cooperation Council, Committee on Foreign Affairs. Available at http://www.europarl.europa.eu/sides/getDoc.do?pubRef=-//EP//TEXT+REPORT+A7-2011-0042+0+DOC+XML+V0//EN. El Said, M. (2012), The Compatibility of Modern Intellectual Property Protection Norms with Islamic Principles: Lessons from History, The WIPO Journal, Analysis of Intellectual Property Issues, Volume 4, Issue 1, page 121.

317 The universality of intellectual property will always be problematic as unlike human rights which are steeped in international law making history, intellectual property is quintessentially a territorial being and inevitably remains the preserve of domestic law. For further analysis see Murumba, S. (2012), Foxes and hedgehogs at the intersection of human rights and intellectual property, Monash University Law Review, Volume 38, Number 1.

318 Warner Bros. Entertainment, Inc. and J. K. Rowling v. RDR Books, 575 F.Supp.2d 513 (SDNY 2008).

319 For further comments see, http://www.nytimes.com/packages/pdf/nyregion/20080909_POTTER.pdf. Reid, D. (2012), Intellectual Property Rights: A Comparative Perspective on Asia, the EU, and North America, Norteamérica Volume 7, Number 1, México ene. / jun. 2012 and Dinwoodie, G. (2013), Methods and Perspectives in Intellectual Property, ATRIP Intellectual Property Series, Edward Elgar Publishing at page 41 deliberating on the developments the Rowling case made to the fair use doctrine.

320 Other areas of law include human rights and criminal law. Human Rights are enshrined in the Universal Declaration of Human Rights since 1948. Available at http://www.un.org/en/documents/udhr/ and for criminal law, the International Criminal Court has been established since 1998.

321 Kimbrough, A. (2012), Transformative use vs. Market impact: why the fourth fair use factor should not be supplanted by transformative use as the most important element in a fair use analysis, Alabama Law Review, Volume 63 Issue 3, page 625.

322 See T 201/ 04 Microsoft Corporation v. Commission of the European Communities. The case involved the US software giant, Microsoft, losing its patented right to refuse interoperability information. Microsoft asserted intellectual property rights over its interoperability information. The Court of First Instance assessed Microsoft's intellectual property rights against its abuse of a dominant position in the common market and found Microsoft to be in violation of competition law. The change made by the Microsoft decision was that the existence of an intellectual property right can be challenged under exceptional circumstances. It is however unrealistic to expect the GCC States to develop as sophisticated an intellectual property legal system that has the capacity to deal with very fragmented case by case specific intellectual property assets. For further details on intellectual property law and competition law see Korah, V. (2006) Intellectual Property Rights and EC Competition Rule, Hart Publishing.

323 Liu, H. (2005) The Coming Trade War, Part 5 Intellectual property rights: Bad TRIPS.

324 Leo, B. (2010), Where are the BITs? How U.S. Bilateral Investment Treaties with Africa Can Promote Development, Centre for Global Development. Available at http://www.cgdev.org/sites/default/files/1424333_file_Leo_BITs_FINAL.pdf.

325 See Chapter 6 (8)-(14).

326 Pugatch, M. (2007) A Transatlantic Divide? The US and EU's Approach to the International Regulation of Intellectual Property Trade-Related Agreements", ECIPE Working Papers and Chu, Y. (2010), The Evolution of US and EU Approaches to Intellectual Property Provisions Related to Public Health in Free Trade Agreements:

Are They Responding to Public Health Concerns? Available at SSRN: http://ssrn.com/abstract=1739488.

327 The flexibilities are found at Article 1.1 of the TRIPS Agreement.

328 Mehta, P. (2004), TRIPS Plus: Enhancing Right Holders' Protection, Eroding TRIPS flexibilities, Briefing Paper, CUTS Centre for International Trade, Economics & Environment.

329 U.S. International Trade Commission, (2004), U.S.-Bahrain Free Trade Agreement: Potential Economywide and Selected Sectoral Effects, Chapter 18, Diane Publishing Company.

330 Fink, C. and Reichenmiller, P. (2006) Tightening TRIPS: Intellectual Property Provisions of U.S. Free Trade Agreements, World Bank Organization. Also see Abbott, F. (2010), Intellectual Property Provisions of Bilateral and Regional Trade Agreements in Light of U.S. Federal Law, UNCTAD - ICTSD Project on IPRs and Sustainable Development and Deere, C. (2008), The Implementation Game: The TRIPS Agreement and the Global Politics of Intellectual Property Reform in Developing Countries, Oxford University Press.

331 Saudi Arabia is the biggest GCC trader with the US, latest figures show trade in services, both imports and exports, exceeded $61 billion making Saudi Arabia the 12th biggest trading partner for the US. Trade with Kuwait for the US stands at $10.5 billion a year, with the UAE annual trade is at $18.3 and UAE is the 34th largest goods trading partner for the US. Qatar also has trading ties with the US trading in the region of $4 billion. See http://www.ustr.gov/countries-regions/europe-middle-east/middle-east/north-africa/qatar.

332 The Report: Kuwait 2013, Trading up: Both internal and external GCC imports and exports have increased considerably Available at http://www.oxfordbusinessgroup.com/news/trading-both-internal-and-external-gcc-imports-and-exports-have-increased-considerably.

333 Economist Intelligence Unit, (2011), GCC trade and investment flows the emerging-market surge, The Economist Intelligence Unit Limited 2011.

334 See for example the Statute of Anne from Britain which was the first copyright Act in the world, dated back to 1710. A facsimile is at the British Library, 8 Anne c. 19. Also see John Feather, The Book Trade in Politics: The Making of the Copyright Act of 1710, Publishing History, 19(8), 1980, page 39 (note 3).

335 Available at http://www.wipo.int/wipolex/en/profile.jsp?code=EU#a1.

336 EU legislation on copyright covers; copyright in the knowledge economy, management of copyright and related rights in the internal market, copyright and related rights: term of protection, resale right for the benefit of the author of an original work of art, rental right and lending right, orphan works, copyright and related rights: satellite broadcasting and cable retransmission, legal protection of databases, legal protection of services based on, or consisting of, conditional access, legal protection of computer programs, copyright and related rights in the information society and management of online rights in musical works. Available at http://europa.eu/legislation_summaries/internal_market/businesses/intellectual_property/index_en.htm.

337 Key areas for EU inventions covers; the European patent system, Community patent, establishment of the Community Patent Court, legal protection of biotechnological inventions and genetic engineering and legal protection of topographies of semiconductor products. http://europa.eu/legislation_summaries/internal_market/businesses/intellectual_property/index_en.htm.

338 The Trademark law covers; The European trademark law, community trademark regulation and trademark directive. Available at European Commission, official website (europa.eu).

339 Other areas include; counterfeit goods and piracy, European anti-counterfeiting and anti-piracy plan, industrial property rights strategy, enforcement of intellectual property rights, combating counterfeiting and piracy in the single market, customs response to latest trends in counterfeiting and piracy, goods infringing intellectual property rights, technology transfer agreements, defence-related products: rules on transfer within the EU, geographical indications and designations of origin and traditional specialities.

340 In total the EU has the highest number of statutes in the area of intellectual property law. These are broken down into; intellectual property laws, implementing rules and regulations, geographical Indications, treaty approvals intellectual property legal literature and jurisprudence, administered intellectual property-related treaties and treaty memberships. All are available at http://www.wipo.int/wipolex/en/profile.jsp?code=EU.

341 The EU has extensive resources and policies governing intellectual property within the EU such as; the European Patent Office (EPO), European Commission Internal Market and services and the Office for Harmonization in the Internal Market (OHIM). Also the EU has a strong presence in intellectual property business initiatives, namely, React the Anti Counterfeiting Network and Business Action to Stop Counterfeiting and Piracy (BASCAP). All available at http://ec.europa.eu/trade/policy/accessing-markets/intellectual-property/.

342 The EU has pioneered and steered many international rules in intellectual property. For example, in 2004, a Strategy for the Enforcement of Intellectual Property Rights in Third Countries was set up by the EU and it set out an enforcement framework dealing with intellectual property infringement outside the of the EU. Other enforcement regimes are developed by the EU through bilateral activities. These include; bilateral agreements, intellectual property dialogues, intellectual property and working groups. The bilateral agreements contain extensive intellectual property rights chapters. The chapters aim to offer similar levels of protection as is in the EU, while taking into account where a particular country or union of countries is at within the global market and its level of development. All available at http://ec.europa.eu/trade/policy/accessing-markets/intellectual-property/

343 European Commission, 2013, Report on the protection and enforcement of intellectual property rights in third countries, Commission staff working document at page 19.

344 Barnier, M. (2013), European Commission in charge of Internal Market and Services, Intellectual Property Rights, Europe's asset, Europe's priority, European Commission.

345 European Patent Office and the Office for Harmonization in the Internal Market,2013, *"Intellectual property rights intensive industries: contribution to economic performance and employment in the European Union"*

346 The Unitary Patent will come into force once 13 of the 38 member states, that includes the UK, France and Germany have ratified the Agreement on a Unified Patent Court, although current plans forecast the unitary patent to be made available by the end of 2015. See http://www.ipo.gov.uk/pro-types/pro-patent/p-policy/pro-p-upandupc/pro-p-up.htm.

347 The two institutions were set up under the EPC at Article 4 which states; (1) A European Patent Organisation, hereinafter referred to as the Organisation, is established by this Convention. It shall have administrative and financial autonomy. (2) The organs of the Organisation shall be: (a) the European Patent Office; (b) the Administrative Council. (3) The task of the Organisation shall be to grant European patents. This shall be carried out by the European Patent Office supervised by the Administrative Council.

348 Not all members of the EPC are members of the EU; therefore EPC can offer intellectual property protection across a larger number of individuals than the EU. See Wild, J. (2005), European Patent Office, Patents in Europe Helping Business Compete in Global Economy, Intellectual Asset Management Magazine Supplement.

349 Treaty of the European Union states at Article 5 (1-2): the limits of Union competences are governed by the principle of conferral. The use of Union competences is governed by the principles of subsidiarity and proportionality. Under the principle of conferral, the Union shall act within the limits of the competences conferred upon it by the Member States in the Treaties to attain the objectives set out therein. Competences not conferred upon the Union in the Treaties remain with the Member States. For further detail see Geiger, C. (2013), Constructing European Intellectual Property Achievements and New Perspectives, Edward Elgar publishing at page 6.

350 OHIM deals with registration of community trademarks and designs. Available at https://oami.europa.eu/ohimportal/en/. Accessed on 05.02.2015.

351 The history of the EPO: A look back at the history of the European Patent Convention, the Organisation and the Office.

352 *Re Astron Clinica Ltd and others* [2008] EWHC 85 (Pat); [2008] WLR (D) 12. The UK High Court augment the situations under which a computer program can be granted a patent to be more in line with the EPO and reversed the UK practice on computer programs to allow computer program claims that unequivocally refer to admissible methods. Claims resumed being granted by examiners at the UK Intellectual Property Office, as they have been at the EPO, but with the stipulation that the UK test for patentability must be consistent with the Aerotel/Macrossan four step test in preference to the 'technical character' test at the EPO. In *Re Astron Clinica Ltd*, the UK High Court broadened the circumstances under which a computer program can be granted a patent. This is very significant. In Re Astron a category that was previously exempt from patent protection was given the right to be patented.

353 Human Genome Sciences Inc. v. Eli Lilly and Company, [2011] UKSC 51. The five UK Supreme Court collectively reversed the Court of Appeal decision that Human Genome Sciences (HGS) Neutrokine-α was invalid as it lacked industrial application. This is further evidence the UK courts are conscious that in order to uphold international intellectual property rights they need to make judicial decisions that are in line with the (EPO) and in HGS the Supreme Court adopted EPO'S interpretation of industrial applicability. The UK Supreme Court ruled that Article 57 of the EPC does not require patent application for new genes to go as far as providing clinical tests to meet the burden of proof of industrial application.

354 See Torremans, P. (2013), Holyoak and Torremans Intellectual Property Law, Seventh Edition, Oxford University Press at page 150. Ayadi, R. and Gadi, S. (2013), EU-GCC Trade and Investment Relations: What Prospect of an FTA between the Two Regions? Sharaka Enhancing Understanding and Cooperation in EU-GCC Relations.

355 Luciano, G. and Schumacher, T. (2004), Relations Between the European Union and the Gulf Cooperation Council, Record and Promises for the Future, Gulf Research Center.

356 Commission Of The European Communities, 1995, Communication From The Commission To The Council, Improving Relations Between The European Union And The Countries Of The Gulf Cooperation Council (GCC).states "*the original premises of EU-GCC cooperation, namely a high degree of economic and energy inter-dependence, have not changed*". Available at http://eurlex.europa.eu/LexUriServ/LexUriServ.do?uri=COM:1995:0541:FIN:EN:PDF.

357 Kostadinova, V. (2013), What is the Status of the EU-GCC Relationship? Gulf Research Center.

358 Preamble to the EU-GCC Cooperation Agreement, Official Journal of the European Communities No L 54/3 of 25 February 1989, pages 3-15.

359 Koch, C. and Stenberg, L. (2010), The EU and the GCC: Challenges and Prospects under the Swedish EU Presidency, Gulf Research Center.

360 See for example, Hashmni, M. and Al-Eatan, F. (2014), Is There A Need For A Free Trade Agreement Between The European Union And Gulf Cooperation Council? International Business & Economics Research Journal, Volume 13, Number 1.

361 Ali, J. (2014) GCC looks east for win win trade deals, http://www.bilaterals.org/?gcc-looks-east-for-win-win-trade#sthash.HcAFUifL.dpuf. Other agreements include the GCC-Malaysia framework agreement on economic, commercial, investment and technical cooperation in 2011. The GCC trade agreements with other countries will be a further research area as it will be a point of interest to investigate whether the integrated approach recommended in this research is fit for purpose for all the GCC trading partners.

## Chapter 5

362 See Chapter 2 (3), Table 1.

363 WTO Analytical Index: TRIPS, Agreement on Trade-Related Aspects of Intellectual Property Rights, Article 9.1. Available at http://www.wto.org/english/res_e/booksp_e/analytic_index_e/trips_01_e.htm#article9B1.

364 Article 1, Berne Convention. The Berne Convention has been amended several times; September 9, 1886, May 4, 1896, November 13, 1908, March 20, 1914, June 2, 1928, June 26, 1948, July 14, 1967, July 24, 1971 and September 28, 1979. Initially, the Union was composed of the main developed countries pioneering intellectual property right protection and included Switzerland, Belgium, Spain, Italy, United Kingdom, Tunisia, France and Germany. This can be compared to the GCC States ascension to the Berne Convention with the first State joining in 1996 (Bahrain), followed by Oman in 1999, Qatar 2000, Saudi Arabia 2003, UAE 2004 and Kuwait is yet to join.

365 The Paris Convention was needed as prior to the enactment of the Convention patent applications had to be made at the same time in each country the property right holder was seeking a monopoly. This was mainly because if the patent applications were made at different times in different countries, then the requirement of novelty in the invention would be lost as a patent cannot be granted if the invention is made public in any way, anywhere in the world. The Paris convention addressed this hurdle and created a uniform law to avoid destroying the novelty of the invention in other countries.

366 WIPO was established as a UN Agency responsible for administering intellectual property issues for its member states. See Tejan-Cole, A. (2011), International Copyright Law- Part I: The Berne Convention for the Protection of Literary and Artistic Works, 1886.

367 For the Paris Convention see Paris Convention for the Protection of Industrial Property (wipo.int). For the Berne Convention see Berne Convention for the Protection of Literary and Artistic Works (wipo.int).

368 Vrins, O. and Schneider, M. (2006), Enforcement of Intellectual Property Rights Through Border Measures, Oxford University Press.

369 World Intellectual Property Organization, Berne Convention for the Protection of Literary and Artistic Works, May 4, 1896.

370 See the TRIPS Agreement, Annex 1C of the Marrakesh Agreement Establishing the World Trade Organization, signed in Marrakesh, Morocco on 15 April 1994. See also Article 64, TRIPS Agreement, dispute settlement procedures.

371 Trade Related Intellectual Property Rights, Part V. Nair, M. (2009), TRIPS, WTO and IPR – How Effective is the Dispute Settlement Process? Journal of Intellectual Property Rights, Volume14, pages 346 to 348. Available at http://nopr.niscair.res.in/bitstream/123456789/5351/1/JIPR%2014%284%29%20346-348%20%28Opinion%29.pdf.

372 Land, M. (2012), Rebalancing TRIPS, Michigan Journal of International Law, Volume 33, Issue 3. Available at http://repository.law.umich.edu/cgi/viewcontent.cgi?article=1019&context=mjil.

373 Yu, P. (2009), The Objectives and Principles of the TRIPs Agreement, Drake University Law School, Houston Law Review, Volume 46, pages 797 to 1046.

374 Deere, C. (2009), Developing Country Perspectives on Intellectual Property in the WTO: Setting the Pre-Trips Context. See more at http://ssrn.com/abstract=1405430.

375 El-Said, M. (2005), The Road from TRIPS-Minus, to TRIPS, to TRIPS-plus, Implications of IPRs for the Arab World, The Journal of World Intellectual Property, page 53.

376 Onley, J. (2005), Britain's Informal Empire in the Gulf, 1820—1971, Journal of Social Affairs, Volume 22, Number 87, American University of Sharjah, pages 29 to 45.

377 Peterson, J. (2009), Britain and the Gulf: At the Periphery of Empire, Chapter 14, Edited by Lawrence G. Potter. The Persian Gulf in History. [Online] Available at http://www.palgraveconnect.com/pc/doifinder/10.1057/9780230618459.

378 See Chapter 2 for further details in relation to the legal development of each individual state.
379 Hassanien, M. (2008), Bilateral WTO-Plus free trade agreements In the Middle East: A case Study of OFTA in the Post-Trips Era, Intellectual Property Law Journal, pages 161 to 197.
380 Noland, M. (2008), Arab Economies at a Tipping Point, Peterson Institute for International Economics. Davis, W. and Hayashi, C. (2007), The Gulf Cooperation Council (GCC) Countries And The World: Scenarios To 2025: Implications For Competitiveness, World Economic Forum. Momani, B. (2007), A Middle East Free Trade Area: Economic Interdependence and Peace Considered, World Economy, Volume 30, Issue 11, pages 1682 to 1700. Habibi, N. (2011), Growth in economic relations of China and India with the GCC countries, Asian-Pacific Economic Literature, Volume 25, Issue 2, pages 52 to 67. PenubartI, M. and Maskus, K. (1995), How trade-related are intellectual property rights?, Journal of International Economics Volume 39, Issues 3-4, pages 227 to 248. Kim, Y. (2012), Appropriate Intellectual Property Protection and economic growth in countries at different levels of development, Research policy, Volume 41, Number 2, pages 358 to 375, Elsevier Publications.
381 Seznec, J. (2011), Industrialization in the Gulf - A Socioeconomic Revolution, Routledge Studies in Middle Eastern Economies, Routledge Taylor and Francis Group, page 25, where the interdependence of East and West States and their respective international economies has been described by Seznec as the "rayon route" to replace the original "silk route".
382 Maskus K. (2000), Intellectual Property Rights and Economic Development.
383 Carvalho, N. (2010), The TRIPS Regime of Patent Rights, Kluwer Law International, page 36. Musungu, S. and Dutfield, G. (2003), Multilateral Agreements and a TRIPS – plus world: The World Intellectual Property Organisation (WIPO), TRIPS Issues Papers 3, Quaker United Nations Office and Quaker International Affairs Programme. Biadgleng, E. and Maur, J. (2011) The Influence of Preferential Trade Agreements of Intellectual Property Rights in Developing Countries, A First Look, UNCTAD – ICTSD Project on IPRs and Sustainable Development, Issue Paper, Number 33.
384 Butcher, A. (2004), US – Bahrain Free Trade Agreement: Political Economywide and Selected Sectoral Effects, United States International Trade Commission Publication 3726.
385 Hassanien, R. (2010), United States Bilateral Free Trade Agreements: Consistencies Or Conflicts with Norms in the Middle East?, Chapter 1, page 33, Kluwer Law International. Available at https://books.google.co.uk/books?id=40BLy5XT2mAC&pg=PA33&dq=OMAN+US+FTA+TRADE+CONCESSIONS&hl=en&sa=X&ei=b9_9VIvTJsHiO8qugJAJ&ved=0CDMQ6AEwAQ#v=onepage&q=OMAN%20US%20FTA%20TRADE%20CONCESSIONS&f=false.
386 Hvidt, M. (2013), Economic diversification in GCC countries: Past record and future trends. Kuwait Programme on Development, Governance and Globalisation in the Gulf States pages 1-55. Al-Yousif, Y. (2002), Oil Economies and Globalization: The Case of the GCC Countries. Polczynski, M. (2008), Protecting Intellectual Property in a Global Environment. Maskus, K. (2000), Intellectual Property Rights In The Global Economy, Chapter 3. Arewa, O. (2006), TRIPS and Traditional Knowledge: Local Communities, Local Knowledge, and Global Intellectual Property Frameworks. Case Research Paper Series in Legal Studies Working Paper. Dahrendorf, A. (2009), Global Proliferation of Bilateral and Regional Trade Agreements: A Threat for the World Trade Organization and/or for Developing Countries, Maastricht Faculty of Law Working Paper Number 6. Drahos, P. (2003), The Global Intellectual Property Ratchet: Why it Fails as Policy and What Should be Done About It. Birnhack, M. (2008), Trading Copyright: Global Pressure On Local Culture.
387 European Union, EU relations with the Gulf Cooperation Council (GCC). Available at http://eeas.europa.eu/gulf_cooperation/index_en.htm.

388 The Economic Agreement between the GCC States Adopted by the GCC Supreme Council (22nd Session; 31 December 2001). Also, EU, US and China are all offering to finalise FTA's with the GCC states.
389 GCC Charter, Foundations and Objectives. Available at http://www.gcc-sg.org/eng/index895b.html?action=Sec-Show&ID=3. Accessed on 15.03.2015.
390 Adolf, H. (2001), Trade-Related Aspects of Intellectual Property Rights And Developing Countries, The Developing Economies. Kernohan, D. (2004), Measuring the Economic Impact of an EU-GCC Free Trade Agreement, Centre for European Policy Studies, pages 1 to 68. Lindstrom, B. (2010), Scaling Back TRIPS-Plus an Analysis of Intellectual Property Provisions in Trade Agreements and Implications for Asia and the Pacific. Social Science Research Network. Maur, E. (2011), The Influence of Preferential Trade Agreements on the Implementation of Intellectual Property Rights in Developing Countries: A First Look, World Bank; Groupe d'Economie Mondiale (GEM) UNCTAD-ICTSD Project on IPRs and Sustainable Development Paper Number 33. Mercurio, B. (2006), TRIPS-Plus Provisions in FTAs: Recent Trends, Regional Trade Agreements and the WTO Legal System, pages 215 to 237. Mohamadieh, K. (2006), Free Trade Agreements in the Arab Region, The Arab NGO Network for Development. Ruse-Khan, H. G. (2011), The International Law Relation between TRIPS and Subsequent TRIPS-Plus Free Trade Agreements: Towards Safeguarding TRIPS Flexibilities?, Journal of Intellectual Property Law Volume 18, Number 2. Gervais, D. (2007), IP Trade and development, Strategies to optimize economic development in a TRIPS plus Era.
391 Khanna, N. (2002), Trade Related Intellectual Property Rights and Their Effects on World Trade, The Saskatchewan Economics Journal, Volume 4. Available at http://artsandscience.usask.ca/economics/skjournal/2002edition4.php.
392 Landes, W. (2009), The Economic Structure of Intellectual Property Law, Harvard University Press, page 414. Available at http://books.google.co.uk/books?id=L2P3EHagf8cC&dq=free+market+ideology+intellectual+property&source=gbs_navlinks_s.
393 Treaty on Intellectual Property in Respect of Integrated Circuits and International Convention for the Protection of Performers, Producers of Phonograms and Broadcasting Organizations.
394 Editor Stamatoudi, I. (2010), Copyright Enforcement and the Internet, Kluwer Law International, Part 1, Taylor, M. The Global System of Copyright enforcement: Regulation, Policies and Politics, page 73.
395 UNDP and the UNDP Special Unit for South-South Cooperation, (2008), The Challenge of Assessing the Creative Economy: towards Informed Policy-making, Creative Economy Report 2008.
396 Price, D. (2009), The Development of Intellectual Property Regimes in the Arabian Gulf States: Infidels at the Gates, Chapter 5, Routledge.
397 See Chapter 1 (4).
398 Business Software Alliance, Global Software Survey, 2018. Available at 2018 BSA Global Software Survey | BSA | The Software Alliance.
399 Wati, R. (2012), Study on Specialized Intellectual Property Courts, joint project between the International Intellectual Property Institute (IIPI) and the United States Patent and Trademark Office (USPTO). Available at http://iipi.org/wp-content/uploads/2012/05/Study-on-Specialized-IPR-Courts.pdf.
400 Saudi Arabia 2014 Crime and Safety Report: Riyadh. Available at https://www.osac.gov/pages/ContentReportDetails.aspx?cid=15563.
401 International intellectual property alliance (IIPA) 2013 special 301 report on copyright protection and enforcement. The reason as to why Saudi Arabia does not have a public repository links back to its political structure as discussed in Chapter 2 (6). Saudi Arabia lacks transparency in its judicial system and a public repository would be an area of development.

402 World Trade Review, (2011), Saudi Arabia, Contributing firm United Trademark & Patent Services in association with Dr Hasan Al Mulla Law Office, Page 191.

403 The full powers of the Violations Review Committee are stated in the Saudi Arabia Copyright Law (2003) at Article 25 which states at least one member shall be a Sharia advisor. See Article 25: Violation Review Committee (1) *A Committee to review the violation shall be formed by the Minister's decision, with a minimum of three members, provided that one of them is a legal advisor and the other a Shari'ah advisor. (2) Decisions of the Committee shall be made by majority vote, which shall be endorsed by the Minister.*

404 World Trade Organization, (2011), Trade Policy Review, Report by The Kingdom Of Saudi Arabia, Page 12.

405 World Intellectual Property Review, (2014), More than 70 Saudi shops closed for copyright violations. Available at http://www.worldipreview.com/news/more-than-70-saudi-shops-closed-for-copyright-violations-6525.

406 Beltrametti, S. (2010), The Legality of Intellectual Property Rights under Islamic Law, The Prague Yearbook of Comparative Law, pages 55 to 94 and El-Bialy, N. (2011), Enforcing IPR Through Informal Institutions: The Possible Role of Religion in Fighting Software Piracy.

407 Intellectual Copyright Committee of The Ministry of Culture and Information in Jeddah, found that Al-Qarni had copied some chapters from a book written by the female Saudi author, Salwa Aededan. See http://www.saudigazette.com.sa/index.cfm?method=home.regcon&contentid=20120125116308.

408 According to the Saudi Gazette, Sheikh Ayad al-Qarni responded by saying, ""People of knowledge usually benefit from each other without referring to the source," and "I need not mention that Ibn Taimiyya had copied tens of scholars without referring to them. Does this mean he was incapable? I'm not incapable. I can author one complete book without referring to a single reference".

409 The case is unusual as firstly, both the Applicant and Respondent are Saudi nationals and there is no Western intellectual property right holder seeking remedies and secondly, the Applicant was female and the Respondent male. Although gender issues in the Gulf State are beyond the scope of this research, it is an underlying issue for national born female intellectual property right holders. For further details see Sidani, Y. (2005), Women, work, and Islam in Arab societies, Women In Management Review, Volume 20, Issue 7, pages 498 to 512 and Abou, E. (2001), Speaking in God's Name: Islamic Law, Authority and Women, Oxford, Oneworld.

410 Beltrametti, S. (2010), The Legality of Intellectual Property Rights under Islamic Law, The Prague Yearbook of Comparative Law, pages 55 to 94.

411 See Chapter 7 (17) and Chapter 8 (4).

412 Saudi Arabia Law of Patents (2004), Article 4. The full article covers exemption for conflicts with Sharia, plant and human life and the environment. Article 4: *"(a) The protection document shall not be granted if its commercial exploitation violates the Shari'ah. (b) The protection document shall not be granted if its commercial exploitation is harmful to life, to human, animal or plant health, or is substantially harmful to the environment"*.

413 The Berne Convention, section 2 sets rules for the protection of moral rights, that is, the right to claim authorship of the work and the right to object to any mutilation, deformation or other modification of, or other derogatory action in relation to, the work that would be prejudicial to the author's honour or reputation.

414 Beltrametti, S. (2010), The Legality of Intellectual Property Rights under Islamic Law, The Prague Yearbook of Comparative Law, pages 55 to 94.

415 Uruguay Round Agreement, TRIPS, Part III, Section 4, Articles 51-60. Available at http://www.wto.org/english/docs_e/legal_e/27-trips_05_e.htm.

416 Aljehani, K. (2013), Better protection: the KSA's fight against counterfeiters at the border, World Intellectual Property Review. Available at http://www.worldipreview.com/article/better-protection-the-ksa-s-fight-against-counterfeiters-at-the-border.

417 Annual Report, Saudi Customs, (2012), Sixth Chapter: Commercial Fraud & Counterfeiting and Protecting of Intellectual Property Rights (IPR), page 84.
418 See Chapter 2 (6).
419 Saudi Arabia, International Intellectual Property Alliance (IIPA) 2014 Special 301 Report On Copyright Protection and Enforcement.
420 Saudi Arabia, International Intellectual Property Alliance (IIPA) 2014 Special 301 Report On Copyright Protection and Enforcement.
421 O'Connell, N. (2010), United Arab Emirates: Working With Dubai Customs To Fight The Infringement Of IP Rights, Al Tamimi & Company, Available at http://www.mondaq.com/x/113760/Trademark/Working+With+Dubai+Customs+To+Fight+The+Infringement+Of+IP+Rights.
422 See Dubai Customs at http://www.dubaicustoms.gov.ae/en/NewsCenter/Pages/NewsDetail.aspx?NewsID=334.
423 See Fourth Global Congress on Combating Counterfeiting and Piracy Dubai Declaration, held in Dubai, U.A.E, 3-5 February 2008. Available at http://www.wcoomd.org/en/about-us/legal-instruments/~/media/8B70762244B74C3BB2CB40F2BBA0668D.ashx.
424 Obeidat, O. and Suboh, M. (2011), United Arab Emirates, Al Tamimi and Co, World Trade Review.
425 United Arab Emirates, International Intellectual Property Alliance (IIPA), 2014 Special 301 Report On Copyright Protection And Enforcement.
426 See Chapter 2 (9).
427 UK Trade and Investment, (2014), Guidance Exporting to Qatar.
428 See Chapter 2 (9).
429 Drahos, P. (2013), Emerging Markets and the World Patent Order, Edward Elgar Publishing, Page 338.
430 See Law No. (17) of 2011, Article 3 which states: *"a right holder can lodge an application with the Customs Department to stop the clearance process and request suspension of the release into free circulation of the imported goods which involve an infringement of the right holder's rights."*.
431 Trade Policy Review, (2014), Report by the Secretariat Qatar, Page 41. Available at http://www.wto.org/english/tratop_e/tpr_e/s296_e.pdf.
432 Mina, W. (2010), Do Bilateral Investment Treaties Encourage FDI in the GCC Countries?" African Review of Economics and Finance 2(1) and Ramady, M. and Saee, J. (2007), Foreign direct investment: A strategic move toward sustainable free enterprise and economic development in Saudi Arabia, Thunderbird International Business Review, pages37-56.
433 Braga, P. (1998), Reforming Intellectual Property Rights Regimes: Challenges for Developing Countries, Journal of International Economic Law Volume 1, pages 537 to 554.
434 Cullen, C. (2010), Can TRIPS Live in Harmony with Islamic Law: An Investigation of the Relationship between Intellectual Property and Islamic Law?
435 See for example Qatar, Bahrain and Oman who have installed a Software for the Management of Automated Systems of Arab Industrial Property Offices which is the implementation of automated information systems for the national intellectual property offices in order to improve the performance of services and to satisfy the automation requirements in the framework of modernization of the intellectual property systems. Also, Bahrain and Oman both have bilateral trade agreements with the US and the intellectual property provisions accede those specified by TRIPS as the agreements require ratification to further international treaties. For example the 2006 Bahrain bilateral agreement requires Bahrain s to ratify or accede to the International Convention for the Protection of New Varieties of Plants, the Trademark Law Treaty, the Brussels Convention Relating to the Distribution of Programme-Carrying Satellite Signals, the Protocol Relating to the Madrid

Agreement Concerning the International Registration of Marks, the Budapest Treaty on the International Recognition of the Deposit of Microorganisms, the Patent Cooperation Treaty, the WIPO Copyright Treaty and the WIPO Performances and Phonograms Treaty.

436 Sundaram, J. (2008), Economic liberalization and constraints to development in sub-Saharan Africa, Working Papers 67.

437 Thirwall, A. (2000), Trade, Trade Liberalisation and Economic Growth: Theory and Evidence, Economic Research Papers, Volume 63, Issue 30.

438 Berg, H. (2007), International trade and economic growth, M E Sharpe Incorporated.

439 International Institutions and Global Governance Program 2012.

440 Kuwait is still on the United States Trade Representative (USTR) Special 301 Watch List whereas Saudi Arabia has been removed from the list in February 2010.

441 Drahos, P. (2003), When the Weak Bargain win the Strong, Kluwer Law, pages 79 to 109.

442 Maskus, K. (2000), Intellectual Property Rights in the Global Economy, Institute for International Economics, US. Winter, S. (1989), Patents in Complex Contexts: Incentives and Effectiveness, In Weil and Snapper, Owning Scientific and Technical Information. New Brunswick, NJ: Rutgers University Press, pages 41 to 60. Braga, C. (1995), Trade-Related Intellectual Property Issues: The Uruguay Round Agreement and Its Economic Implications, The Uruguay Round and Developing Economies, Washington, DC, W. Martin and L.A. Winters Editions, World Bank, Discussion Paper, Chapter 12, pages 381 to 412.

443 See for example, Ferris, K. (2012), The Compliance with Intellectual Property Laws and their Enforcement in Jordan - A post - WTO Review & Analysis. The analysis of Jordan's intellectual property laws by Ferris shows intellectual property laws are incompatible with Jordan's economic stage of development, having little economic impact on the Jordanian economy. This he states is mainly due to the majority of technologies used in Jordan being unrelated to intellectual property right issues. The GCC countries have similar systems to Jordan, taking on several intellectual property laws to gain more foreign direct investment without fully measuring the economic impact of these new laws over certain time intervals. Also see, Olwan, R. (2013), The History of International Intellectual Property and Development, Chapter 2, where the author states at page 35 that there is no evidence that the development of developing countries has been encouraged by intellectual property laws.

444 Yu, P. (2009), The Objectives and Principles of the Trips Agreement, Houston Law Review, Volume 46, pages 797 to 1046, Social Science Research Network. Available at http://papers.ssrn.com/sol3/papers.cfm?abstract_id=1398746.

445 TRIPs covers copyright and related rights (i.e. the rights of performers, producers of sound recordings and broadcasting organizations); trademarks including service marks; geographical indications including appellations of origin; industrial designs; patents; the protection of new varieties of plants; the layout-designs of integrated circuits; and undisclosed information including trade secrets and test data. The trips agreement has three main strands; standards, enforcement and dispute settlement. The standards set out the minimum standards of protection to be provided by each Member in respect of each of the main areas of intellectual property covered by the agreement. This covers a definition of the minimum protection required for intellectual property assets, a definition of the subject-matter, the minimum duration of protection, the rights to be granted and the exceptions to those rights. The TRIPS Agreement contains enforcement obligations. The main set of provisions includes domestic procedures and remedies for the enforcement of intellectual property rights that are applicable to all intellectual property rights enforcement procedures. The provisions are; civil procedures and remedies, administrative procedures and remedies, measures, special requirements related to border measures and criminal procedures. TRIPs have a powerful enforcement mechanism. States which do not adopt TRIPs compliant intellectual property systems can be disciplined through the WTO's dispute settlement

mechanism, which is capable of authorising trade sanctions against nonconformist states. Thirdly, the Agreement has incorporated a dispute settlement procedure as part of the minimum TRIPS requirements to deal with disputes between members. See World Trade Organisation at http://www.wto.org/english/tratop_e/trips_e/intel2_e.htm.

446 Yu, P. (2009), The Objectives And Principles Of The TRIPS Agreement." Houston Law Review, Volume 46, pages 797 to 1046, Social Science Research Network. Available at http://papers.ssrn.com/sol3/papers.cfm?abstract_id=1398746.

447 Summary of the Berne Convention for the Protection of Literary and Artistic Works (1886). Available at http://www.wipo.int/treaties/en/ip/berne/summary_berne.html.

448 Price, D. (2009), The Development of Intellectual Property Regimes in the Arabian Gulf States Infidels at the Gates, Chapter 6, Routledge.

449 Hassanein, M. (2008), Bilateral WTO-Plus Free Trade Agreements in The Middle East: A Case Study of OFTA in the Post Trips Era, Wake Forest Intellectual Property Law Journal, pages 161 to 197. Dahrendorf, A. (2009), Global Proliferation of Bilateral and Regional Trade Agreements: A Threat for the World Trade Organization and/or for Developing Countries, Maastricht Faculty of Law, Working Paper Number 6. Ranjan, P. (2010), Bilateralism, MFN and TRIPS: Exploring Possibilities of Alternative Interpretation, International Trade Law and Regulation, Volume 13, Number 4, pages 67 to 78.

450 The GCC has a number of free trade agreements pending. The GCC-EFTA agreement was signed in 2009 but is yet to come into force, the GCC-India agreement is not finalised and the EU-GCC agreement is currently stated as 99% complete. See more at http://www.tax-news.com/news/GCCEU_Free_Trade_Agreement_Is_99_Percent_Complete____61559.html. Ayadi, R. and Gadi, S. (2013), EU-GCC Trade and Investment Relations: What Prospect of an FTA between the Two Regions? Sharaka Enhancing Understanding and Cooperation in EU-GCC Relations.

451 Turk, M.(2010), Bargaining and IP Treaties: The case for a pro-development interpretation of TRIPS but not TRIPS Plus, New York University Journal of International Law and Politics, Volume 42, pages 981 to 1030, The New York University Law School. Also see Price, D. (2009), The Development of Intellectual Property Regimes in the Arabian Gulf States Infidels at the Gates Chapter 5 and Said, E. (2007), The European Trips Plus Model and the Arab World, Liverpool Law Review.

452 Alexander, D. (2002), Integrating Intellectual Property Rights and Development Policy.

453 See Yaqub, D. (2009), Intellectual Property and Developing Countries, A review of the literature, RAND Cooperation, Said, E. (2007), The European Trips Plus Model and the Arab World, Liverpool Law Review, Cottier, T. and Foltea, M. (2012), Global Governance in Intellectual Property Protection: Does the Decision-making Forum Matter? The WIPO Journal Volume 3 Issue 2. Price, D. (2009), The Development of Intellectual Property Regimes in the Arabian Gulf States Infidels at the Gates, Chapter 1, Routledge. Rizk, N. and Shaver, L. (2010), Access to Knowledge: Economic, Global and Local Perspectives. Hassanein, M. (2008), Bilateral WTO-Plus Free Trade Agreements In The Middle East: A Case Study Of OFTA In The Post Trips Era, Wake Forest Intellectual Property Law Journal, Volume 8, pages 161 to 197. Khoury, A. (2003), The Development of Modern Trademark Legislation and Protection in Arab Countries of the Middle East, The Transnational Lawyer. Tamimi, E. (1999), Current U.A.E. Copyright Law and how it Compares and Contrasts with WTO's Trips-Agreement and the Berne Convention, The Journal of World Intellectual Property, pages 371 to 391. Said, E. (2005), The Road from TRIPS-Minus, to TRIPS, to TRIPS-Plus Implications of IPRs for the Arab World, The Journal of World Intellectual Property, Volume 8, pages 53 to 65. Lai, E. (2001), The economics of intellectual property protection in the global economy. OseiTutu, J. (2010), A Sui Generis Regime for Traditional Knowledge: The Cultural Divide in Intellectual Property Law, Legal Studies Research Paper Series. Malbon, J. (2008), TRIPS-plus Treaty

Terms: Dealing with Coercion, Chapter 8: In Interpreting and Implementing the TRIPS Agreement: Is it fair? Ruse–Khan, H. (2011), The International Law Relation Between Trips And Subsequent Trips-Plus Free Trade Agreements: Towards Safeguarding Trips Flexibilities? Journal of Intellectual Property Law, Volume 18. Yu, P. (2011), Are Developing Countries Playing a Better TRIPS Game? Legal Studies Research Paper Series Drake University Research Paper, Number 12. Morin, J. (2008), Multilateralising TRIPs-Plus Agreements: Is the US Strategy a Failure. Mohamadieh, K. (2007), The Arab Region And Trade Liberalization Policies A Look into Sectoral Implications, Arab NGO Network for Development Working Paper. Yu, P. (2011), TRIPS and Its Achilles ' heel, Journal Of Intellectual Property Law. Frankel, S. (2012), Challenging Trips-Plus Agreements: The Potential Utility of Non-Violation Disputes, Victoria University of Wellington Faculty of Law Research Papers.

454 Pastor, R. (2006), The Impact of Free Trade Agreements on Intellectual Property Standards in a Post-TRIPS World , Pastor highlights three main areas of TRIPS compliance which require analysis in intellectual property and international trade; The following issues should always be followed when dealing with IPR and international trade: to firstly ensure effective competition and avoid the risk of limitations in competition in smaller developing countries because of the monopolising nature of patent protection, secondly to give greater weight to public health inventions and the cost reflecting the financial situation in the specific developing countries, thirdly addressing the knowledge gap in technological advances between developed and developing countries and lastly ensuring protection of traditional knowledge, recognizing the complications in establishing patents in this area. Available at http://www.bilaterals.org/spip.php?article4311#sthash.YOQ4kVgY.dpuf.

455 Business Software Alliance News Release, Business Software Alliance urges Gulf countries to further intensify campaign against piracy. Available at http://portal.bsa.org/globalpiracy2010/downloads/press/pr_gulfregion.pdf.

456 Business Software Alliance for 2012 showed improvement in software piracy in the six Gulf States from 2000 to 2006; Oman 16%, Qatar, 23%, Saudi Arabia, 7%, UAE, 9%, Kuwait, 16% and Bahrain, 20%. However from 2006 to 2012, there have been little or no improvements; Oman 0%, Qatar, 9%, Saudi Arabia, 0%, UAE, -1%, Kuwait, 4% and Bahrain, 6%.

457 Vivas, D. (2003), Regional and bilateral agreements and a TRIPS-plus world: the Free Trade Area of the Americas (FTAA), TRIPS Issues Papers 1, QUNO/QIAP/ICTSD, 2003, page 4.

458 Unctad and the UNDP Special Unit for South-South Cooperation, (2008), The Challenge of Assessing the Creative Economy: towards Informed Policy-making, Creative Economy Report 2008.

459 Said, E. (2007), The European Trips Plus Model and the Arab World, Liverpool Law Review. Sakmar, S. (2008), Globalization and Trade Initiatives in the Arab World: Historical Context, Progress to Date, and Prospects for the Future, University of San Francisco School of Law. Mohamadieh, K. (2006), Free Trade Agreements in the Arab Region, The Arab NGO Network for Development and Morin, J. (2009), Multilateralizing TRIPs-Plus Agreements: Is the US Strategy a Failure? The Journal of World Intellectual Property.

460 TRIPS Plus is not a defined concept, it is not a minimum standard that must be adhered by all WTO Member States and therefore the TRIPS Plus requirements for the GCC States may not necessarily be the same as other developing countries.

461 Santa Cruz, M. (2007), Intellectual Property Provisions in European Union Trade Agreements, ICTSD Intellectual Property and Sustainable Development Series, page 12.

462 Said, E. (2007), The European TRIPS Plus Model and the Arab World: from co-operation to association – a new era in the Global IPRS regime? Liverpool Law Review, Volume 28, Number 1, pages 143-174, Springer Science and Business Media and Said, E. (2005), From

TRIPS-minus to TRIPS to TRIPS-plus: Implications of IPRs for the Arab world, The Journal of World Intellectual Property, Volume 8, Number 1.

463 Arab Development Challenges Report and Staff of the International Monetary Fund (2012), Arab Countries in Transition: Economic Outlook and Key Challenges, International Monetary Fund. Hvidt. M. (2013), Economic diversification in GCC countries: Past record and future trends, Kuwait Programme on Development, Governance and Globalisation in the Gulf States. Fassano, U. (2003), GCC Countries: From Oil Dependence to Diversification, International Monetary Fund. Devaux, P. (2013), Economic diversification in the GCC: dynamic drive needs to be confirmed, BNP Paribas.

464 Arab Human Development Report 2009. Available at http://www.arab-hdr.org/.

465 Exploration in Falkland Islands by a number of British firms such as Rockhopper, Desire Petroleum and Argos Resources.

466 The transition to a knowledge-based economy relies on the privatisation of information. For examples see Khoury, A. (2009), Dubai's New Intellectual Property-Based Economy: Prospects for Development without Dependency, The John Marshall Review of Intellectual Property Law and the Arab World Competitiveness Report, (2013), World Economic Forum.

467 Each GCC State has produced official documentation with an emphasis on developing knowledge-based economies. See for example; http://www.insead.edu/facultyresearch/centres/innovation_policy_initiative/breakfasts/upcoming/documents/measuring_innov_RD_uae. Also see Rasem, H. (2011), Saudi Arabia's economic development: entrepreneurship as a strategy, International Journal of Islamic and Middle Eastern Finance and Management. Available at http://www.arabnews.com/news/451416. Brinkley, I. (2012), Kuwait and the Knowledge Economy, The Work Foundation and the Kuwait Programme on Development, Governance and Globalisation in the Gulf States, The London School of Economics and Political Science. Hertog, S. (2007) The GCC and Arab economic integration: a new paradigm, Middle East policy, pages 52 to 68. Economist Intelligence Unit, 2010, The GCC in 2020: Broadening the economy, report from the Economist Intelligence Unit, Sponsored by Qatar Financial Centre Authority and Ahmad, E. and Al Faris, A. (2010), Fiscal Reforms In The Middle East, Edward Elgar Publishing Limited.

468 Fabry, E. (2013), Think Global – Act European v Thinking Strategically about the EU's External Action, Centre for European Policy Studies and Elasrag, H. (2008), Enhancing The Competitiveness Of The Arab SMES, Open Journal of Economic Research.

469 Endeshaw, A. (2006), Intellectual Property and the WIPO Development Agenda, Maur, E. (2011), The Influence of PTAs-on the implementation of intellectual property rights in developing countries, International Centre for Trade and Sustainable Development (ICTSD) and Rizk, N. and Shaver, L. (2010), Access to Knowledge: Economic, Global and Local Perspectives.

470 Correa, C. (2000), The Strengthening Of IPRS In Developing Countries And Complimentary Legislation, DFID, Yaqub, D. (2009), Intellectual Property and Developing Countries A review of the literature, RAND Cooperation and Foray, D. (2007), Patents and Development In The Knowledge Economy, International Centre for Trade and Sustainable Development (ICTSD).

471 Joint Action Programme for Implementation of the GCC-EU Cooperation Agreement of 1988, 2010-2013 part 9 "Exchange of views and experience in the area of intellectual property rights. Establish cooperation between the EU and the GCC in the field of patents in order for the GCC to benefit from the EU experience. Such cooperation could include exchange of expertise and technical assistance in various fields such as capacity building, training, expert missions, patent databases, IT and seminars. In this respect, cooperation between the European Patent Office and the GCC Patent Office will be encouraged." Also see Jaruzelski, B. (2013), Strengthening Innovation Hubs in the GCC, The Role

of Enterprise Champions, The Global Innovation Index 2013: The Local Dynamics of Innovation, INSEAD. Driouchi, A. (2008), Domestic Institutions, Intellectual Property Rights & Development in the EU-Mediterranean Partner Countries, The Political Economy of Governance in the Euro-Mediterranean Partnership and the World Intellectual Property Organization. Ulrichsen, K. (2011), Knowledge Economies in the GCC States, The Political Economy of the Gulf, Summary Report, Center for International and Regional Studies Georgetown University School of Foreign Service in Qatar.

472 Said, E. (2007), The European Trips Plus Model and the Arab World, Liverpool Law Review and Turk, M. (2011), Bargaining And Intellectual Property Treaties: The Case For A Pro-Development Interpretation of Trips But Not Trips Plus, Journal of International Law & Politics.

473 Kim, Y. (2012), Appropriate Intellectual Property Protection and economic growth in countries at different levels of development, Research policy, Volume 41, Number 2, pages 358 to 375, Elsevier Science B V Amsterdam.

474 Said, E. (2008), The development of intellectual property protection in the Arab world, Edwin Mellen Press. Ruse-Khan, H. (2011), The International Law Relation between TRIPS and Subsequent TRIPS-Plus Free Trade Agreements: Towards Safeguarding TRIPS Flexibilities? Journal of Intellectual Property Law, Volume 8, Number 2.

475 Muhaisen, W. (2009), Share'a: Intellectual Theft or Intellectual Infringement? Journal of International Commercial Law and Technology, Volume 4, pages 71 to 74.

476 The Dubai International Financial Centre (DIFC) is governed by the Law of Obligations DIFC Law No. 5 of 2005. Articles 37 and 38 make provisions for breach of confidence and passing off however to date no case has been brought in the DIFC under Article 37 or 38.

477 For the GCC and its states there is a clear recognition of the protection of intellectual property to its continued development as a dominant trading hub in the Middle East. It is the development of international trade and services via multilateral and bilateral trade agreements which allows the GCC States to act as a hub between Eastern and Western markets.

478 The Gulf Cooperation Council Customs Union was formed in 2003.

479 See Common Customs Law of the Cooperation Council for the Arab States of the Gulf

480 Qatar Law Number (17) of 2011 on the Border Measures for the Protection of Intellectual Property Rights, the law reflects on the wording of section 4 of TRIPS on "special requirements related to border measures".

481 Ramdy, M. (2012), The GCC Economies: Stepping Up To Future Challenges, Springer Science and Business Media, Chapter 11, Price D, The GCC Intellectual Property Regimes: Global Harmonization or Regional Integration? Page 133 Available at http://books.google.co.uk/books?id=W98WDUkV0OUC&pg=PA133&lpg=PA133&dq=gcc+and+trips+plus&source=bl&ots=jXtx65LfmJ&sig=siofs9v09jQnD_THZCv5xAbPwGc&hl=en&sa=X&ei=Ddt2Uq7HN4Sf0QX32oDYDQ&ved=0CC4Q6AEwAA#v=onepage&q=gcc%20and%20trips%20plus&f=false.

482 El-Bialy, N. (2011), Can Shari'a be a Deterrent for Intellectual Property Piracy in Islamic Countries? The Journal of World Intellectual Property, pages 441 to 466.

483 Price, D. (2009), The Development of Intellectual Property Regimes in the Arabian Gulf States: Infidels at the Gates, Routledge Research in Intellectual Property.

484 Ballantyne, W. (1986), Commercial Law in the Arab Middle East, Lloyds of London Press.

485 Gulf states have been described as having little influence in the intellectual property standard-setting process, see for example, Drahos, P.(2003), Developing countries and International Intellectual Property Standard Setting Process, http://www.iprcommission.org/papers/pdfs/study_papers/sp8_drahos_study.pdf.

486 Charafeddine, R. (2011), The Economic and Financial Impacts of the Arab Awakening.

487 Beltrametti, S.(2010), The Legality of Intellectual Property Rights under Islamic Law, The Prague Yearbook of Comparative Law 2009, pages 55 to 94.

488 Ministry of Economic Development, UAE Departments of Economic Development, Articles 37 and 38 Available at http://www.uibm.gov.it/attachments/article/2006096/judicial_protection_of_ipr_in_the_uae.pdf.

489 The GCC states differ in their approaches. The UAE has established a number of free zones, each with customised regulatory and federal legal requirements that provide incentives for organisations operating in specific sectors such as Dubai's Internet City offering free zone incentives to a number of high profile companies to operate their business including IBM and Microsoft. Saudi Arabia on the other hand doesn't have free zones but has heavily invested in the King Abdulaziz City for Science and Technology for Scientific Research Support and the King Abdullah University of Science and Technology, therefore the university-focused model adopted in Saudi Arabia is different from the free zone model adopted in the UAE.

490 Each GCC state has set up its own associations to raise awareness of intellectual property. For instance, the Dubai eGovernment signed memorandum of understanding with Emirates Intellectual Property Association (EIPA) in January 2013 for raising awareness of intellectual property rights and reducing software piracy.

491 See Manto, S. (2009), United Arab Emirates, Anti-counterfeiting 2009 – A Global Guide, pages 199 to 202.

492 Economist Intelligence Unit 2011 states 30 years ago the Organisation for Economic Co-operation and Development, (OECD), accounted for 85% of GCC trade, however with the influx of emerging markets, by 2009 45% of GCC trade stems from emerging markets. Also see Habibi, N. (2011), Growth in economic relations of China and India with the GCC countries. Asian-Pacific Economic Literature, Volume 25, pages 52 to 67.

## Chapter 6

493 United Nations Conference On Trade And Development, World Investment Report, 2013, Global Value Chains: Investment and Trade for Development, Chapter 3, page 110. Available at http://unctad.org/en/publicationslibrary/wir2013_en.pdf.

494 Drahos, P. (1996), A Philosophy of Intellectual Property, Aldershot, UK, Dartmouth Publishing Company. Menell, P. (1999), Intellectual Property: General Theories, Berkeley Centre for Law and Technology, pages 129 to 188.

495 Drahos, P. (1996), A Philosophy of Intellectual Property, Aldershot, UK, Dartmouth Publishing Company.

496 Gordon, W. (2003), Intellectual Property, Chapter 28, Boston University School of Law Working Paper Series, Law and Economics Working Paper, Number 3.

497 See Chapter 3 (8).

498 Locke, J. (1690), Second Treatise on Civil Government, Chapter 5, Section 28.

499 Maskus, K. (2005), Intellectual Property and Development, Lessons from Recent Economic Research, The International Bank for Reconstruction and Development / The World Bank and Oxford University Press.

500 Menell, P. (1999), Intellectual Property: General Theories, Berkeley Centre for Law and Technology, University of California at Berkeley.

501 Hughes, J. (1988), The Philosophy of Intellectual Property, Georgetown Law Journal, Volume 77.

502 Locke, J. (1690), Second Treatise on Civil Government, Chapter 5.

503 Drahos, P. (1996), A Philosophy of Intellectual Property, Aldershot, UK, Dartmouth Publishing Company.

504 Hollinrake v Truswell (1894), 3 Ch 420; 63 LJ Ch 719.

505 TRIPS Agreement, Article 9.2 states that copyright protection shall extend to expressions and not to ideas, procedures, methods of operation or mathematical concepts as such. Available at https://www.wto.org/english/tratop_e/trips_e/intel2_e.htm.

506 Braga, P. (1996), Trade-Related Intellectual Property Issues: The Uruguay Round Agreement and its Economic Implications, in W. Martin and L.A. Winters Editions, The Uruguay Round and the Developing Economies, World Bank Discussion Paper Number 307, pages 381 to 411, Washington, DC, the World Bank.

507 World Trade Organization, (2015), Overview: the TRIPS Agreement, Substantive standards of protection, Copyright. Available at https://www.wto.org/english/tratop_e/trips_e/intel2_e.htm.

508 Alikhan, S. (2009), Intellectual Property and Competitive Strategies in the 21st Century, Chapter 1, page 10, Kluwer Law International. Available at https://books.google.co.uk/books?id=QvKDZ8_YWh8C&pg=PA10&dq=A+design+right+registered+or+unregistered?&hl=en&sa=X&ei=wX4UVZSlNYjyPO3SgJgP&ved=0CD4Q6AEwBQ#v=onepage&q=A%20design%20right%20registered%20or%20unregistered%3F&f=false.

509 Waelde, C. (2013), Contemporary Intellectual Property: Law and Policy, Chapter 8, Oxford University Press. Available at https://books.google.co.uk/books?id=PaicAQAAQBAJ&pg=PA299&lpg=PA299&dq=A+design+can+be+protected+as+a+registered+design+if+the+design+is+new,+has+individual+character+or+constitutes+a+component+part+of+a+complex+product.&source=bl&ots=fr57-TGgl3&sig=OFPzQwUD8IIrtU1IEmtLURhD5H4&hl=en&sa=X&ei=tn8UVcLgOJLuaKn1gcgD&ved=0CD4Q-6AEwBQ#v=onepage&q&f=false.

510 Grove, P. (1997), Sourcebook on Intellectual Property Law, Chapter 5, Cavendish Publishing.

511 TRIPS: Agreement On Trade-Related Aspects Of Intellectual Property Rights, (1995), Part II— Standards concerning the availability, scope and use of Intellectual Property Rights, Section 4, Articles 25 and 26.

512 Menell, P. (1999), Intellectual Property: General Theories, Berkeley Centre for Law and Technology, University of California at Berkeley. Drahos, P. (1996), A Philosophy of Intellectual Property, Aldershot, UK, Dartmouth Publishing Company.

513 Maurer, E. (2001), An Economic Justification for a Broad Interpretation of Patentable Subject Matter, Northwestern University Law Review , Volume 95, Number 3. Fink, C. (1999), How Stronger Protection of Intellectual Property Rights Affects International Trade Flows, Policy Research Working Papers, The World Bank.

514 Dollinger, J. (2008), Entrepreneurship Strategies and Resources, Fourth Edition, Kelley School of Business, Indiana University, Marsh Publications Lombard, Illinois USA.

515 Gordon, W. (2003), Intellectual Property, Chapter 28, Boston University School of Law Working Paper Series, Law and Economics Working Paper, Number 3.

516 Paepke, O. (1987), Economic Interpretation of the Misappropriation Doctrine: Common Law Protection for Investments in Innovation, Berkeley Technology Law Journal, Volume 2, Issue 1, Article 2. Available at http://scholarship.law.berkeley.edu/cgi/viewcontent.cgi?article=1057&context=btlj. Accessed on 23.03.2015.

517 Munari, F. (2005), Review of Literature on the Use and Impact of IPRs at the Firm Level: Patents, Trademarks and Designs, University of Bologna, EU Observatory.

518 TRIPS Agreement, (1995), Uruguay Round Agreement, Part II, Section 5, Article 27, Patentable Subject Matter. Available at https://www.wto.org/english/docs_e/legal_e/legal_e.htm#TRIPs.

519 TRIPS Agreement, (1995), Uruguay Round Agreement, Part II, Section 5, Article 33, Terms of Protection. Available at https://www.wto.org/english/docs_e/legal_e/legal_e.htm#TRIPs.

520 TRIPS Agreement, (1995), Uruguay Round Agreement, Part I — General Provisions and Basic Principles, Article 8, Principles.

521 Dinwoodi, G. (2008), Trademark Law and Theory: A Handbook of Contemporary Research, Chapter 4, Edward Elgar Publishing Limited.
522 Schechter, F. (1927), The Rational Basis of Trademark Protection, Harvard Law Review, Volume 40, Number 6, pages 813 to 833. Available at http://www.jstor.org/stable/1330367.
523 Gielen, C. (2014), Trademark Dilution Under European Law, The Trademark Reporter, Volume 104, Number 3.
524 TRIPS Agreement, Part II — Standards concerning the availability, scope and use of Intellectual Property Rights, Section 2: trademarks, Article 15, Protectable Subject Matter. Available at https://www.wto.org/English/docs_e/legal_e/27-trips_04_e.htm#2.
525 Protocol Relating to the Madrid Agreement Concerning the International Registration of Marks. (1989). Available at http://www.wipo.int/treaties/en/text.jsp?file_id=283530.
526 Morison v. Moat (1851), 9 Hare 492.
527 Prince Albert v. Strange [1849], 1 Mac & G 25.
528 Aplin, T. (2012), Gurry on Breach of Confidence: The Protection of Confidential Information, Oxford University Press.
529 See Saltman Engineering Co. Ltd. v. Campbell Engineering Co. Ltd. (1948) 65 R.P.C. 203; Terrapin Ltd. v. Builders' Supply Co. (Hayes) Ltd. [1960] R.P.C. 128 and Seager v. Copydex Ltd. [1967] 1 W.L.R. 923; [1967] R.P.C. 349 and Coco v A.N. Clark (Engineers) Limited [1968] F.S.R. 415.
530 The elements of a confidential information action were set out by Meggary, J. in Coco v. A.N. Clark (Engineers) Ltd [1969] RPC 41.
531 Irish, V. (2003), Disclosing Confidential Information, World Intellectual Property Office.
532 TRIPS: agreement on trade-related aspects of intellectual property rights, part II — Standards concerning the availability, scope and use of Intellectual Property Rights, Article 39.
533 See Chapter 5 (5).
534 Patent Regulation of the Cooperation Council for the Arab States of the Gulf, Article 15.
535 TRIPS: agreement on trade-related aspects of intellectual property rights, part II — Standards concerning the availability, scope and use of Intellectual Property Rights, Article 33. Available at https://www.wto.org/English/docs_e/legal_e/27-trips_04d_e.htm.
536 US-Oman FTA, Article 15.8, 6(b) states "with respect to patents covering pharmaceutical products or their method of use:(i) each Party shall make available an adjustment of the patent term to compensate the patent owner for unreasonable curtailment of the effective patent term". Available at http://www.ustr.gov/sites/default/files/uploads/agreements/fta/oman/asset_upload_file715_8809.pdf.
537 Kerry, V. (2007), TRIPS, the Doha declaration and paragraph 6 decision: what are the remaining steps for protecting access to medicines?, Globalization and Health. Available at http://www.globalizationandhealth.com/content/3/1/3. Castro, S. (2009), Compulsory Licensing and Public Health: TRIPS-Plus Standards in Investment Agreements, Social Science Research Network. Available at http://ssrn.com/abstract=2101574.
538 TRIPS Agreement, Article 31. Available at http://www.wto.org/english/tratop_e/trips_e/wtl641_e.htm.
539 US-Jordan FTA, Article 4.20. Available at http://tcc.export.gov/Trade_Agreements/All_Trade_Agreements/exp_005607.asp.
540 Minister of Domestic Trade and Consumer Affairs, Malaysia, (29 October 2003), Authorisation for exploitation of patented invention in Malaysia. Available at http://www.cptech.org/ip/health/c/malaysia/arv-license.html. Also see El Said, M. (2013), Patent-Related Flexibilities in Multilateral Treaties and their Importance for Developing Countries and LDCs, 2nd WIPO Inter-Regional Meeting on South-South Cooperation on Patents, Trademarks, Geographical Indications, Industrial Designs and Enforcement.
541 See Chapter 3 (8) "Sharia Principles on Mutual Consent".

542 Compulsory licensing and pharmaceutical products will be a further area of research as further analysis is outside the scope of the current research.
543 See Chapter 3 (11).
544 See Chapter 3 (10).
545 GCC Quarterly Review, Quarter 4, (2014). Available at http://www.linklaters.com/Insights/GCC/Q4-2014/Pages/Index.aspx.
546 Price, D. (2012), The Development of Intellectual Property Regimes in the Arabian Gulf States: Infidels at the Gates, Routledge.
547 Vizcaino, B. (2015), Islamic finance looks to outgrow bad habits as it expands, Thomson Reuters News. Available at http://www.ifsc.ie/article.aspx?idnews=299168.
548 See further analysis in Chapter 7.
549 A detailed analysis of Islamic finance and the potential of Islamic finance structures to offer an alternative approach to intellectual property protection in the GCC is discussed in Chapter 7.
550 See Chapter 2.
551 See Khan, A. (2001), Islam as Intellectual Property My Lord! Increase Me In Knowledge, Cumberland Law Review, Volume 31, Part 3, pages 631-684. See Chapter 2.
552 In relation to property law a quranic reference is made in the Surah An-Najm, Verse 39, linking Locke's labour theory to Islamic proprietary rights; "And that man hath only that for which he maketh effort", Quran at 53:39 Sahih International Translation available at www.quran.com. Islam allows a person to own property, possess and enjoy wealth which has been acquired through lawful means and effort.
553 Quranic references attributed to contract law include Surah Al-Mā'idah, Verse 1, "O you who have believed, fulfill [all] contracts". See the Quran at 5:1 Sahih International Translation.
554 El-Bialy, N. (2011), Enforcing IPR Through Informal Institutions: The Possible Role of Religion in Fighting Software Piracy, Joint Discussion Paper Series in Economics by the Universities of Aachen, Gieben, Gottingen, Kasel, Marburg and Siegen.
555 For the full analysis of sharia law and intellectual property see Chapter 2.
556 Azmi, I. (1997), Authorship and Islam in Malaysia: Issues in Perspective, International Review of Intellectual Property and Competition Law.
557 Beltrametti, S. (2010), The Legality of Intellectual Property Rights under Islamic Law, The Prague Yearbook of Comparative Law, pages 55 to 94.
558 Geraghty, E. and Cingotti, N. (2014), The hidden cost of EU trade deals: Investor-state dispute settlement cases taken against EU member states, Friends of The Earth Europe. Available at http://www.foeeurope.org/sites/default/files/publications/hidden_cost_of_eu_trade_deals.pdf.
559 Egypt - Qatar Bilateral Investment Treaty, (1999). Available at http://investmentpolicyhub.unctad.org/Download/TreatyFile/1103. Also see Donnan, S. (2014), Al Jazeera sues Egypt for $150m after crackdown on journalists, Financial Times. Available at http://www.ft.com/cms/s/0/7ff2210c-cec0-11e3-ac8d-00144feabdc0.html#axzz3CNLGmNPk.
560 Eli-Lilly highlights the debate around ISDS and affordable medicines especially the impact the TPP will have however although this is outside the scope of the current research, it will be a further research area.
561 MENA-OECD Investment Programme, Assessing Investment Policies Of Member Countries Of The Gulf.
Cooperation Council Stocktaking analysis, page 57. Available at http://www.oecd.org/mena/investment/Preliminary%20assessment%20GCC%20invt%20policies.pdf.
562 Riba is the doctrine on the prohibition of interest payments, undue profits or excessive gain from a transaction and gharar deals with risk, speculative transactions, ambiguity or excessive uncertainty in contracts. See Wilson, R. (2009), The development of Islamic finance in the GCC Working Paper, Kuwait Programme on Development, Governance and Globalisation in the Gulf States at page 27.

563 In relation to the impact of ISDS on the Al Jazeera case see French, A. (2014), Investor-State Dispute Settlement — A Cut Above the Courts? Supreme and Federal Courts Judges' Conference. Available at frenchcj09jul14.pdf (hcourt.gov.au). For further analysis of the Islamic principles of riba and gharar see Chapter 3 (9)-(10).
564 Khalaf, A. and Luciani, G. (2006), Constitutional Reform and Political Participation, Gulf Research Center.
565 Beblawi, H. and Luciani, G. (1987), The Rentier State, Croom Helm, page 1.
566 International Centre for the Settlement of Investment Disputes, (2012), Background Paper on Annulment
For the Administrative Council of ICSID, World Bank.
567 See Documents of the Fifth Session Including the Report of the Commission to the General Assembly, [1953] 2 *Yearbook of the International Law Commission* 211, Article 30 of the Draft Convention on Arbitral Procedure and Broches, A. (1995), Observations on the Finality of ICSID Awards in Selected Essays: World Bank, ICSID, and Other Subjects of Public and Private International Law.
568 French, A. (2014), ISDS: A cut above the courts? Speech delivered by the Chief Justice of Australia on 9 July 2014 in Darwin at judges' conference. Available at http://www.cla.asn.au/News/isds-a-cut-above-the-courts/.
569 See Khan, A. (2001), Islam as Intellectual Property My Lord! Increase Me In Knowledge, Cumberland Law Review, Volume 31, Part 3, pages 631-684.

## Chapter 7

570 Wilson, R. (2009), Kuwait Programme on Development, Governance and Globalisation in the Gulf States: The development of Islamic finance in the GCC, The Centre for the Study of Global Governance. KPMG, (2007), Growth and Diversification in Islamic Finance, Financial Series. Reeve, J. (2014), GCC Trade and Investment Flows, The Economist Intelligence Unit Limited.
571 Hayat, U. (2014), Islamic Finance: Ethics, Concepts, Practice (a summary), The Chartered Financial Analyst (CFA) Institute Research Foundation.
572 Ahmad, A. (2012), The Time Value of Money Concept in Islamic Finance, The American Journal of Islamic Social Sciences, pages 66 to 89.
573 Saeed, A. (2012), Islamic Banking and Interest: A Study of the Prohibition of Riba and Its Contemporary Interpretation, Studies in Islamic Law and Society, Volume 2, Brill Academic Publishers.
574 Elasrag, H. (2011), Principals of the Islamic Finance: A Focus on Project Finance, Munich Personal RePEc Archive. Available at http://mpra.ub.uni-muenchen.de/30197/1/MPRA_paper_30197.pdf.
575 Fisho-Oridedi, A. (2010), The Prohibition Of Riba Under Islamic Law: What Are The Implications For International Contracts? Centre for Energy, Petroleum and Mining Law and Policy.
576 Elasrag, (2011), Principals of the Islamic Finance: A Focus on Project Finance, Munich Personal RePEc Archive. Available at http://mpra.ub.uni-muenchen.de/30197/1/MPRA_paper_30197.pdf.
577 Mirakhor, A. (2006), Profit-and-loss sharing contracts in Islamic finance, Handbook of Islamic banking.
578 Khalid, M. (2013), Fundamental of Islamic Banking - Framework of Islamic Financial System and Historical Development of Islamic Banking and Finance in Malaysia, Universiti Teknologi Mara. Beck, T. (2013), Islamic vs. conventional banking: Business

model, efficiency and stability, Journal of Banking & Finance, Volume 37, Issue 2, February 2013, Pages 433–447.

579 Primary and secondary sources of Islam are discussed in Chapter 3.

580 Nisar, S. (2003), The Practices of Islamic Banking and Finance: A Historical Perspective. Ariff, M. (1988), Islamic Banking , Asian-Pacific Economic Literature, Volume 2, Number 2, pages 46 to 62. Asutay, M. (2013), Reflecting on the Trajectory of Islamic Finance: From Mit Ghamr to the Globalisation of Islamic Finance, Afro Eurasian Studies, Volume 2, Issues 1 & 2, Spring & Fall 2013, pages 5 to 14.

581 Wilson, R. (2009), Kuwait Programme on Development, Governance and Globalisation in the Gulf States: The development of Islamic finance in the GCC, The Centre for the Study of Global Governance. Presley, R. (2012), Directory of Islamic Financial Institutions, Routledge: Banking and Finance, Croom Helm Limited.

582 PriceWaterHouseCoopers, (2009), Shariah-compliant funds: A whole new world of investment, PricewaterhouseCoopers Global Financial Services Islamic Finance programme.

583 World Finance, (2014), Oil boom in GCC region shifts economic landscape. Warde, I. (2000), Islamic Finance in the Global Economy, Edinburgh University Press, Redwood Books, Trowbridge, Wilts. Clement, M (2004), The Politics of Islamic Finance, Edinburgh University Press Limited, page 39. Grais, W. (2006), Corporate Governance and Shariah Compliance in Institutions Offering Islamic Financial Services, World Bank Policy Research Working Paper 4054.

584 Khan, I. (2009), Islamic Banking, Global Islamic Finance. Also see Garbois, C. (2012), The Future of Islamic Banking, AT Kearney. Wilson, R. (2009), Kuwait Programme on Development, Governance and Globalisation in the Gulf States: The development of Islamic finance in the GCC, The Centre for the Study of Global Governance.

585 Majwood, S. (2007), The Biography of Imam Iba Al Qayim, Translated by Abdul Rafi-Adewala, Darussalam Publishers & Distributors. Also quoted in Thomas, A. (2004), Interest in Islamic Economics: Understanding Riba, Routledge Publishers, 2006, page 63.

586 Usmani, T. (2004), An Introduction to Islamic Finance, Arham Shamsi.

587 This includes direct or indirect investment with certain types of business areas that involve profit making from alcohol, pork products, betting and gambling. See Quran at 2:173, 2:219, 5:3, 5:90, 6:145 and 16:115. Available at www.quran.com.

588 See the Quran at 2:275. Available at www.quran.com.

589 Shafaat, A. (2005), Islamic Perspectives, Chapter 1, Riba in the Quran. Thomas, A. (2004), Interest in Islamic Economics: Understanding Riba, Routledge Publishers. Ghias, S. (2009), Contemporary Islamic Finance: Innovations, Applications and Best Practices, Chapter 6, Edited by Ahmed, John Wiley & Sons. Warde, I. (2000), Islamic Finance in the Global Economy, Edinburgh University Press, Redwood Books, Trowbridge, Wilts.

590 See the Quran at 2:275-280, 3:130, 4:161 and 30:39. Available at www.quran.com.

591 Hussain, I. (2006), Islamic Finance Industry: Positioned for Growth, 2nd Pakistan Islamic Banking Conference held at Karachi on November 8, 2006.

592 Fiqh is the consensus opinion of a group of scholars and exists in all aspects of sharia. For Islamic finance fiqh is concerned with consensus opinions pertinent to sharia compliant financial products.

593 See the Quran at 2:129, 2:159, 2:231 and 62:2. Available at www.quran.com.

594 Schoon, N. (2010), Islamic Banking and Finance, Chapter 14, page 144, Spiramus Press Limited.

595 Dow Jones Islamic Market Indices. Available at Dow Jones Islamic Market World Index | S&P Dow Jones Indices (spglobal.com)

596 See Chapter 5 (5).

597 There are a number of other sharia compliant frameworks such as Bai' al-Inah, known as a sale with a buy back agreement, however this is outside the scope of the research. The Various other types of Islamic finance products will provide the framework for further

research and will include safeguarding property for another known as wadia, a surety known as kafala and loan agreements known as qard hasssan.
598 Jobst, A. (2007), Monetary and Capital Markets Department - The Economics of Islamic Finance and Securitization, International Monetary Fund (IMF) Working Paper. Available at https://www.imf.org/external/pubs/ft/wp/2007/wp07117.pdf.
599 Ghias, S. (2009), Contemporary Islamic Finance: Innovations, Applications and Best Practices, Chapter 6, Edited by Ahmed, John Wiley & Sons.
600 See Musharaka on Shariah Ruling, The institute of Islamic Banking and Insurance (IIBI).
601 Hamzah, Z. (2011), Shariah-compliant Intellectual Property based Financing, Talk by Zaid Hamzah at INCEIF.
602 Amin, S. (1986), Islamic Banking and Finance – The Experience of Iran, Vahid Publications, page 33.
603 Heck, G. (2006), Charlemagne, Muhammad, and the Arab Roots of Capitalism, Chapter 3, Islamic "Free Market" Doctrine Paradigm Applied, page 104, Walter De Gruyter GmbH and Co.
604 Rahman, Z. (2007), Accounting Treatment For Mudarabah Regarding Unrestricted Investment Deposits in Malaysian Islamic Banks, Islamic Business Research Center.
605 See Murabaha on Shariah Ruling, The institute of Islamic Banking and Insurance (IIBI).
606 Iqbal, Z. (2011), An Introduction to Islamic Finance: Theory and Practice, John Wiley & Sons.
607 See Chapter 3 (9).
608 Karim, R. (2013), Islamic Finance: The New Regulatory Challenge, Wiley Finance Series.
609 See Chapter 3 (9).
610 Bank Negara Malaysia, (2010), Principles and Practices of Shariah in Islamic Finance, page 21.
611 Balala, M. (2010), Islamic Finance and Law: Theory and Practice in a Globalized World, Chapter 3, page 29, IB Tauris Company Limited.
612 Eisenberg, D. (2012), Islamic Finance: Law and Practice, Chapter 4 at 4.174, Oxford University Press.
613 Godlewski, C. (2011), Do markets perceive sukuk and conventional bonds as different financing instruments? Bank of Finland, BOFIT Institute for Economies in Transition.
614 Ali Qayyum, M. (2008), New Horizon Global Perspective on Islamic Banking and Insurance, Institute of Islamic Banking and Insurance.
615 Garg, S. (2012), Sukuk and its Growth across Major Islamic Financial Markets, Infosys Limited.
616 Afshar, T. (2013), Compare and Contrast Sukuk (Islamic Bonds) with Conventional Bonds, Are they Compatible? The Journal of Global Business Management, Volume 9, Number 1, pages 44-52.
617 Islamic Finance Resource, (2010), How Sukuk works: Introduction, structuring and application of Sukuk bonds.
618 HM Treasury, (2014), Government issues first Islamic bond.
619 Strohecker, K. (2014), After Western sukuk debuts, Islamic finance looks to emerging sovereigns, Thomson Reuters.
620 Ghuddah, A. (2007), Ijarah [Lease], Dallah Al-Barakah Group.
621 Further details on FWU AG Group are available at http://www.fwugroup.com/cms/index.php?id=23.
622 Ali Qayyum, M. (2013), New Horizon Global Perspective on Islamic Banking and Insurance, Institute of Islamic Banking and Insurance.
623 Rizvi, M. (2013), Islamic finance gains popularity across the globe, Khaleej Times.
624 Takaful Islamic Insurance, Institute of Islamic Banking and Insurance.
625 Htay, S. (2012), Accounting, Auditing and Governance for Takaful Operations, Wiley Limited. Ahmed, A, (2009), Theory and Practice of Modern Islamic Finance: The Case Analysis from Australia, Universal Publishers.

626 Anthony, D. (2011), Standard & Poor's Analysis of Sharia-Compliant Cooperative And Takaful Insurers In The Middle East Focuses Primarily On Financial Strength, Chapter 5, pages 36-49, Standard & Poor's Islamic Finance Outlook 2012.
627 Caprio, G. (2012), Handbook of Key Global Financial Markets, Institutions, and Infrastructure, Chapter 42, page 469, Academic Press.
628 Ramadan, H. (2006), Understanding Islamic Law: From Classical to Contemporary, page 101-2, Roman Altimira.
629 Schoon, N. (2010), Islamic Banking and Finance, Chapter 16, page 104, Spiramus Press Limited. Also see Elasrag, H. (2014), Islamic Finance: Basic concepts and Issues, Chapter 2, page 49.
630 Elasrag, H. (2014), Islamic Finance: Basic concepts and Issues, Chapter 2, page 49. Available at https://books.google.co.uk/books?id=-coXBAAAQBAJ&pg=PA49&dq=types+of+istisna&hl=en&sa=X&ei=NDDAVIX5G-nX7QakgoHwDw&ved=0CDcQ6AEwBA#v=onepage&q=types%20of%20istisna&f=false. Accessed on 27.03.2015.
631 Malkawi, B. (2014), A Bright Future: Towards an Enhanced Shariah Supervision in Islamic Finance, The European Financial Review.
632 Malkawi, B. (2013), Shari'ah Board in the Governance Structure of Islamic Financial Institutions, The American Society of Comparative Law, The American Journal of Comparative Law.
633 Jaffer, S. (2004), Islamic Asset Management: Forming the Future for Shari'a-compliant Investment Strategies, Chapter 17, page 247, Euromoney Books. Also see Htay, S. (2012), Accounting, Auditing and Governance for Takaful Operations, John Wiley and Sons Singapore Pte Limited. Available at https://books.google.co.uk/books?id=s9fDavp4zqEC&pg=RA2-PT64&dq=structure+of+a+sharia+board&hl=en&sa=X&ei=c6u6VOWCGNHjaMyqgoAO&ved=0CFMQ6AEwCQ#v=onepage&q=structure%20of%20a%20sharia%20board&f=false.
634 Malkawi, B. (2014), A Bright Future: Towards an Enhanced Shariah Supervision in Islamic Finance, The European Financial Review. Available at http://www.europeanfinancialreview.com/?p=487. Also see Shari'ah Supervisory Board [Religious Board], Institute of Islamic Banking and Insurance.
635 Further details on the World Database of Islamic finance and banking is available at http://www.wdibf.com/index.html.
636 The full background to the Islamic Financial Services Board (IFSB) is available at http://www.ifsb.org/background.php. The IFSB has over 184 members comprising of 59 regulatory and supervisory authorities, 8 international inter-governmental organisations, 112 financial institutions and 5 self-regulatory organisations operating in 44 jurisdictions.
637 Islamic Financial Services Board, (2009), Guiding Principles On Shari`Ah Governance Systems For Institutions Offering Islamic Financial Services. Available at http://www.ifsb.org/standard/IFSB-10%20Shariah%20Governance.pdf.
638 Grais, W. (2006), Corporate Governance and Shariah Compliance in Institutions Offering Islamic Financial Services, World Bank Policy Research Working Paper 4054. Available at http://elibrary.worldbank.org/doi/pdf/10.1596/1813-9450-4054. Obid, S. (2014), Towards a comprehensive theoretical framework for sharia governance in Islamic financial institutions, Journal of Financial Services Marketing, pages 304 to 318, Palgrave McMillan.
639 See Chapter 3 (5).
640 Mufti Muhammad Taqi Usmani is a chairman of the following sharia boards; Central Bank of Bahrain, Abu Dhabi Islamic Bank, U.A.E., Meezan Bank Ltd., Karachi, Pakistan, International Islamic Rating Agency, Bahrain, Pak-Kuwait Takaful, Karachi, Pak-Qatar Takaful, Karachi, JS Investments Islamic Fund, Karachi, JS Islamic Pension Savings Fund, President and Shaikul-Hadith, Centre for Islamic Economics, Pakistan, Jamia Darul Uloom

Karachi, International Shariah Standard Council set up by the Accounting and Auditing Organization for Islamic Financial Institutions, Bahrain, Arif Habib Investments, Pakistan International Element Islamic Fund, Karachi. He is a member of the following shariah boards; Guidance Financial Group, USA, Arcapita Bank, Bahrain, Islamic Corporation for the Development of the Private Sector (ICD), an organ of IDB Jeddah, Islamic Fiqh Academy of Rabita-al-'Alam-e-Islami, Makkah and International Islamic Fiqh Academy, Jeddah. Available at http://muftitaqiusmani.com/index.php?option=com_content&view=article&id=2&Itemid=5.

641 Executive Profile, Sheikh Mohamed Bin Ali Elgari PhD, Former President and Director, Wafa Insurance states he is connected to 85 board members in 10 different organisations across 10 different industries. Available at Sheikh Dr Mohammed Ali Bin Ibrahim Elgari Bin Eid - IslamicMarkets.com.

642 Siddique, R. (2010), A Sharia scholar's place on the board, Gulf News. Available at http://gulfnews.com/business/features/a-sharia-scholar-s-place-on-the-board-1.625445. Visser, H. (2013), Islamic Finance: Principles and Practice, Second Edition, Chapter 5, page 123. Available at https://books.google.co.uk/books?id=Y30tAgAAQBAJ&pg=PA123&dq=many+sharia+boards+have+same+members&hl=en&sa=X&ei=xw-zVOnJGJHgatPigsAO&ved=0CCAQ6AEwAA#v=onepage&q=many%20sharia%20boards%20have%20same%20members&f=false.

643 Ali, A. (2014), Business Ethics in Islam, Edward Elgar Publishing Limited, Chapter 6, The Ethics of Banking and Financial Services, page 109. Warde, I. (2010), Islamic Finance in the Global Economy, Chapter 12, Religious Issues and Challenges: Defining Islam and Interpreting the Sharia, page 235, Edinburgh University Press. Available at https://books.google.co.uk/books?id=4jDMQd7yVX4C&pg=PA235&dq=many+sharia+boards+have+same+members&hl=en&sa=X&ei=xw-zVOnJGJHgatPigsAO&ved=0CFUQ6AEwCQ#v=onepage&q=many%20sharia%20boards%20have%20same%20members&f=false.

644 Davies, A. (2012), Rock star scholars a risk for Islamic finance, Thomson Reuters, Edited by Torchia, A.

645 Gruening, H. (2008), Risk Analysis for Islamic Banks, Chapter 11, page 189, The International Bank for Reconstruction and Development, The World Bank. Available at https://books.google.co.uk/books?id=Ejl-sEs4yPMC&printsec=frontcover&dq=scrutiny+and+checks+and+balances+of+shariah+boards+islamic+finance&hl=en&sa=X&ei=6Rq0VMDjEImAU-vcg-gF&ved=0CDMQ6AEwAw#v=onepage&q&f=false. Warde, I. (2010), Islamic Finance in the Global Economy, Chapter 12, Religious Issues and Challenges: Defining Islam and Interpreting the Sharia, page 235, Edinburgh University Press. Available at https://books.google.co.uk/books?id=4jDMQd7yVX4C&pg=PA235&dq=many+sharia+boards+have+same+members&hl=en&sa=X&ei=xw-zVOnJGJHgatPigsAO&ved=0CFUQ6AEwCQ#v=onepage&q=many%20sharia%20boards%20have%20same%20members&f=false.

646 Alkhamees, A. (2013), The impact of Shari'ah governance practices on Shari'ah compliance in contemporary Islamic finance, Journal of Banking Regulation, Palgrave McMillan. Obid, S. (2014), Towards a comprehensive theoretical framework for sharia governance in Islamic financial institutions, Journal of Financial Services Marketing, pages 304 to 318, Palgrave McMillan.

647 See the Quran at 82:10-12 and 84:6-9. Available at www.quran.com.

648 Van Gruening, H. (2008), Risk Analysis for Islamic Banks, Chapter 4, Key Stakeholders, The International Bank for Reconstruction and Development, World Bank Publications. Available at https://books.google.co.uk/books?id=Ejl-sEs4yPMC&pg=PA51&lpg=PA51&dq=islamic+finance+institutions+internal+auditing+systems&source=bl&ots=b9STSI1yMw&sig=nPppBcYGPyKMWZjwH2mAw1CjYHI&hl=en&sa=X&ei=bES-VKnEJsHaUrXugfgJ&ved=0CEcQ6AEwCA#v=onepage&q=islamic%20finance%20institutions%20internal%20auditing%20systems&f=false.

649 See Chapter 7 (18)-(21).
650 Bahrain has five pieces of legislation regulating its financial sector; Central Bank of Bahrain and Financial Institutions Law 2006, the Bahrain Stock Exchange Law 1987, the Commercial Companies Law 2001, The Anti-Money Laundering Law 2001 and the Financial Trust Law 2006. Available at http://www.lexadin.nl/wlg/legis/nofr/oeur/lxwebah.htm.
651 Further information on the AAOIFI is available at http://www.aaoifi.com/.
652 Further information on the IIFM is available at http://www.iifm.net/.
653 Hassan, R. (2010), A Comparative Analysis of Shari'ah Governance in Islamic Banking Institutions Across Jurisdictions, International Shari'ah Research Academy for Islamic Finance.
654 Central Bank of Bahrain (2012), CBB seeking lasting solutions for banks, The Review. Available at http://www.cbb.gov.bh/assets/The%20Review/The%20Review%20March%202012.pdf.
655 Garas, S. (2010), Shari'a supervision of Islamic financial institutions, Journal of Financial Regulation and Compliance, Volume 18, Number 4, pages 386-407, Emerald Group Publishing Limited.
656 Islamic Finance Resource, Sharia Scholars, Sheikh Nizam Yaquby. Available at http://ifresource.com/shariah-specialists-in-islamic-finance/.
657 Alim, E. (2013), Global Leaders in Islamic Finance: Industry Milestones and Reflections, John Wiley & Sons Limited. Karim, A. (2011), Islamic Finance: The Regulatory Challenge, John Wiley & Sons Limited. Andreasyan , T. (2010), New Horizon Global Perspective on Islamic Banking and Insurance, The institute of Islamic Banking and Insurance. Barreh, I. (2013), Scholar shortage threatens Islamic financing industry, Muslim Link. Available at http://muslimlink.ca/biz-tech/islamic-finance/scholar-shortage-threatens-islamic-financing-industry. Pasha, S. (2010), Islamic finance relies on too few of its scholars, Thomson Reuters.
658 Vizcaino, B. (2014), Bahrain to develop central sharia board for Islamic banks, Thomson Reuters.
659 Further details on the liquidity management centre are available at http://www.lmcbahrain.com/.
660 Hasan, Z. (2010), Regulatory Framework of Shari'ah Governance System in Malaysia, GCC Countries and the UK, Kyoto Bulletin of Islamic Area Studies, PAGES 82-115. Available at http://www.asafas.kyoto-u.ac.jp/kias/1st_period/contents/pdf/kb3_2/07zulkifli.pdf.
661 Al Rajhi Bank was the first modern Islamic financial institute in Saudi Arabia in 1987. Prior to this, Saudi Arabia opened the Islamic Development Bank in 1975, to bring international institutions together and give Islamic finance a platform for development.
662 Fleihan, T. (2013), Saudi Arabia is identified as one of the most developed Islamic finance countries, Thomson Reuters Zawya.
663 The Report, (2010), Saudi Arabia, Oxford Business Group. Available at https://books.google.co.uk/books?id=z6d_3NJj-uUC&pg=PA102&dq=sharia+law+islamic+finance+saudi+arabia&hl=en&sa=X&ei=nhm7VJbhHoXxavTZgrgL&ved=0CDMQ6AEwAA#v=onepage&q=sharia%20law%20islamic%20finance%20saudi%20arabia&f=false.
664 Financial based legislation exists in Saudi Arabia and includes; Cooperative Insurance Companies Control Law, (2003), Royal Decree Number M/32, Electronic Transactions Law, (2007),Royal Decree Number M/8 and Law of Cooperative Associations, (2008), Royal Decree Number M/14. However, these laws are for conventional financial system and not specific to Islamic finance.
665 Dubai Chambers of Commerce, Dubai Chamber report highlights growing popularity of Islamic finance over conventional sector.
666 Islamic Finance Resource, Sharia Scholars, Dr. Abdul Sattar Abu Ghuddah, Dr. Mohamed A. Elgari, Sheikh Al-Manea and Sheikh Al-Atram. Available at http://ifresource.com/shariah-specialists-in-islamic-finance/.
667 See Chapter 1 (3).
668 The Economist, (2014), Big interest, no interest - The market for Islamic financial products is growing fast, Islamic finance, The Economist Newspaper Limited. Available at http://

www.economist.com/news/finance-and-economics/21617014-market-islamic-financial-products-growing-fast-big-interest-no-interest.

669 McBain, S. (2012), Islamic Finance's 'Scholar Problem': Why Are Shariah Scholars Paid So Much? Spears Wealth Management. Available at http://www.spearswms.com/news/islamic-finances-scholar-problem-why-are-shariah-scholars-paid-so-much.

670 Federal laws include; UAE Federal Law No. 5 of 1985 Concerning Civil Transactions, Federal Law No. 18 of 1993 concerning the Commercial Transaction Law, Federal Law No. 6 of 1985 concerning Islamic Banks and Financial Institutions, Federal Law No. 8 of 1984 concerning Commercial Companies, Federal Law No. 10 of 1980 concerning the Central Bank, The Monetary System and Organization of Banking and Dubai Law No 9 of 2004 concerning the Law Establishing the Dubai International Financial Centre.

671 Al Tamimi & Company, (2009), Islamic Finance A UAE Legal Perspective

672 Details of the sharia supervisory committee are available at https://www.sc.com/ae/islamic/shariah-supervisory-committee.html.

673 Article 6, Federal Law No.6 of 1985 concerning Islamic Banks and Financial Institutions.

674 Further details on the Central Bank of the UAE is available at Home Page | CB UAE (centralbank.ae).

675 Further details on the Dubai International Financial Centre are available at http://www.difc.ae/.

676 Nazir, M. (2012), Sharia governance at the Central Bank of the UAE, International Financial Law Review, Euromoney Institutional Investor PLC Investor. Available at http://www.iflr.com/Article/3110470/Shariah-governance-at-the-Central-Bank-of-UAE.html. The Report, Dubai, (2013), Oxford Business Group. Available at https://books.google.co.uk/books?id=pX3emdScFHkC&pg=PA82&dq=THE+REPORT:+DUBAI+SHARIA+BOARDS+2010&hl=en&sa=X&ei=3VO9VLGENIWp7AaNrICYDw&ved=0CDYQ6AEwAQ#v=onepage&q=THE%20REPORT%3A%20DUBAI%20SHARIA%20BOARDS%202010&f=false.

677 Vizcaino, B. (2013), UAE plans Islamic finance authority backed by legislation, Thomson Reuters.

678Al Awar, A. (2013), Dubai as the world's capital of Islamic Economy: The roadmap ahead, Islamic finance news, Dubai Islamic Economic Roundtable, Dubai International Finance Center.

679 Central Bank of Kuwait Law 32/1968, Chapter 3, Islamic Banking, Section 10, Articles 86-100. The legislation provides for the self-regulation of Islamic financial institutions and requires each Islamic financial institution to have its own sharia supervisory board.

680 Further details on the Ministry of Awqaf and Islamic Affairs fatwa board can be found at http://islam.gov.kw/Pages/en/NewsDetails.aspx?newsId=533.

681 Basher, S. (2009), Islamic finance lacks government support in some GCC countries, Business and Banking, Gulf News. Available at http://gulfnews.com/business/banking/islamic-finance-lacks-government-support-in-some-gcc-countries-1.499863. Hancock, M. (2013), Oman hopes to open Islamic finance floodgates, The Banker, Financial Times Limited. Available at http://www.thebanker.com/Comment/Viewpoint/Oman-hopes-to-open-Islamic-finance-floodgates?ct=true.

682 Legislation available at the World Law Guide, Legislation Oman. Available at http://www.lexadin.nl/wlg/legis/nofr/oeur/lxweoma.htm.

683 Further details on Bank Nizwa are available at http://www.banknizwa.om/.

684 Further details on Al Izz Bank are available at http://alizzislamic.com/Home.

685 Reuters, (2014), Oman sets up sharia board to boost Islamic finance, Trade Arabia, Middle East Association.

686 Central Bank of Oman, (2014), Islamic Banking Regulatory Framework. Available at http://www.cbo-oman.org/.

687 Hussain, A. (2012), Oman adopts strict Islamic banking rules, Global Islamic Finance. Available at http://www.global-islamic-finance.com/2012/12/oman-adopts-strict-islamic-banking-rules.html.

688 Oman Islamic Finance Report, (2015), Building On A Strong Start, Islamic Finance Country Report: Oman. Available at http://www.irti.org/English/Research/Documents/Report-6.pdf.

689 The Report, Qatar, (2012), Oxford Business Group, page 56. Available at https://books.google.co.uk/books?id=1JsAZouLOVQC&pg=PA56&dq=Qatar++sharia+authority+awqaf+ministry&hl=en&sa=X&ei=3sqVOTwPIbY7AbIooH4BQ&ved=0CCcQ6AEwAQ#v=onepage&q=Qatar%20%20sharia%20authority%20awqaf%20ministry&f=false.

690 Hassan, K. (2011), Islamic Capital Markets: Products and Strategies, Chapter 15, page 324, John Wiley & Sons Limited. Available at https://books.google.co.uk/books?id=Yeyo3tE-2NMC&pg=PT352&dq=central+bank+of+Qatar+does+not+have+a+higher+sharia+authority+awqaf+ministry&hl=en&sa=X&ei=i8e-VPjMEqWt7gbp-YDABw&ved=0CC4Q6AEwAA#v=onepage&q=central%20bank%20of%20Qatar%20does%20not%20have%20a%20higher%20sharia%20authority%20awqaf%20ministry&f=false.

691 Anani, A. (2014), How Greater Regulation Will Lead to Islamic Finance Growth in Qatar, Latham and Watkins.

692 The Report, (2012), Qatar, Islamic Financial Services Overview, page 100, Oxford Business Group. Available at https://books.google.co.uk/books?id=BT1gIeuQq6wC&pg=PA100&dq=qatar+has+4+islamic+banks&hl=en&sa=X&ei=QX6_VJ7NJNDuaM2PgfgD&ved=0CDkQ6AEwAQ#v=onepage&q=qatar%20has%204%20islamic%20banks&f=false.

693 Wigglesworth, R. (2011), Islamic directive shocks Qatari banks, The Financial Times Limited. Available at http://www.ft.com/cms/s/0/0ab164e0-3858-11e0-8257-00144feabdc0.html#axzz3PSjdVoSy. Mejia, A. (2014), Regulation and Supervision of Islamic Banks, International Monetary Fund (IMF) Working Paper, International Monetary Fund states Malaysian Islamic banking system has isolated sharia compliant banking to Islamic banks only. Available at http://www.imf.org/external/pubs/ft/wp/2014/wp14219.pdf.

694 Anani, A. (2014), How Greater Regulation Will Lead to Islamic Finance Growth in Qatar, Latham and Watkins.

695 Anderson, S. (2014), GCC Islamic finance prospects bright in spite of growth hiccups, Saudi Gazette. Available at http://www.saudigazette.com.sa/index.cfm?method=home.regcon&contentid=20141012220943. Kassem, M. (2014), GCC to lead growth in sukuk market, The National. Colombo, S. (2014), Bridging the Gulf: EU-GCC Relations at a Crossroads, Chapter 7, page 270, Edizioni Nuova Cultura. Available at https://books.google.co.uk/books?id=n9qrAwAAQBAJ&pg=PA270&dq=islamic+finance+growing+industry+gcc&hl=en&sa=X&ei=UnHBVMSNOore7Abp_oCoBw&ved=0CEcQ6AEwBQ#v=onepage&q=islamic%20finance%20growing%20industry%20gcc&f=false.

696 Further details on FWU AG Group are available at http://www.fwugroup.com/cms/index.php?id=23.

697 See Chapter 3 (7) "Inferential Reasoning for Intellectual Property Law".

698 A detailed analysis of the shortcomings in Islamic finance and recommendations to better regulate the Islamic finance sector will be a further research interest area that will be an off shoot of the current research. The further research will deal specifically with the criticisms of sharia boards and propose changes to further enhance the regulation of the Islamic finance sector.

699 See Chapter 2.

700 See Chapter (4) and Table 2 and Chapter 3 (1).

701 See Chapter 4 (9)-(10), Chapter 5 (5)-(8) and (12)-(14). Also see Chapter 6 (11)-(16).

702 See Chapter 2 (5)-(11).

703 See Chapter 6 (3).

704 See Chapter 7 (6) and (6).
705 See Chapter 4 (6) and Chapter 5 (6) "Saudi Arabia's Copyright Law".
706 See Chapter 4 (6).
707 See Chapter 5 (12).
708 Endeshaw, A. (2006), Intellectual Property and the WIPO Development Agenda, Maur, E. (2011), The Influence of PTAs-on the implementation of intellectual property rights in developing countries, International Centre for Trade and Sustainable Development (ICTSD) and Rizk, N. and Shaver, L. (2010), Access to Knowledge: Economic, Global and Local Perspectives.
709 Alternative dispute mechanisms have been considered at Chapter 6 (12).
710 See Chapter 7 (7)-(8) and (18).
711 See Chapter 3 (15).

## Chapter 8

712 Hassanein, M.(2008),Bilateral WTO-Plus Free Trade Agreements In The Middle East: A Case Study Of OFTA In The Post-Trips Era,Wake Forest Intellectual Property Law Journal, Volume 8, pages 161-197, Said, E. (2007), The European Trips Plus Model and the Arab World, Liverpool Law Review, Said, E. (2005), The Road from TRIPS-Minus, to TRIPS, to TRIPS-Plus
Implications of IPRs for the Arab World, Tamimi, E. (1999),Current U.A.E. Copyright Law and how it Compares and Contrasts with WTO's Trips-Agreement and the Berne Convention, The Journal of World Intellectual Property, Volume 2, pages 371-391, Price, D. (2011). Politics, Piracy and Punishment: Copyright Protection in the Arabian Gulf, Journal of World IP Volume 14, Numbers 3-4, pages 276-300 and Deere, C. (2009), The implementation game: the TRIPS agreement and the global politics of intellectual property reform in developing countries.
713 Jamar, S. (1992), The Protection of Intellectual Property under Islamic Law, Capital University Law Review, Khoury A. (2003), Ancient and Islamic Source of Intellectual Property protection in the Middle East: A focus on Trademarks, The Journal of Law and Technology at 153 and 154, Raslan H. (2009), Shari'a And The Protection Of Intellectual Property—The Example Of Egypt, The Intellectual Property Law Review 47 (4), pages 497-559, Mahafzah Q.(2009), The Perspective of Moral and Financial Rights of Intellectual Property in Islam, Arab Law Quarterly, Volume 23, Issue 4, pages 457-468, Loutfi, M. (2003), The Protection of Intellectual Property Rights: The views of the Pharos, Islamic Jurisprudence and Masters of Poetry and Literature, pages 232–233, Cullen, C. (2010), Can TRIPS Live in Harmony with Islamic Law: An Investigation of the Relationship between Intellectual Property and Islamic Law? Beltrametti, S. (2010), The Legality of Intellectual Property Rights under Islamic Law. The Prague Yearbook of Comparative Law, pages 55-94.
714 See the Quran for example at; 2:188, 2:220, 2:275, 2:278-279, 4:2, 4:5-6, 4:95, 4:161, 6:152, 9:41, 9:88, 49:15 and 61:11. Available at www.quran.com.
715 See the Quran 3:77. Available at www.quran.com.
716 See Chapter 3 (8).
717 See the Quran at 2:195, 2:254, 2:267 and 9:103. Available at www.quran.com.
718 See Chapter 3 (8) "Linking Theft of Property to Intellectual Property Infringement". Also see the Quran at 4:29. Available at www.quran.com.
719 Adam, M. (2005), Remarks about the TRIPS Agreement with Particular Reference to Compulsory Licensing.

720 See the Quran at 59:7. Available at www.quran.com. See Usmani, M. (2009), Present Financial Crisis Causes And Remedies From Islamic Perspective. Available at http://www.muftitaqiusmani.com/index.php?option=com_content&view=article&id=41:present-financial-crisis-causes-and-remedies-from-islamic-perspective-&catid=12:economics&Itemid=15. Also see Chaudhry, M. Islam and Other Economic Systems, Chapter 20.

721 For an analysis on riba and gharar see Chapter 3 (9)-(10).

722 See Chapter 3 (8) "Quranic Reform on Property Law".

723 See Chapter 3 (9).

724 See the Quran at 4:29. Available at www.quran.com.

725 See the Quran at 9:1, 9:4, 9:7, 9:8, 9:10, 9:12 and 13:20. Also see Beltrametti, S. (2010), The Legality of Intellectual Property Rights under Islamic Law. The Prague Yearbook of Comparative Law, pages 55 to 94.

726 Olwan, R. (2013), Intellectual Property and Development: Theory and Practice, Springer Publishing. See Quran at 11:15. Available at www.quran.com.

727 The Book of Virtue, Good Manners and Joining of the Ties of Relationship (Kitab Al-Birr was-Salat-I-wa'l-Adab) Translation of Sahih Muslim, Book 32 at Chapter 27.

728 See Chapter 3 (10). Drahos, P. (2003), When the Weak Bargain win the Strong, Kluwer Law, pages 79 to 109.Penubarti, M. and Maskus, K. (1995), How trade-related are intellectual property rights? Journal of International Economics, Volume 39, Issue 3, pages 227 to 248.

729 See the Quran at 2:275, 3:130, 4:29, 4:161,5:1, 5:62, 5:90, 9:4-12, 13:20 and 30:39 at www.quran.com.

730 See Chapter 3 (14).

731 See the Quran at 16:90 states; *"Indeed, Allah orders justice and good conduct and giving to relatives and forbids immorality and bad conduct and oppression. He admonishes you that perhaps you will be reminded."* Available at www.quran.com.

732 The Book of Virtue, Good Manners and Joining of the Ties of Relationship (Kitab Al-Birr was-Salat-I-wa'l-Adab) Translation of Sahih Muslim, Book 32 at Chapter 27. See Chapter 3 (9)-(12).

733 Kamali, M. (1989), Principles of Islamic Jurisprudence, 1-2 Pelanduk Publications and Raslan, H. (2007), *Sharī'a* and the Protection of Intellectual Property: The Example of Egypt ,The Intellectual Property Law Review, page 497.

734 See Chapter 3 (11).

735 See Chapter 2 (4)-(9).

736 See Chapter 2 (2).

737 The Basic Law of Government, (1992), Saudi Arabia, Article 1.

738 Khan, A. (2000-2001), Islam as Intellectual Property My Lord! Increase Me in Knowledge, Cumberland Law Review Volume 31, pages 1-46, Gattje, H. (1997), The Qur'an and its exegesis, [English trans. & ed. Alford T. Welch], Oxford Oneworld and Price, D. (2012), The Development of Intellectual Property Regimes in the Arabian Gulf States: Infidels at the Gates, Routledge.

739 Legislation includes; Law Of Trade Names (2010), Law of Patents, Layout-Designs of Integrated Circuits, Plant Varieties, and Industrial Designs (2004), Copyright Law (2003), Law of Trademarks (2002), Commercial Register Law and its Explanatory Memorandum and Implementing Regulations (2011), Electronic Transactions Protection Law (2007), Regime of E-Transactions (2007), GCC Common Law on Anti-dumping and Countervailing Measures and Safeguards (2006), Retail Business Regime (2005), Competition Law (2004), Law Against Dissimulations (2004), Law of Commercial Data (2002), Law on Trade in Agricultural Fertilizers (2002), Law on Private Laboratories (2002), Law of Criminal Procedure (2001), Telecommunication Law (2001), Printing and Publishing Law (2000), Chartered Accountants Law (1991), Law against Commercial Fraud (1984), Arbitration Law (1983) and Saudi Arabia's Regime of commercial agencies (1962)

740 Saudi Arabia became a member of the Berne Convention and Paris Convention in 2004, WIPO in 1982 and the Patent Co-operation Treaty in 2013. Available at http://www.wipo.int/wipolex/en/profile.jsp?code=SA.

741 WatiZuallcobley, R. (2012), Study on Specialized Intellectual Property Courts, joint project between the International Intellectual Property Institute (IIPI) and the United States Patent and Trademark Office (USPTO). Available at http://iipi.org/wp-content/uploads/2012/05/Study-on-Specialized-IPR-Courts.pdf.

742 See Chapter 5 (6). Also see World Trade Review, (2011), Saudi Arabia, Contributing firm United Trademark & Patent Services in association with Dr Hasan Al Mulla Law Office, page 191.

743 The full powers of the Violations Review Committee are stated in the Saudi Arabia Copyright Law (2003) at Article 25 which states at least one member shall be a Sharia advisor. See Article 25: Violation Review Committee (1*) A Committee to review the violation shall be formed by the Minister's decision, with a minimum of three members, provided that one of them is a legal advisor and the other a Shari'ah advisor. (2) Decisions of the Committee shall be made by majority vote, which shall be endorsed by the Minister.*

744 See Chapter 5 (6) "Border Measures in Line with TRIPS".

745 Chapter 1, Article 1 (b), Constitution of the Kingdom of Bahrain (2002).

746 Constitution of Bahrain, WIPO Lex.

747 Constitution of the Kingdom of Bahrain, Part 1, Article 2 states *"The Islamic Sharia is a principal source for legislation"*.

748 Law No. 6 of 2014 Approving the Law (System) of Trade Marks of the GCC (Gulf Cooperation Council) Countries (2014), Act No. 22 of the Year 2006 Relating to the Protection of Copyright and Neighbouring Rights (2006), Law No. 12 of 2006 Amending some Provisions of Law No. 7 of 2003 Pertaining to Trade Secrets (2006), Law No. 14 of 2006 Amending some Provisions of Law No. 1 of 2004 in Respect of Patents and Utility Models (2006), Legislative Decree No. 11 of 2006 in Respect of Trade Marks (2006), Law No. 5 of 2006 on Designs of Integrated Circuits (2006), Law No. 6 of 2006 on Industrial Designs and Models (2006), Law No. 16 of 2006 Amending Law No. 16 of 2004 on the Protection of Geographical Indications (2006), Law No. 35 of 2005 Pertaining Amendment of Article No. 5 of Law No. 7 of 2003 on Trade Secrets (2005), Law No. 16 of the Year 2004 Relating to the Protection of Geographical Indications (2004), Law No. 1 of 2004 on Patents and Utility Models (2004), Ministerial Decree No. 1 of 2010 Issuing the Executive Regulations for the Law of Industrial Designs and Models No. 6 of 2006 (2010), Decree-Law No. 47 of 2002 on the Organisation of the Press, Printing and Publishing (2002), Decree-Law No. 21 of 2001 Promulgating Commercial Companies Law (2001), Legislative Decree No. 10 of June 7, 1993 in Respect of Copyright Law (1993) and Law No. 7 of 2003 on Trade Secrets (2003).

749 Budapest Treaty on the International Recognition of the Deposit of Micro-organisms for the Purposes of Patent Procedure (November 20, 2012), Brussels Convention Relating to the Distribution of Programme-Carrying Signals Transmitted by Satellite (May 1, 2007), Patent Cooperation Treaty (March 18, 2007), Trademark Law Treaty (March 18, 2007), Rome Convention for the Protection of Performers, Producers of Phonograms and Broadcasting Organizations (January 18, 2006), Nice Agreement Concerning the International Classification of Goods and Services for the Purposes of the Registration of Marks (December 15, 2005), Patent Law Treaty (December 15, 2005), Protocol Relating to the Madrid Agreement Concerning the International Registration of Marks (December 15, 2005), WIPO Copyright Treaty (December 15, 2005), WIPO Performances and Phonograms Treaty (December 15, 2005), Paris Convention for the Protection of Industrial Property (October 29, 1997), Berne Convention for the Protection of Literary and Artistic Works (March 2, 1997) and Convention Establishing the World Intellectual Property Organization (June 22, 1995).

750 Agreement between the Government of the United Kingdom of Bahrain and the Government of the United States of America on the Establishment of a Free Trade Area (January 11, 2006) and Treaty between the Government of the United States of America and the Government of the State of Bahrain concerning the Encouragement and Reciprocal Protection of Investment (May 31, 2001).
751 Bahrain and the US Free Trade Agreement, (2006), Chapter 14, Intellectual Property Rights. Available at https://ustr.gov/sites/default/files/uploads/agreements/fta/bahrain/asset_upload_file211_6293.pdf.
752 Power, G. (2012), The difficult development of parliamentary politics in the Gulf - Parliaments and the process of managed reform in Kuwait, Bahrain and Oman.
753 Federal Law No. 7 of the Year 2002 Concerning Copyrights and Neighbouring Rights (2002).
754 Federal Law No. 37 of 1992 on Trademarks amended by Law No. 19 of 2000 and Law No. 8 of 2002 (1992).
755 Federal Law No. 31 for the Year 2006 Pertaining to the Industrial Regulation and Protection of Patents, Industrial Drawings, and Designs (2002).
756 Federal Law No. 17 of 2009 on the Protection of New Plant Varieties (2010), Federal Law No. 6 of 2008 on establishing a national council for tourism and Antiquities (2008), Federal Decree No.85 of 2007 on The Common Customs Law for the Arab States of the Gulf (2007), Federal Law No. 24 of 2006 Concerning Consumer Protection (2006), Law No. 1 Of 1992 Of the Emirate of Sharjah On Antiquities (1992), Federal Law No. 15 of 1980 on the Press and Publication (1980), Federal Law No. 8 of 1980, on Regulation of Labour Relation (1980) and Law No. 5 of 1973 on Commercial Register (1973).
757 Latham and Watkins LLP, (2013), Doing Business in the United Arab Emirates, Middle East and Africa Technology, IP and Sourcing Focus.
758 See Chapter 2 (3), Table 1.
759 See Chapter 2 (3), Table 1.
760 See Dubai Customs at http://www.dubaicustoms.gov.ae/en/NewsCenter/Pages/NewsDetail.aspx?NewsID=334.
761 See Fourth Global Congress on Combating Counterfeiting and Piracy Dubai Declaration, held in Dubai, U.A.E, 3-5 February 2008. Available at http://www.wcoomd.org/en/about-us/legal instruments/~/media/8B70762244B74C3BB2CB40F2BBA0668D.ashx
762 See Chapter 2 (9) and also see the Constitution of Qatar, (2004), Part 1, Article 1.
763 The Report Qatar 2012, Oxford Business Group, page 42, Oxford Business Group.
764 See Chapter 2 (9).
765 See Chapter 1 (7).
766 See Chapter 5 (8) and also see Drahos, P. (2013), Emerging Markets and the World Patent Order, Edward Elgar Publishing, page 338.
767 See Law No. (17) of 2011, Article 3 which states: *"a right holder can lodge an application with the Customs Department to stop the clearance process and request suspension of the release into free circulation of the imported goods which involve an infringement of the right holder's rights."*.
768 US-Oman FTA, (2009), Chapter Fifteen, Intellectual Property Rights. Available at https://ustr.gov/sites/default/files/uploads/agreements/fta/oman/asset_upload_file715_8809.pdf.
769 US-Oman FTA, (2009), Chapter Fifteen, Intellectual Property Rights. Available at https://ustr.gov/sites/default/files/uploads/agreements/fta/oman/asset_upload_file715_8809.pdf.
770 Omani Constitution Article 2 reads, "*The State's religion is Islam and Islamic Sharia is the basis for legislation*".
771 See Omani Royal Decree No. 65/2008 promulgating the Law on Copyright and Related Rights (2008), Omani Industrial Property Rights and their Enforcement for the Sultanate of Oman (Royal Decree No. 67/2008) (2008), Omani Royal Decree No. 49/2009 promulgating the Law on the Protection of Breeders' Rights in New Varieties of Plants (2010), Omani Royal Decree No. 81/2002 promulgating the Law on Consumer

Protection (2002), Omani Royal Decree No.29/2002 promulgating the Law on Civil and commercial procedure (2002) and Omani Royal Decree No. 6/80 promulgating the Law on the Protection of National Heritage (1980).

772 Kuwaiti Constitution, Part 1, Article 2 states "*The religion of the State is Islam, and the Islamic Shari'a shall be a main source of legislation*".

773 Kuwait gained independence from Britain in 1961 and approved its first constitution in 1962.

774 Price, D. (2012), The Development of Intellectual Property Regimes in the Arabian Gulf States Infidels at the Gates, Chapter 2, page 30.

775 Power, G. (2012), The difficult development of parliamentary politics in the Gulf - Parliaments and the process of managed reform in Kuwait, Bahrain and Oman. The Kuwait Programme on Development, Governance and Globalisation in the Gulf States.

776 Kuwaiti Constitution, Part II, Article 18, Private Property, Inheritance states "*private property is inviolable. No one shall be prevented from disposing of his property except within the limits of the law. No property shall be expropriated except for the public benefit under the circumstances and in the manner specified by law, and on condition that just compensation is paid*".

777 Decree-Law No. 68 of 1980 on Trademarks, as amended by Decree-Law No. 10 of 1987 and Law No. 1 of 2001 (2001), Law No. 4 of 1962 relating to Patents, Designs and Industrial Models as amended by Law No. 3 of 2001 (2001), Law No. 64 of 1999 concerning Intellectual Property Rights including Explanatory Memorandum (1999) and Law No. 56 of 1996 promulgating the Industrial Law (1996).

778 http://www.ustr.gov/sites/default/files/05012013%202013%20Special%20301%20Report.pdf.

779 See Chapter 3 (15). Also see Abu-Ghazaleh, T. (2001), Challenges to Arab Industries in Acquiring and Selling Appropriate Technologies, Beltrametti, S. (2009), The Legality of Intellectual Property Rights under Islamic Law. In: The Prague Yearbook of Comparative Law and Jamar, S. (1992), The Protection of Intellectual Property under Islamic Law, Capital University Law Review, Carroll, J. (2001), Intellectual Property Rights in the Middle East: A Cultural Perspective, Fordham Intellectual Property, Media and Entertainment Law Journal Volume 11, Issue 3 and Cullen, C. (2010), Can TRIPS Live in Harmony with Islamic Law: An Investigation of the Relationship between Intellectual Property and Islamic Law?

780 See Chapter 3 (4)-(5).

781 Jamar, S. (1992), The Protection of Intellectual Property under Islamic Law. Capital University Law Review and Beltrametti, S. (2010), The Legality of Intellectual Property Rights under Islamic Law. The Prague Yearbook of Comparative Law, pages 55-94.

782 See Chapter 3 (8).

783 See Chapter 3 and El-Bialy, N. and Gouda, M. (2011), Enforcing IPR Through Informal Institutions: The Possible Role of Religion in Fighting Software Piracy, Joint Discussion Paper Series in Economics, by the Universities of Aachen, Gießen, Göttingen, Kassel, Marburg and Siegen.

784 See Chapter 3 (14).

785 Price, D. (2009), The Development of Intellectual Property Regimes in the Arabian Gulf States Infidels at the Gates, Wiley & Sons Limited.

786 See Chapter 3 from (3) onwards for an analysis of primary and secondary sharia sources relevant to intellectual property protection.

787 See the Quran at 12:40. The full translation of the verse is; "*You worship not besides Him except [mere] names you have named them, you and your fathers, for which Allah has sent down no authority. Legislation is not but for Allah. He has commanded that you worship not except Him. That is the correct religion, but most of the people do not know*". Available at http://quran.com/12.

788 The US has many bilateral agreements in place with several countries around the globe including; Jamaica, Mongolia, Panama, Columbia, Korea, Peru, Oman, Uruguay, Bahrain, Morocco, Mozambique, Australia, Singapore, Chile, Jordan, Vietnam, Lithuania, Azerbaijan,

Croatia, Bolivia, Korea, Bulgaria, Grenada, Cameroon, Bangladesh, Zaire, Poland, Congo, Ukraine, Trinidad and Tobago, Czech, Slovakia, Argentina, Hungary, Cambodia, Turkey, Sri Lanka, Albania, Ecuador, Kyrgyzstan, Tunisia, Kazakhstan, Armenia, Egypt, and Senegal. Each agreement can be found at http://www.wipo.int/wipolex/en/profile.jsp?code=US.

789 Patent Law Treaty, Beijing Treaty on Audio-visual Performances , Marrakesh Treaty to Facilitate Access to Published Works for Persons Who Are Blind, Visually Impaired or Otherwise Print Disabled, Singapore Treaty on the Law of Trademarks, Protocol Relating to the Madrid Agreement Concerning the International Registration of Marks, WIPO Performances and Phonograms Treaty, WIPO Copyright Treaty, Trademark Law Treaty, Berne Convention for the Protection of Literary and Artistic Works, Brussels Convention Relating to the Distribution of Programme-Carrying Signals Transmitted by Satellite, Budapest Treaty on the International Recognition of the Deposit of Micro-organisms for the Purposes of Patent Procedures, Patent Cooperation Treaty, Strasbourg Agreement Concerning the International Patent Classification, Convention for the Protection of Producers of Phonograms Against Unauthorized Duplication of Their Phonograms, Nice Agreement Concerning the International Classification of Goods and Services for the Purposes of the Registration of Marks, Convention Establishing the World Intellectual Property Organization and Paris Convention for the Protection of Industrial Property. Available at http://www.wipo.int/wipolex/en/profile.jsp?code=US.

790 Kaminski, M. (2014), The Capture Of International Intellectual Property Law Through The U.S. Trade Regime, Southern California Law Review.

791 See http://tcc.export.gov/Trade_Agreements/Bilateral_Investment_Treaties/index.asp for each individual bilateral investment treaty.

792 US-Oman FTA available at Oman Free Trade Agreement | United States Trade Representative (ustr.gov)and US-Bahrain FTA available at http://www.ustr.gov/trade-agreements/free-trade-agreements/bahrain-fta/final-text.

793 EU legislation on copyright covers; copyright in the knowledge economy, management of copyright and related rights in the internal market, copyright and related rights: term of protection, resale right for the benefit of the author of an original work of art, rental right and lending right, orphan works, copyright and related rights: satellite broadcasting and cable retransmission, legal protection of databases, legal protection of services based on, or consisting of, conditional access, legal protection of computer programs, copyright and related rights in the information society and management of online rights in musical works. Available at http://europa.eu/legislation_summaries/internal_market/businesses/intellectual_property/index_en.htm.

794 Key areas for EU inventions covers; the European patent system, Community patent, establishment of the Community Patent Court, legal protection of biotechnological inventions and genetic engineering and legal protection of topographies of semiconductor products. http://europa.eu/legislation_summaries/internal_market/businesses/intellectual_property/index_en.htm.

795 Other areas include; counterfeit goods and piracy, European anti-counterfeiting and anti-piracy plan, industrial property rights strategy, enforcement of intellectual property rights, combating counterfeiting and piracy in the single market, customs response to latest trends in counterfeiting and piracy, goods infringing intellectual property rights, technology transfer agreements, defence-related products: rules on transfer within the EU, geographical Indications and Designations of Origin and traditional specialities.

796 The EU has extensive resources and policies governing intellectual property within the EU such as; the European Patent Office (EPO), European Commission Internal Market and services and the Office for Harmonization in the Internal Market (OHIM). Also the EU has a strong presence in intellectual property business initiatives, namely, React the Anti Counterfeiting Network and Business Action to Stop Counterfeiting and

Piracy (BASCAP). All available at http://ec.europa.eu/trade/policy/accessing-markets/intellectual-property/.

797 The EU has pioneered and steered many international rules in intellectual property. For example, in 2004, a Strategy for the Enforcement of Intellectual Property Rights in Third Countries was set up by the EU and it set out an enforcement framework dealing with intellectual property infringement outside the of the EU. Other enforcement regimes are developed by the EU through bilateral activities. These include; bilateral agreements, intellectual property dialogues, intellectual property and working groups. The bilateral agreements contain extensive intellectual property rights chapters. The chapters aim to offer similar levels of protection as is in the EU, while taking into account where a particular country or union of countries is at within the global market and its level of development. All available at http://ec.europa.eu/trade/policy/accessing-markets/intellectual-property/.

798 See Chapter 6 (7).

799 Egypt - Qatar Bilateral Investment Treaty, (1999). Available at http://investmentpolicyhub.unctad.org/Download/TreatyFile/1103. Also see Donnan, S. (2014), Al Jazeera sues Egypt for $150m after crackdown on journalists, Financial Times. Available at http://www.ft.com/cms/s/0/7ff2210c-cec0-11e3-ac8d-00144feabdc0.html#axzz3CNLGmNPk.

800 See Chapter 6 (3).

801 US-Oman FTA, Article 15.8, 6 (b) states "with respect to patents covering pharmaceutical products or their method of use:(i) each Party shall make available an adjustment of the patent term to compensate the patent owner for unreasonable curtailment of the effective patent term". Available at http://www.ustr.gov/sites/default/files/uploads/agreements/fta/oman/asset_upload_file715_8809.pdf.

802 Kerry, V. (2007), TRIPS, the Doha declaration and paragraph 6 decision: what are the remaining steps for protecting access to medicines?, Globalization and Health. Available at http://www.globalizationandhealth.com/content/3/1/3. Castro, S. (2009), Compulsory Licensing and Public Health: TRIPS-Plus Standards in Investment Agreements, Social Science Research Network. Available at http://ssrn.com/abstract=2101574.

803 Compulsory licensing and pharmaceutical products will be a further area of research as further analysis is outside the scope of the current research.

804 See more at Chapter 3 (11).

805 Hayat, U. (2014), Islamic Finance: Ethics, Concepts, Practice (a summary), The Chartered Financial Analyst (CFA) Institute Research Foundation. Available at http://www.cfainstitute.org/learning/foundation/research/Documents/islamic_finance_ethics_concepts_practice.pdf

806 This includes direct or indirect investment with certain types of business areas that involve profit making from alcohol, pork products, betting and gambling. See Quran at 2:173, 2:219, 5:3, 5:90, 6:145 and 16:115. Available at www.quran.com.

807 See the Quran at 2:275. Available at www.quran.com.

808 Malkawi, B. (2014), A Bright Future: Towards an Enhanced Shariah Supervision in Islamic Finance, The European Financial Review. Available at http://www.europeanfinancialreview.com/?p=487.

809 Further details on FWU AG Group are available at http://www.fwugroup.com/cms/index.php?id=23.

810 Ali Qayyum, M. (2013), New Horizon Global Perspective on Islamic Banking and Insurance, Institute of Islamic Banking and Insurance.

811 See Chapter 7 for an in-depth analysis on Islamic finance.

812 Full analysis of Islamic finance products and the potential application to intellectual property rights is covered in detail in Chapter 7.